Maybe God Was an Irishman

Bernie Donnelly

And he shall come again, with glory.

New York

Easter Thursday - 2017

Lee Thomas buttoned up his shirt as he stared at himself in the mirror. He looked at his craggy face, his bubbly nose, his receding hairline, and his jowly skin. He wondered what his beloved wife ever saw in him. Okay, he had a brain and a decent personality, but he was considered cranky at work, although highly respected. He knew he could make people laugh whenever he felt like it, which wasn't very often. Then again, he hadn't felt like laughing himself in such a long, long time.

'Oh, Joanna,' he whispered at the mirror. 'Why did you leave me? Why couldn't I have been the one to have left you?'

Putting some paste on his toothbrush, Lee thought about his life pre- and post-Joanna. His pre- life was nothing compared to his post-one. In his pre-Joanna days, he was a totally different person – full of life, even when he thought the world sucked. He had enthusiasm for everything. He would drown Joanna in his opinions about his latest stories while at the same time relishing in her always wise and considered responses.

One time he had taken the view in an article he was writing about people's social behaviors that it was impossible to have a society whose foundations were not built on proper social behavior; in other words, that people these days were so caught up in themselves and their selfishness to the detriment of everybody and everything else that nothing seemed to matter anymore. Gone were the good social graces, the good manners that previous generations had instilled in their children and that society no longer cared about.

Joanna unsettled Lee at first when she argued, 'People these days are no different from us when we were growing up. It is the ever-changing world that molds people differently. It is up to us older generations to show more patience than we did before, more understanding about people's behaviors than we did before. Just because somebody doesn't comply with what you consider to be the "norm" doesn't mean that they are wrong. What if the person doesn't show the "correct considered behavior" when they, because of the unknown pressures that society has dealt them, had to forego the "considered rules of engagement" in order to survive in today's modern world, just as we had to when we were growing up?!'

Joanna's argument had made Lee reconsider his approach. As a result, he posted a totally different perspective to his Sunday *Times* readers, a perspective that sent plaudits his way like never before. But Joanna was gone, taken by that maddening, unrelenting, destructive killer called breast cancer.

They never saw it coming. They never thought it could happen to them. Everything went unobserved until it came knocking at their door, the door that had welcomed saviors and sinners alike in equal measure. The people had knocked looking for Joanna's guidance as she worked relentlessly for the good of mankind, whether it was in New York City or around the world. Everybody knew of Joanna's work – her dedication to helping minorities. She had an ability to gather together the known and the unknown – the celebrities who willingly gave of their time to raise money for whatever cause or causes her attention was on, the university graduates and the professors and businesspeople had no issue when Joanna came calling looking for their help. She had that personality, that persona to which you quite simply could not say no. Joanna asked, and Joanna received – it was that simple.

She always called on God for assistance. God was the one, as she put it, who never tired of hearing from her about her missions, whether they were going well or not going well at all. She had supreme confidence in His spiritual presence. She never blamed God for anything. She trusted His divine spirit implicitly. She was the one who never lost her cool. She had time for everyone. Even when Lee had reached the end of his tether – which was often – she was the model of calmness, the one who said that it would work because she had God on her side. She had the direct line, and God could always be counted upon to give her what she needed.

Joanna had also pulled Lee into her religious corral. He had been a self-proclaimed agnostic when they first met, but she had over time, and with no subtle design, managed to cajole her way into his inner mind and unlock some buried sanctities that he had been totally unaware he possessed. Even as she drew her last breath, she reached out to hold Lee's hand and asked him to say Joanna's prayer.

He had looked in her eyes, which seemed to sparkle as he shed tear after tear. He said, 'Of course,' and striking up the courage, he spoke – 'Heavenly Father, grant us the wisdom to do your will and the strength to see it through. Have mercy on us and grant us eternal life through Jesus Christ, our Savior. Amen.'

With that, Joanna passed from this world into her eternal world, a world that Lee had no time for. His newfound spirituality had been built entirely around his reliance on Joanna's constant state of grace, and it blew apart immediately following her demise. It was a reborn faith that had suffered an immediate abortion. He had never even bothered to do any soul-searching following Joanna's death. Why should he ask the clichéd questions that everybody asks when somebody good is taken from a world in such short supply of these rich human veins of goodness? He was angry, and he would remain angry for whatever future time he had been allotted.

Joanna would have been proud of his achievement since her death back in 2009, some eight years ago now – or was it eighteen years? It seemed like a lifetime ago in a parallel universe. Trying not to miss her and knowing that he felt her supporting him and rallying him, Lee immersed himself in his work, doing what he had always done best – exposing the rats of society, the big rats, the ones who seemed to crawl through the sewers of every town and city in every part of the world, taking – always taking – from the foolish, the narcissists, the egomaniacs, the good and the bad for their own selfish pleasures, always at the expense of the ignorant and foolish citizens who blindly voted them into existence in the first place.

Lee Thomas was the acolyte whom the innocent taxpayer followed these past eight years in his weekly Sunday *Times* exposés, sometimes running into the Monday editions and being syndicated around the world after having rocked whatever city was the den for whatever rat happened to be living there. Of course, that was ever since his Pulitzer-winning destruction of the Boston Catholic hierarchy, which had taken him some two and a half years of in-depth reporting. It brought him tides of new fans and new readers, so much so that he had earned the nickname 'the Skeptic.' Lee was proud to wear that mantle, and he knew that his Joanna would have been proud also. He took particular delight in seeing the Boston hierarchy squirm their way through lie after compounded lie, only to find themselves thwarted at every turn as Lee brought his reporting to bear down on them and their expensive lawyers, resulting in the knockout punch of their admitting their injustices against the innocent children they ruined but of course never admitting liability.

The *New York Times* lauded and protected him just as they protected all of their major assets. Lee Thomas was their treasure, and whatever he asked for, he got. He had been interviewed so often and asked for his views on so many topics since his exposé that he had become a regular contributor to PBS, CNN, and all the major TV networks, making him quite the celebrity. But he shunned most of the limelight and had made himself a routine that he could cope with, a routine without his soul mate.

Lee liked working for the *Times*. He had been working there for over thirty years. He and Dick Martin had been junior reporters together and had become the best of friends. Dick covered the political side while Lee liked to concentrate on social affairs. Joanna had always steered him in that direction, giving her opinion forthrightly on whatever topic he was working on. She more than satisfied Lee's need to bounce his research off somebody he could trust implicitly in order to get a qualified opinion and not some 'yes man' approval from one of the suck-up kiddos back in the office.

After twenty-odd years of hard graft, Dick had worked his way up to the editorial level while Lee decided to stay relatively under the radar. When Dick eventually became desk editor, Lee was more than happy for him. They always worked well together. They had equal respect for each other's work, and nobody was more delighted than Dick when Lee won the Pulitzer. As far as Dick was concerned, the Skeptic was the man who set the *Times* apart from its competitors. The *Times* needed a couple of more reporters just like him.

Lee closed his front door, climbed into his SUV, and made his way over to his daughter's house, the same as he had done for the past ten days, ever since his beautiful Maggie had told him she had stage three Hodgkin's disease. Having dragged himself from the oblivion of a joyless life over these past eight years, immersing himself in his work and giving himself a new lease on wanting to live, Lee was being dragged down screaming into his isolated and soulless world – again! His only child, who was not yet forty years old and who had given him the pleasure of two grandchildren, was being struck down as Joanna had been.

Maggie's husband, Barry, had been devastated by the news. Lee did not show any sign of being depressed when he was in their company. Instead, he rallied, using all of his considerable influence to find the very best oncologist who would give his or her undivided attention to his daughter. He found Dr. Des Murphy, working over at the NYU cancer center, one of the foremost cancer specialists in Hodgkin's lymphoma. Lee knew him well, having helped during a lawsuit against the hospital that he had managed to expose as a fraud, thereby exonerating the hospital and putting another feather in the Skeptic's hat. Des wasted no time in taking on Maggie's case.

The MRIs revealed an active lymphoma spreading towards the lungs and the liver. Des treated her with radiation and chemotherapy immediately. He told Lee that he needed a few more days to be certain about the prognosis. He explained that while Hodgkin's was totally curable in a lot of cases, the best outcome, as with all cancers, was dependent upon early diagnosis. He didn't know if he had caught Maggie's in time. The important thing now was to stop the spread of the disease to the vital organs. He reckoned she had been lucky so far, but they needed to get control of it. It was going to be very rough on her, but she was young and strong and in very good health, so she was certainly able and was willing to fight it.

Lee had asked Des not to pull any punches. He wanted the truth. Des assured him he would tell him everything just as soon as he knew anything. He said that sometimes the cure can be worse than the disease itself, but only time would reveal all.

Lee arrived at Maggie's to be met by Barry holding his five-year-old granddaughter while his seven-year-old grandson ran to greet him with his boyish screams that always sent a shiver of delight up his granddad's back. Maggie had been pregnant with young Bill when Joanna died. He was born that same year. His wife had never gotten to see her grandchild. Nancy was born two years later and completed the set. Joanna had talked about expecting her first grandchild nonstop during her illness, never realizing she would not be around to enjoy any of them.

Lee whipped little Bill up in the air and swung him around as the boy screamed with delight. Lee looked at Barry, and he could see how troubled and worried he was. He liked Barry a lot. He was a good man who adored Maggie just as much as he did. He worked as the financial director of the local GE plant and had been promoted at least twice in the last four years. He was a good provider. Lee mouthed, *'How is she?'* to which Barry responded, 'Not good.'

'Look what Granddad has brought my precious grandchildren,' said Lee as he reached inside his bag to reveal a Lego set for Bill and a drawing set for Nancy. 'Now go into the playroom, and let me see what you can make and draw while your daddy and granddad go upstairs and see your mom.'

'I'm going to make an airplane!' screamed Bill.

'I want to draw Mommy and Daddy!' yelled Nancy as they rushed into the playroom.

'How did you manage to buy those?' quizzed Barry.

'One of the neighbors dropped them over. She's great. She knew I'd be hopeless at shopping for anything appropriate.'

'That's terrific, Lee. I'm afraid we had a rough night again. Maggie has been throwing up practically on the hour, but she never complains, and the doctor said that this was normal. He told me to make sure she had plenty of liquids. For some reason, he suggested flat Diet Coke or ginger ale, and it seems to be helping her.'

'How is her weight?'

'She's losing pounds with every passing day. She looks very fragile, yet she still has her appetite. She's eating everything I put in front of her, so I expect that's a good sign.'

'Yes, that's good. Des told me that as long as she's eating, that's good. It's vitally important that she keep her strength up while she's battling the drugs. I'm expecting to hear from Des later on today. He said he'll have the results of the latest MRI scans and that he'll have a better indication of whether or not there has been any progression.'

'Wouldn't she be better off in the hospital?' asked Barry. 'I mean; the nurses would know what they're doing. I'm just fighting fires not knowing if what I'm doing is right or wrong.' Barry seemed to be not really thinking straight.

'No, don't worry about that. Just be there for her like you always are. That's what's important. If she were in the hospital, she'd be surrounded by strangers. There's nothing anybody can do except to be there for her, show her how much we love her. That's what's important.'

'Okay, Lee. Thanks. It's just that I seem so helpless. I shouldn't be moaning to you.'

'Hey, moan away. It keeps me busy, and I appear important,' he chuckled, trying to ease the temperature.

They knocked on the bedroom door.

'Hi, baby girl. Daddy's home,' said Lee, as he had always done all of her life.

'Hi, Dad. Come on in,' said Maggie, stifling a cough.

Maggie was sitting up, looking blankly at the muted television set hanging on the wall.

'How are you today, precious?' asked Lee, not needing any reply as he could see for himself how drawn and tired she looked. He smiled his best smile anyway.

'I'm not bad. Feeling just a little better,' she lied, but they both knew it.

She looked even weaker than yesterday. She was a lot paler than before, and the anguish showed on Lee's face.

'Don't be worrying, Dad. I'm going to get through this, you'll see,' she said, giving him her best smile.

'I know you will, honey. You're a fighter just like your mother. Doctor Murphy is due to call me today with the latest results from your MRI. Let's not worry too much before we hear from him. The kiddies probably have no idea what's happening, huh?'

'No, thank goodness. Barry has been wonderful. He's taken them to school, bathed them, and fed them. He's a wonderful man, Dad,' Maggie said, looking over in Barry's direction.

'It's easy for me, darling. I just want you to get better,' assured Barry.

'What about we say a little prayer?' asked Maggie.

'Of course, honey, whatever you want,' said Barry as Lee shifted his position on the chair rather awkwardly.

'Come on, Dad, you can do this – for Mom,' prodded Maggie.

'I know, honey. Sure, lead away,' Lee replied, knowing they felt his mood.

'Heavenly Father, look down upon us in our anguish. Give me the strength to beat this sickness. Mother, I know you're up there and that you are fighting for me all the way. Dad is here too, Mom.' Maggie smiled in his direction. 'Help me, Mom.' The tears flowed as she lost control. Lee reached out to hold her hand.

'I'm sorry, Dad. I'm sorry to bring this upon you. I can't believe you have to suffer for me the way you've suffered so much already over Mom. I wish I could be well. I don't want to die.' With that, Lee lost control himself, and the tears flowed down as he choked, unable to respond coherently.

'Say Joanna's prayer for me, Dad.' Maggie looked at Lee, stretching out her hand in his direction, wanting him to take it.

'I don't think I remember it,' Lee choked, taking her hand gently in his and rubbing it.

'Sure you do. I'll help you.'

They held each other's hand as they recited, 'Heavenly Father, grant us the wisdom to do your will and the strength to see it through. Have mercy on us and grant us eternal life through Jesus Christ, our Savior. Amen.'

'Hey, guys,' interjected Barry. 'Hey, come on, now. We're winning this thing. Let's not let this son of a bitch take us down. We're stronger than it. Come on, pull ourselves together,' he insisted.

'You're right, Barry. I'm sorry,' said Lee. 'Honey, don't think for a moment that I'm angry, because I'm not. I'm only ever thinking of you. Your mom is gone, but I know she's watching over us all. Okay, I don't follow the God thing and I guess I never will, but that doesn't mean I'm not a believer in *you!* You are my life, as is Barry, as are my grandchildren. Never think that way about me. Think only of yourself. Be selfish in the extreme.'

'Thank you, Dad. I'll try to be stronger. It's just that sometimes . . .'

With that, Lee's phone rang. It was Des.

'Des,' said Lee shakily. 'What's the news?'

'It's good – well, better than I first thought, Lee. It looks like it's stopped growing, at least for the time being. Are you with Maggie and Barry?'

'Yes, they're both here beside me.'

'Put me on speaker, Lee. I'd like to talk to all of you at the same time.'

Lee pressed the speaker button. Maggie sat up, biting her well-chewed fingernails. Barry tensed.

'Look,' said Des, 'we're not by any stretch of the imagination out of the woods yet, but as I told Lee, it appears the growth has stabilized. We never know why these things happen. They always appear to have a mind of their own, but stopping its growth is always a good thing. It means that the treatment is working, or at least we are using the right strain, or mix, if you like, of medicines. I can't say when it's going to start again or even if it will restart. We never know. But let's take it one day at a time. How are you feeling, Maggie, at this present time?'

Maggie fell back on her pillow and blew out some air. 'Eh, doctor, I'm fine. I'm still eating. I'm getting sick a lot more than I was, but you said that would happen anyway.'

'I'm going to reduce your dosage. I'd like for you to come over and see me tomorrow. Bring Barry – and you can come too, Lee. I have a suggestion to make that I think you should take me up on. How does eleven o'clock sound?'

'I'm fine with that,' said Lee. 'What about you, honey?'

'Well, what about my chemo doctor?'

'Don't take any more medicine until you come in to see me tomorrow. You'll be fine until then. Being off the hard dosage will relieve your nausea, and you won't want to retch so much.'

'That'll be great, doctor. Thanks.'

'Okay, I'm going to leave you now until I see all of you tomorrow morning,' said Des. 'Until then, get a good night's sleep – all of you – and remain positive.'

'Thanks, Des. I really mean that. I don't know what we would have done without you.'

'It's my pleasure, Lee – my pleasure.' With that, he hung up.

'Tell me how you managed to get one of the leading oncologists in the country, Dad,' asked Maggie.

'We came across each other some years back. Let's say we helped each other out.'

'I think you should get some rest. You've got a big day tomorrow, and you'll need all of your strength,' said Barry.

'Yes, Barry's right, kiddo. You get some sleep. We've had great news. I'll meet you both over there tomorrow at eleven.'

Lee kissed Maggie on the cheek. She grabbed him and pulled him in closer to her, digging her fingers into his back and saying, 'I love you so much, Dad.'

'I know, honey. Everything's going to be okay. You'll see.'

Barry led Lee outside and closed the bedroom door. 'I'll let her sleep for as long as she can, and hopefully she won't be interrupted by her vomiting. I'll see you tomorrow, Lee.'

'Yes, until tomorrow, Barry. I'll just say goodbye to the kids, and then I'll be off.'

Maggie stared blankly at the television and tried to remember what normality was like before last week had enveloped her. What had she been doing before the grim reaper came crawling into her life? She thought back to when she was so happy, having obtained her bachelor's degree and certification as a teacher, how she was all set to enter Harvard when Joanna came calling.

A local school in a rundown part of the Upper East Side was due to close because of lack of funds. Joanna had heard about it having been approached by some of the mothers and fathers whose children were attending that school. Joanna took up the mantle to 'Save Hannaford High.' In her usual extroverted way, she managed to raise enough funds to get it back on its feet. But Joanna didn't stop there. No, siree. She immediately raised the ante by encroaching on her political contacts to pull out all the stops, ensuring that they got a development grant to renovate the building as well as funding for new teachers. She had explained to those with influence that the school was the only reason that crime in the area was as low as it was, even though it was still higher than in most other areas. But the children were off the streets, had at least two square meals a day, and were learning. She pointed out that some of these students went on to bigger and better things, that all students had a future, because of Hannaford High.

Then Maggie's mom asked her – in her none-too-subtle way – if she would help out for a time, just until things got sorted out. She had asked Maggie to look after her interests because she didn't want to give some of the politicians any reason to deny them future funding, as one or two of them would have liked to have seen Joanna fall flat on her face. They had looked upon her as a threat to their own political ambitions. Of course Maggie said she'd stay and help out, but only for six months or so. Ten years later, she was now head of the new 'Hannaford High' – pre- and middle school. She never did get to go to Harvard, but she never missed it, having relished the challenges that had arisen and still arose – well, up until the last week, that is.

Then Maggie thought about the bizarre consequences leading up to her own diagnosis. Never for a moment had she or Barry noticed that anything was physically wrong with her. She worked out on her gym equipment every morning, she ran a few days every week, and she ate well and rarely ate junk food because she wanted her children to develop good diets. They had few money problems since Barry's job paid very well. He had been promoted a couple of times, while her own salary was reasonable and pensionable. The children were healthy, normal kids. Then last week, while she was going through the teacher's time rosters, Angela, the senior preschool teacher, knocked on her door, telling her that little Rosa Hernandez was complaining of severe tummy cramps and that she felt she needed to bring the girl to the hospital. Angela's problem was that she had to look after Emma's class as well as her own because Emma hadn't shown up for work that morning.

'I know,' Maggie had said. 'Emma called. She has the flu or something. You can't leave the two classes unattended. I'll take Rosa to my own doctor once I get her parent's approval. He's only a few miles away. I'm sure he won't mind looking at her.'

So off Maggie went with little Rosa Hernandez in tow, the preschool girl whining and moaning the whole time while Maggie tried to pacify her as best she could.

Doctor Maydew had been her doctor for as long as Maggie could remember. She would never forget the way he looked at her as he examined Rosa.

'How are you feeling, Maggie?' he inquired.

'I've never been better, doctor,' she said, explaining how they were planning their vacation, hoping to spend a week in Orlando. 'It's time our kiddies experienced the one and only Mickey Mouse,' she said, totally oblivious to what was coming her way.

Doctor Maydew inquired about her children's ages. 'Five and seven,' she said, telling him that both were doing great.

'When was the last time you had a checkup with me?' he asked her sort of out of the blue, which startled her a little.

'Can't remember. Must be a few years,' she responded, becoming a little apprehensive and wanting to leave his examination room.

'Well, little Rosa here is going to be fine. Just some tummy cramps. You hop up on the table there while I get my nurse to look after little Rosa. I'll give you a quick once-over checkup,' the doctor said as if it were the norm.

So if little Rosa hadn't been sick and if Emma hadn't been out with the flu, then Maggie probably wouldn't have been disturbed, and she would never have had to see Doctor Maydew – and she would be dead.

The doctor felt the lump after he had examined her breathing. He had her cough a number of times and decided to take her blood and get it analyzed. That's when the trouble started, as the jokes always say. Then the past week became surreal as she was whisked from one doctor to another hospital, finally taken under Doctor Murphy's wing, courtesy of her dad.

Maggie reached over for her box of tissues. Putting her hands to her face, she pleaded, 'Please, God, don't let me die.' And with that, the tears cascaded down her face in uncontrollable bursts and lasted some minutes.

She finally stopped crying, blew her nose, and stared blankly at the TV. She saw Anderson Cooper miming something while the CNN red breaking news banner displayed something about a priest in Ireland. She turned off the television and fell into a deep sleep.

New York

Good Friday - 2017

Lee opened his eyes. He checked the clock and saw it was still only five a.m. He'd barely slept even though he had downed nearly half a bottle of bourbon before climbing into bed. He never used to drink that much, particularly the hard stuff, preferring instead to have a couple of glasses of wine with his dinner. Then again, these past few days had been anything but normal. He had barely slept all week since hearing Maggie's news. He hadn't been in touch with anybody at work other than to keep Dick informed as he had requested him to. He hadn't turned on a TV or read anything. His life amounted to nothing over the past number of days. *It's funny,* he thought, *how everything becomes insignificant when something really significant takes over. All the 'must-do' important stuff is immediately forgotten when people's lives are threatened, people who mean everything to you.*

Lee tried to remember what he had been working on last week before his life came crashing down around him. Oh yes, that piece about the Methodists. He had unearthed something shady about one of the larger New York Methodist branches, deciding to give the Catholic church a rest – for the time being. What was it? Oh yes, some definite financial skullduggery. He sighed. *Ah, who gives a crap anyway?* he thought. Throwing his papers down on the side table, he lay on his back and wondered how he was going to fill in the next few hours.

His cell phone rang. Lee awoke with a start. 'Hello, hello?!' he shouted.

'Lee, it's Barry. Just letting you know we have to drop off the kids at my mother's house before heading for the hospital. We're leaving a little earlier, so we'll see you there.'

'What time is it now?' Lee gasped, trying to find his watch, not registering that his phone showed 10:05.

'It's 10:05. You've plenty of time. See you there.'

He must have dozed off again. Thank God Barry had called; otherwise, he probably would have slept all day. Not to worry – he had plenty of time.

Lee arrived at the hospital to be shown into Doctor Murphy's room by his secretary. Maggie and Barry were already seated.

'I hope I'm not late,' said Lee as he dragged one of the chairs from the corner of the room and pushed up alongside Maggie.

'Not at all, Lee. We were just getting started. Let's make our way over to the new facility. I just have to make a quick call.' Des punched some numbers, lifted the receiver, and announced that he was on his way.

'Are the children okay?' asked Lee.

'They're fine, Dad. Barry's mom loves having them over.'

'Okay, let's go over there, and I'll explain what I have in mind,' said Des as he led them out into the hallway and through the nearest exit. 'We can use this golf cart,' he said, pointing to a new four-seater parked outside the door.

'Is it far?' asked Maggie.

'Takes about five minutes,' responded Des.

'I never realized the property stretched out this far,' said Lee.

'Most people never get to see the rear of the main building. You're going to be surprised.'

They took two turns and arrived at a large circular fountain announcing the entrance. The waters gushed from the fountain, bringing immediate tranquility from the hustle and bustle of the main hospital.

'It's like we've been transported to the countryside,' said Barry.

'Wait until you see inside,' said Des as he guided them through the reception area.

The nurse put Maggie in a wheelchair. 'Just for your own safety, Maggie,' whispered Des. 'Just hang on a moment.' He glanced around the corner, muttering something to someone unseen. 'Okay, we're ready. You first, Barry, and wheel Maggie in front. Then you follow next, Lee,' said Des.

They turned the corner to be met by a fanfare of people who immediately broke into applause as Lee brought up the rear.

'What's all this?' said Maggie and Lee in unison.

'Quiet, everybody,' said Des as he raised his hands. He turned to Lee and said, 'Ladies and gentlemen, it is my great pleasure to introduce Mr. Lee Thomas, *New York Times* senior reporter, Pulitzer Prize winner, and effective founding father of the Lee Thomas Cancer Welfare Center.'

With that, everybody burst into applause again. Maggie and Barry turned to see a very surprised but all-smiling Lee look on in amazement.

'I don't understand,' spouted Lee.

'Maggie, Barry, let me tell you that if it wasn't for your father [he looked at Maggie] and your father-in-law [he looked at Barry], this facility would not exist. Neither would the doctors, nurses, and specialists, nor the very grateful patients who have just started to attend and will continue to attend this fabulous facility. You see, about five years ago, this hospital was in very grave danger of being forced to shut down based on the false testimony of certain bad-minded individuals who were out to cause permanent closure by unscrupulous means. If not for Lee, this would certainly have happened. His doggedness, application, and genius protected us and guided us to where we are today. We were able to use the money that we didn't have to spend on legal defenses and put them to real use in building this facility you see here today. This hospital, its patients, and its board will be eternally grateful and forever indebted to one Mr. Lee Thomas. For this and many more reasons, I am delighted to officially announce the opening of the Lee Thomas Care Center. Lee, will you cut the ribbon?'

Des handed a large pair of scissors over to Lee. Lee was open-mouthed as he walked gingerly towards Des and accepted the scissors.

'Of course I will, but I'm still in shock.'

Everybody clapped once again as the ribbon fell in two.

'I'm sorry to spring this on you like this, Lee, as I know how you hate surprises, but we opened the facility only about two weeks ago, and we were due to officially announce its opening this coming week. When I heard about Maggie, I thought it very appropriate that she be one of the first guests, so I rushed to have the opening ceremony coincide with your visit here today.'

'It's not a problem, Des. I never knew you were even contemplating this project.' Lee grinned with embarrassment.

'It's been something I've wanted to do for so long. Come on, let me show you around and explain.'

Des ushered the three of them through the main hallway into the welcoming area. It was a large lounge-style room with dozens of La-Z-Boy-type armchairs. A couple of people were already snoozing peacefully. There was a large bay window looking out onto magnificently kept manicured lawns and gardens.

'Wow, look at that!' said Maggie. 'It's beautiful.'

'Wait until you see the living quarters. The whole concept is to allow patients to get away from everything that makes up their current lives, to take them to another world where their care and attention are screened and monitored 24/7. It's like the Ritz-Carlton of care. You are surrounded by doctors and counselors, all specialists in their fields. In addition to having access to the main hospital, equipment, and facilities, you are also afforded multiple visits each day from your own personal physicians, oncologists, and so forth. The whole reason is to ensure that each patient gets the best individual attention, ensuring their best possible recovery.'

'But how much does all this cost?' asked Barry.

'I know. It costs a lot,' replied Des. 'But the patients we recommend to use this facility all have one thing in common – they all have cancers that have stabilized or even gone away completely. For that reason, we can do individual tests to try to find out why some patients' cancers neutralize themselves while seemingly better

20

candidates – say, younger, stronger patients – don't react in the same way.'

'And die, doctor – right?' said Maggie.

Lee looked up at Des, hoping he could answer Maggie.

'Yes, some people obviously die, Maggie. But we are more than hopeful that with this new facility, we will have even better results than we were having in the main hospital. Now we have the means to do proper testing and analysis.'

'But just because Maggie's cancer has somehow stopped, it still doesn't mean we can afford to stay here,' suggested Barry.

'Maggie is our guest,' said Des. 'We are only too delighted to be able to repay – in some small way – our gratitude to Lee for what he did for us. There will be no cost to have Maggie here.'

'How long will she have to stay?' asked Lee.

'Only for about a week or so. I know you have two young children, Maggie. We ask that the spouse move into the facility with the patient so that they can be together through all of the tests that we have to perform. Hopefully you can arrange to have your children cared for during this time,' said Des.

'That won't be a problem, doctor,' replied Maggie. 'Besides, I think it might be a good time for your parents to take the kids to Disney using the tickets we bought,' Maggie said to Barry. Barry nodded in agreement.

'Why don't you both take a walk in the gardens and get a feel for the place? Lee, you come with me.'

Barry pushed Maggie in her wheelchair through the automatic doors to the gardens.

'Is this some sort of glorified hospice?' asked Lee when Maggie and Barry were well out of earshot.

'Anything but,' said Des. 'Look, Lee, you asked me to be honest with you, and I promised you I would be. We are going to test the living daylights out of Maggie and do everything in our power to make her better. This is the only way I can do this. I need her beside me. She's young, she's strong, and the cancer has stopped growing. These are all positives. We must act during this stable period while she is strong in order to get some sort of a grip on what's happening inside her body. But I won't lie to you Lee. Maggie is in serious trouble. Unless we are able to rid her body of the disease, then we are talking in terms of years at best.' Lee looked towards the floor taking in the words he had just heard. Shaking himself free of any negative thoughts, he said'

'So Barry stays with her at all times while you do your tests. Correct?'

'Yes, we always recommend that. It helps the patients to know that their loved one is beside them, keeping them company and not letting them get in on themselves.'

'Will I be able to visit?' Lee asked expectantly.

'I'm afraid not. We don't want any more than the immediate partner, as other visitors are a distraction. Rest assured that Maggie is under my personal care. You don't have to worry. Remember, this is 2017 – we've made super advances in curing many cancers compared to even twenty years ago. You get back to work, Lee; occupy yourself. You can call me as often as you'd like. I will keep you updated. How's that?'

'Whatever you say, Des. Thank you again. When will she be admitted?'

'Let's see, today is Thursday. I'd hope she can organize things today, and we'd have her checked in tomorrow morning.'

'As soon as that? Wow, I didn't think it would happen that fast,' said Lee, now looking worried.

'Yes, we have to act fast. The quicker we can get to testing her, the better it will be for her. Come on, let's go talk to them, and you can say your goodbyes,' said Des.

Maggie and Barry were happy to oblige the doctor, knowing that he was doing it for her own good.

'Dad, will you be okay not being able to see me every day?'

'I'll be fine,' Lee lied. 'Besides, I'll be able to see my grandkids every day.'

Barry coughed. 'Lee, I'm sorry, but you know that my mom and dad are taking the kids to Disneyland. You know we had made reservations some weeks back, so they can use part of the booking. Besides, it'll take the kids' minds off all the sadness going on around them.'

'Of course. I completely forgot about that. Don't worry your head about it. I understand completely. It'll be great for your parents and the kiddies. In fact, it's a terrific idea. I'm going to be busy anyway with the paper, and I know Des is going to take personal care of you, and that's all that matters,' said Lee hurriedly, trying to placate everybody while they could see that he was nevertheless a bit upset.

'You can bank on that,' assured Des.

'Goodbye, honey,' said Lee as he reached down to kiss Maggie. Maggie responded by hugging him deeply, and then the tears flowed. 'Come on now, kiddo. Chin up. You must be strong.' Lee smiled as he gave her another hug and kiss.

'I'll be fine, Dad. Look after yourself.'

'We'd better be going if we're to organize everything by tomorrow morning,' interrupted Barry.

They all said their farewells. Lee waited until Barry and Maggie had disappeared. He shook hands with Des and made his way to his car.

Okay, Lee thought. *At least Maggie is in the safest of hands, and Barry is there all of the time. The grandkids are fine. They'll be thrilled to be going to Disney. Now, what the hell am I going to do for the next week?'*

As he drove in the direction of home, Lee contemplated his life at that moment. *What would Joanna have done?* he asked himself. *I suppose she would have started with Joanna's prayer. How did it go?* He hadn't been reminded of it until Maggie had brought it up yesterday. *Oh yes, it went, 'Heavenly Father, grant us the wisdom to do your will and the strength to see it through. Have mercy on us, and grant us eternal life through Jesus Christ, our Savior. Amen.'*

The phone shrilled its maddening ring. Lee knocked over something.

'What the...?' He tried to orient himself. He was in bed. He remembered he had been drinking. He had taken some sleeping pills.

Oh crap, another lost night, he thought. He searched for the phone and his glasses.

'Hello?'

'Where the hell have you been, Lee?' Dick's photo looked up at him from his phone, with that pearly grin that seemed to be permanently across his chubby face.

'What's up, Dick?' Lee asked as he made his way towards the kitchen to put on some coffee.

'First things first. How's Maggie?'

'Better than expected. Des told us yesterday that the lymphoma has stopped growing for now. He's taken her into his care at their new private wing. She's going to be there for about a week.'

'Do you see her every day?'

'I have, but the doctor has taken her into his personal care at the new wing of the hospital. It means I have to leave her and Barry alone for about a week while they do all their tests.'

'That's great news.'

'Well, yes, I suppose it is.'

'No, I mean that's great that you have nothing to do because I need you to go over to Ireland for me.'

'Ireland! Why in blazes would I want to go to Ireland?'

'Because A, I'm asking you to; and B, it's probably the greatest story going on in the world right now; and C, it's right up your alley!'

'What do you mean it's right up my alley?'

'Have you been watching the news?'

'I haven't been watching anything this past week or so. What's going on?'

'Only the biggest thing to hit Ireland since St. Patrick, that's what's going on, my friend. Get yourself a coffee while I explain.'

Lee filled his coffee cup and made his way to his chair. 'Go ahead, shoot.'

Dick began. 'Last Wednesday, an Irish priest went missing. He's on the run, and the police can't find him. I'm not going to bore you with the criminal aspects because Bill Canon has been handling all of that.'

'A good reporter, our Bill. How is he doing?' enquired Lee.

'He's doing fine. Forget about him because we are talking about the Second Coming here!'

'What?!' spat Lee as he spilled his hot coffee down his shirt. 'Oh blast it. I've just scalded myself. This is a load of crap, Dick. Why are you wasting my time?'

'It could be a load of crap. Then again, it might not be. That's what I'm asking you to find out. Look, you know my relations came from the West of Ireland and that I go back there every year on vacation.'

'Yes, for the fishing.'

'And the drink. I'm telling you, my people don't suffer fools gladly. I've been talking to some cousins over the past couple of days, and they're saying that this priest – a Father Sean Robinson – is the genuine article. He's revered to the point that a lot of people consider him a saint.'

'Well, maybe a saint is okay, but not Jesus Christ. Come on, Dick, this is one of those weeping statue stories!'

'There's not a weeping statue to be seen for this story. This guy is credited with doing miracles over the past number of years without any public acclaim. He's kept very much under the radar. Now it's gone ballistic internationally. All the news media are camped out in this tiny rural village in the West of Ireland, all craving to know the truth. But nobody has uncovered anything yet. That's why I want to send my ace reporter – the one, the only Skeptic. I want you to uncover this con man, defrock him, and hang him out to dry. How does that grab you, my super anti-ecclesiastical friend?'

Lee stared at the picture of Maggie, Barry, and the children smiling at him from the framed photo on his kitchen counter. They were doing what they had to do. He would only be in the way. He felt he was going to be incapable of unearthing his own stories. He might as well follow one being given to him on a plate.

'Okay, I'll go. I'll do this crazy exposé!'

'Great,' said Dick. 'You're booked on this evening's Aer Lingus flight to Shannon – departs at nine p.m. You arrive sometime in the early morning local time. It should give you enough time to interview the main protagonists.'

'Jasus, you know me too well, Dick.'

'There you go, and you're even beginning to talk like an Irishman. Grab a call with Bill Canon. He'll bring you up to speed on the crime-reporting side. You concentrate solely on getting inside and behind the main character, this Father Robinson character. I'll keep the front page open in case you break something for me. There's nothing really newsy going on at the moment. I'd like to lead with it in the Sunday edition.'

'Crap, Dick. I'll never be able to make that deadline. Besides, there's probably nothing to this story.'

'Oh, I'm sure you'll dig up something worthwhile.'

Dick hung up. Lee looked at his watch. It was 8:30 a.m. That gave him about ten hours to clean himself up, pack his travel case, get brought up to speed by Bill Canon, and try to find out what this whole story was about!

How in God's name...? He interrupted his thoughts, knowing he had better contact Maggie and let her know what was happening. He pressed the speed dial, and she answered.

'Dad, is everything okay?'

'Yes, darling, everything's fine. How are you?'

'I'm great, Dad. We're just leaving Barry's parents' house, making sure the kiddies are all set. Dad, they are so excited about going to Disneyland. It would do your heart good to see the smiles on their faces.'

'I'm sure, honey. Listen, the office called me. They want me to make a trip to Ireland of all places. There's some story Dick wants me to cover. I'm flying out tonight. I should be gone only a few days, maybe even less. Will you be okay?'

'Ireland! What's going on over there?' Maggie said, surprised.

'Oh, some mad story about some crazy priest. I should have said no, but Dick twisted my arm – as usual.'

'That's great, Dad. I'm delighted. It'll take your mind off me for a while at least.'

'You're always on my mind, honey.'

'Aw, Dad, that sounds like a song.' They both giggled. 'No, seriously, I'm delighted. Go. Do your thing. I'm sure if Dick wants you there, then it's bound to be important. I'll be fine. Besides, I have Barry by my side.'

'Okay, honey, as long as you're sure.'

'I'm positive. I love you, Dad. We'll see you when you get back.' They hung up.

'Right. Better get a move on,' said Lee.

Ireland

In the beginning...

Bridie Robinson shuffled through the papers on her desk, cross-checking the drug stocks with the reports from the previous month. She often thought how she had ended up back in Ballinasloe in the great county of Galway, back to where she was born and going to work at the local St. Brigid's Hospital.

It was a small but busy enough hospital, offering general treatments as well as births. She was particularly proud of their maternity wing. They always passed the most stringent tests that the Department of Health imposed. Her wing was always spick and span, and would pass any hygiene tests with flying colors. Mothers were proud to have their babies there, and Bridie took personal care of every proud mother and mother-to-be.

She had done her training in one of Ireland's largest hospital complexes – at St. James's in Dublin. Having passed all of her exams, she decided, having fallen in love with Dan, that getting back to her roots was best for her. She hadn't bargained for getting promoted to Matron at the tender age of twenty-seven, but the powers that be decided she was the one to look after their hospital. She hadn't disappointed them as she entered her seventh year in charge. She had taken to it like a duck to water, just like her mother before her, although her mother's role had been a lot easier than hers. In those days, things worked a shade differently. Nowadays, you had to account for everything, which was why she was working late trying to balance the books between the goods coming in and those being used. It was a never-ending battle that always eventually worked itself out. She could trust the people who worked around her. They trusted Bridie, and Bridie was no fool.

She looked at her watch and saw that it was – again – beyond clocking off time. She folded her papers and filed those that needed

28

filing, throwing those that needed throwing straight into the wastepaper basket. Any difference in her reconciliation could wait. She was dog tired and needed her sleep. Bridie's two kids, Kevin and Molly, would be well in bed having been nursed to sleep by Rosie as usual, in her own inimitable way. God, what would she have done without Rosie?

Her thoughts were interrupted by Maisie, her second-in-command, who said, 'Bridie, you'd better be getting on home now before Dan gets home. You know he gets more than a little pissed off when you're late.'

'Aw, Dan will be working late. It's the end of the month, and he has to do the stock take, as the auditors will be coming tomorrow. Are we all asleep in the wards?'

'Yes, everything is calm. No major riots, and I put an extra dose of sleepies in Baggie's cocoa just to be sure,' assured Maisie.

'Get Baggie out of here tomorrow, and tell him I don't want to be seein' his ugly face around this hospital again. Are you hearing me, Maisie?'

'Sure, to be sure, Bridie, but you know how it is.'

'That's enough, Maisie. I'm getting sick of him. Out, out of here – do you hear?' she blasted.

'Sure, I'll look after it, Bridie,' smiled Maisie, knowing full well that Bridie had a heart of gold and would never shove poor old homeless Baggie out on the street. *Sure, he had nowhere else to go!* thought Maisie.

'I'm off,' said Bridie. 'I'm totally shattered. Good night, Maisie.'

'Nighty-night, Bridie. Oh, and don't forget to look up in the sky at Halliwell's thingamajiggy thingie,' pressed Maisie.

'It's Halley's Comet, Maisie. I promise I'll have a look skyward before I go home.' She smiled and thought to herself that Maisie would be destroyed if she ever had the inclination to work in one of the Dublin hospitals.

Bridie bid Adam a good night. Adam was the handyman, security man, wheelchair assistant, and general dogs body she employed. He was reliable; that's about all you could credit him with.

29

'Good night, Adam. See you in the morning.'

'Good night, missus – eh, Bridie. I'll be here the night.'

'I know you will, because that's why I pay you such an exorbitant salary,' mused Bridie. Adam scratched his head, not understanding her.

As Bridie stepped outside into the clear September sky, the fresh Galway air filled her lungs as she took a deep breath. She checked her reflection in the glass door and saw that she still had the good looks that had attracted Dan towards her. Though she was only small in height compared to Dan's six feet, she had a great figure enhanced by her long flowing Irish red hair. She looked up before venturing towards her car and saw what Maisie had been going on about for the past couple of nights. Indeed, Halley's Comet had made its regular – what was it? – some seventy-six-year sojourn into our stratosphere. Here it was in 1986 and wouldn't be seen again for another seventy-six years or so. She would be long gone by the time Mr. Halley came around these parts again. She saw its tail and wondered how others reasoned with it, century after century before now. She thought how confused they must have felt, how tribes would have used its appearance to kill, sacrifice, mourn, or celebrate; or used its appearance for their own illegal means, confusing the innocents and taking their hard-earned . . .

Bridie's thoughts were disturbed by the obvious sounds of a baby crying. She turned towards the sound, which was getting louder. The noise abated. She shook her head as if she must have imagined it. *God, I need my sleep more than I thought. I'm hearing babies and seeing comets,* she thought and smiled at the same time.

Bridie moved towards her car. Just as she did so, the definite crying of a baby broke the still air again. 'That's not me imagining, for sure,' she said to herself. She made her way towards the sound. Pushing back the overhung bush that sided up against the entrance pillar and pushing her legs and arms inwards, Bridie sank back as she saw what was obvious to her a newly born baby wrapped in a blanket, looking lost and forlorn.

'What is it we have here?' she cooed as she reached down to lift the baby in her arms. 'There, there now. Don't you be fretting yourself. Bridie has you. I'll take care of you.'

Bridie reached down and lifted the baby carefully. The baby calmed itself almost immediately. Bridie looked around to see if anybody was there. Seeing nobody, she scampered back inside the hospital doorway into the warmth. She hurried past Adam, telling him to get Maisie to meet her down at incubation right away.

'Aye, ma'am, aye,' he said as he lifted the phone and started to punch in some numbers.

Bridie pushed open the door to the incubation room and picked out the nearest incubator. She immediately put her neonatal nurse experience into action. She uncovered the baby and saw that it was a boy. It was barely hours old but seemed to be in good health. She would have to wait until the doctor did his tests, but her immediate opinion was good. Maisie rushed in.

'What's wrong, Bridie?'

'This little fellow was abandoned outside the hospital. He seems to be fine, but I need to run some tests. Help me check his lungs, and find me some clean clothes and a bottle.'

'Right away,' said Maisie as she ran from the room.

Bridie laid the baby down after buttoning up the sheet it was wrapped in. She continued to talk softly to it.

'What have you been doing out at this time of the night? Don't you fret yourself, little fella; Bridie is here for you. I'll look after you. You can be sure of that.'

He gulped at the bottle of infant milk Bridie took from the shelf and instantly fell asleep. Bridie looked at him as Maisie rushed in carrying an assortment of clothing and bottles.

'What do we do with him?' asked Maisie.

Bridie looked down at the infant and smiled. Then, realizing what Maisie had said, she retorted, 'We put an advertisement in the paper tomorrow and sell him to the highest bidder. What do you think we do with him?'

'There's no need for that, Bridie. I was only asking!'

'I'm sorry, Maisie. I'm just bone tired, that's all. I've no idea what happens to him. This is my first abandoned child too.' She looked down at the baby again, who seemed to be already in a deep sleep. 'He seems to be calm enough. Let's look after him for now, and we'll ring the authorities in the morning.'

'You go home, Bridie. I've just come on duty. You must be knackered!'

'If you don't mind, I'll take you up on that offer. Are you sure you'll be all right?'

'Bridie, it's Maisie you're talking to, not Adam.'

'Sorry, Maisie. I'll see you in the morning.'

She took one last look at the new baby. He was fast asleep. He had the most beautiful soft smile. He was so serene.

And you shall name him...

Bridie awoke with a start. She jumped up in the bed and saw that Dan was fast asleep beside her. She hadn't heard him come in last night. She looked at the clock and saw that it was five minutes before her alarm was due to go off at six. She had to get up and help Rosie get the kids ready.

My God, the baby, she thought. 'What am I going to do with the baby?' she said aloud.

Kevin came down the stairs excitedly as he always did, followed by Rosie carrying Molly, who still looked half asleep. Kevin was four and had just started in infant's school whilst Molly had just turned three and was in the local crèche.

'Okay, Kevin, Molly, let's be having you. Mummy has a lot of work down at the hospital, so I don't want any delays.'

Bridie told Rosie about last night's news. 'Who would do that to a newborn baby?' Rosie asked, obviously upset the more she thought about it.

'God only knows, Rosie. There's always a reason. The important thing now is the welfare of the child. The police can do their work finding the mother and the parents.'

Bridie kissed the kids, and Rosie assured her that she would collect them from school later and not to worry herself. She had enough on her plate.

'Tell Dan to ring me later whenever he's ready.'

'Will do, Bridie.'

Bridie checked on the baby as soon as she arrived at the hospital. He seemed to be doing fine. Maisie came in soon after and said that she had fed him again and that everything seemed normal to her.

'Did anybody enquire after him?' asked Bridie.

'No, not a soul. I rang the Gardaí after you left in accordance with procedure,' said Maisie.

'Good girl, Maisie. In all of the excitement, I forgot about any procedure. Okay, I'd better call the authorities and find out what's to happen.' Bridie picked up the phone and dialed.

'Gardaí. How can I help you?'

'This is Bridie Robinson down at the hospital.'

'Hello, Bridie. It's Sergeant Malachy Brown here. I heard all about that abandoned baby boy from Maisie last night. I've been working the phone most of the night, and I've nothing for you, I'm afraid. I circulated all of the Garda stations in the neighboring counties. I'm afraid that nobody is looking for any baby. There are no missing baby reports anywhere across the country.'

'It's very unusual, sergeant. I've never had any experiences like this, have you?'

'No, can't say I have,' Malachy responded. 'I mean, I know the procedures, but having actually experienced it . . . no, can't say I have.'

'What should I do now?' asked Bridie.

'Well, the little baby is in the safest place at your hospital. There's nowhere else to send the poor thing. I've checked the local orphanage, and they simply can't accommodate him. Best to keep it there until I come up with the correct protocol. I'll get on to Dublin head office and find out what I'm supposed to do.'

'Okay, let's stay in touch.'

'Will do. Good luck, Bridie.' With that, he hung up.

Bridie sat in deep thought. She thought how some young mother was distressed right then and possibly suicidal. God, she hoped things worked out well. *Right,* she thought. *Better get some plan together; I've a hospital to run as well.*

The first thing she did was talk to Doctor Luke O'Reilly. He was the senior doctor in charge. She needed him to do a full physical examination of the new baby. They would need blood tests as well as an all-faculty examination. Dr. O'Reilly got on it immediately.

Bridie had around thirty patients in various degrees of hospitalization. Most of them were procedural and would be discharged within a week or so. About ten or so were long term.

Some had just come through the rigors of full-blown operations and were under care. The others were still at the diagnosis stage awaiting their test results.

Bridie had fourteen staff in all – two doctors, nine nurses, and three administrative staff. Most of her nurses were seasoned veterans who had been doing nursing all of their lives. They were so experienced; they could easily do the doctors' work for them. Bridie had the benefit of being able to use three or four of them on a temporary basis so that she could control her wage costs. They all lived locally anyhow, so it suited them as well. They all had great respect for Bridie, none more so than the two doctors. They didn't stand on ceremony and were grateful to be working with professionals. There was none of the acrimony and standoffishness that you experienced in the city hospitals.

Bridie needed to register the baby for a birth certificate. She went back down to the incubation room. There were just two other newborn babies, and they would be released with their mothers by the end of the week. Maisie was changing one of the babies.

'Maisie, I need to register our orphan for a birth certificate. It's the law – although I suppose it'll be only temporary until they find the real mother. In the meantime, the form says I have to give it a name. What should we call him?'

'Gee, Bridie, I don't know. I do know that every time you come into this room, his eyes seem to light up. Perhaps you should be the one to name the poor critter.'

'Don't be imagining things, Maisie. How could a wee thing like that light up? Sure he knows nothing that's going on.'

'I'm just saying that I've been here all morning and he's been fast asleep. Look at him. He's staring at you.'

Bridie looked down at the baby and had to agree with Maisie. He did seem to like the sound of her voice. His eyes were as wide open as a new baby's could be. He was definitely looking straight at her.

'He's probably hungry again,' said Bridie.

'I fed him earlier.'

'Anyway, how about Sean?'

'Sean's a great name.'

'Dan's middle name is Sean. Yes, I like it.'

'I love it,' agreed Maisie.

'Sean it is, then.'

Bridie filled in the name, and for 'date of birth,' she wrote, 'September 8, 1986.'

Dan Robinson opened his eyes and squinted as the sunlight burst through the gap in the curtains. He moved in the bed to escape the direct rays. He had had a late night running the stock figures, shifting and sorting through the bottles, crates, and barrels in lieu of the auditors attending their annual stock take today. He always figured it was a total waste of time doing any sort of stocktaking because it was nearly always impossible to get the numbers to agree. *Ten-twelfths in this bottle and a quarter in that,* he thought to himself. Hadn't he been doing bar work only all of his life? He'd know if there was anything amiss even if he had been down a trench for the past month.

Dan Robinson's Bar and Lounge had been in existence for two generations in Ballinasloe, and Dan was the latest standard-bearer to carry the family name. He had worked there for his father, who had worked there for his father before him. It was known locally as Dan's. Everybody went for a pint to Dan's. They always sold a great pint, and all of the locals knew it. Thank God for the October horse fair – Europe's largest– held every year in Ballinasloe, as it had been since the eighteenth century. Some twenty-thousand extra visitors flooded the town for the event. *God,* he thought, only for it, *I'd never have survived – or my father before me.*

Ballinasloe was nestled in the far eastern side of County Galway. It was the county's largest town, with a population measured only in the thousands. It consisted of one main street and four side streets. It had the usual for a rural Irish town – two supermarkets, three churches, two hospitals, a Garda barracks, a mixture of restaurants and fast food joints, and far too many pubs. This was the week of pure bedlam, unadulterated craic, and oodles of spondoolicks, as the

Dubs would say, when Dan would be forced to take off the doors at the main entrance, allowing as many people to come and go as they felt like it. It was also a time when the Gardaí turned a blind eye to regulations and concentrated on keeping the peace. Dan could liquefy his customer's twenty-fours a day for nine glorious days.

The annual fair made his income for the entire year. It subsidized the rest of the year, and without it, he could not remain in business. The new drink-driving laws were affecting his business like every other publican across the land, so that was another reason to make hay as the drinkers drank. Not that too many would be driving anyway, as most lived nearby or within walking distance of their nightly abode. Anyway, that wasn't his problem. His duty was to serve as many as he could in the shortest period of time. That's why it was best to get the annual stock take with the auditors out of the way before next week's fair, leaving him free to make as much money as he could. Dan had already organized the extra temporary staff to help him and Jimmy, his only full-time staff member. They'd be the usual staff he generally picked upon for this event. He knew them, but he knew how to keep an eye on them too.

Dan assessed that he was a happy man, especially at this time of the year. He also was a very happy man knowing that he was married to his princess, the only woman he had ever loved. Bridie was his dream come true. When she went to work in Dublin, he was devastated. He had courted her and dreamt about her ever since he was a teenager.

Dan drove up to Dublin every weekend, making sure that no 'Dublin Jackeen' was going to take his Bridie away from him. That, he had managed to achieve. She knew he adored her, and the fact that she hated the hustle and mad lifestyle of the big city gave Dan the impetus to enhance Bridie's disquiet. No sooner had she made a reputation for herself as a nurse than she wanted to come home. Dan promised her the world. He promised her everything he could to show her how much he loved her and that he would never let her down. She had taken him at his word and his promise to her was now entering their seventh year of marriage.

He shook his head. It was time to get up. He dragged his 230 pounds into the bathroom. He washed, shaved, and showered and made his way downstairs to be greeted with a breakfast by Rosie.

'Bridie told me to tell you to ring her as soon as you got out of bed.'

'I'll have to ring her when I get into work as I've the auditors waiting on me and I've a lot to do getting ready for the fair.'

'Well, don't say I didn't tell you; otherwise, she'll kill me.'

'Understood.'

With that, Dan kissed little Molly, telling her to be a good little girl. 'Who's Daddy's bestest girl?'

'Molly,' she said giggling.

'That's my girl.'

The next week flew by. Dan was hardly to be seen as customer followed customer, parting with their money, imbibing beyond imbibing, throwing the cash at Dan as fast as he could catch it.

Bridie worked manically until all hours of the night as one drunken casualty followed another with scrapes, cuts, and bruises, sometimes a broken leg or arm, and the occasional stab wound. The police would follow up the morning after, taking names and following leads on the disputes of the day before. Bridie was well used to this week from hell. But she also knew how important it was for Dan's business. She was happy knowing that he was happy.

Baby Sean became part of the furniture. Bridie and Maisie looked after him like mother hens, bowing to his every cry and moan with whatever was needed to keep the abandoned soul happy and safe. Bridie checked with Malachy every day, sometimes twice or three times a day, hoping to hear something, but it always came to nothing.

A week passed after the end of the fair. Bridie made Dan his favorite Irish stew with plenty of tender lamb and his absolute favorite, hot flowery dumplings.

'Holy God, Bridie, is that what I think it is?' said Dan as he walked into the kitchen, taking a big sniff of the pot.

'It is love. Don't go making me think that you're deprived. Sit down and enjoy.'

'It's been one hell of a year this year, Bridie. I'd say we broke all records.' Dan tucked in, slurping down one mouthful after another, interrupting himself only to bring Bridie up to date. 'We should be able to clear off the car loan and a good chunk of the mortgage. Maybe even bring it down to more acceptable levels.'

'That's great, Dan. You deserve it after all the hard work you put into it.'

'The whole town does well at this time of the year. I know all the businesses are more than happy.' He polished off his plate by mopping up the soup with a large chunk of warm homemade bread just out of the oven. 'God, Bridie, that was great. I'm one very happy man.'

'Why don't you go inside and pour yourself a whiskey? Maybe you should have one of those cigarettes you're not supposed to be smoking but the whole town knows you are!'

Dan cocked one eye at her mockingly. 'Hold the phone. Send in the cops. Just a cotton-pickin' moment here. Bridie Robinson, would I be right in assuming that you want to ask me for something? Or am I the total idiot you think I am?'

'Dan, that's a terrible thing to say, me here looking after you and you suspecting something underhanded is afoot.'

'Go on.'

Bridie put on her cutest, most roguish smile and cast her rich brown eyes at him, blinking with comic disdain.

'Ah, I hate it when you do that. Come on, out with it, girl.'

'Well, there is a little something I wanted to discuss with you.'

'Humph. And there was I thinking that this wasn't my last meal before the gallows.'

'Remember I told you about the little orphan?'

'Yes,' said Dan in a *where is this leading to?* tone.

'The Gardaí have no clue who, or what, left the abandoned baby. I've been looking after him in the hospital, but obviously I can't continue to have him there. If that's the case, there's a good chance the authorities will take the boy and put him into a foster home somewhere. However, they can't do that if the boy is being cared for in a suitably qualified home – a qualified home being one recommended by the local clergy and Gardaí.'

'Which of course you've already checked out, and you've established that the Robinsons qualify on every score.'

'Correct. What a smart man you are, Dan Robinson.'

'Let me stop you there, Bridie, before I lose the will to live. Yes, I agree that we should take in said orphan. Yes, I agree that it is totally your responsibility and that I will have nothing to do with its rearing. Yes, I agree that I can go now and have said cigarette together with said whiskey – said I.'

'Dan Robinson, I love you.'

'Yeah, yeah, yeah. I'm outta here.'

With that they embraced and gave each other a big kiss on the lips.

Dan checked himself outside, drew out a cigarette, and puffed away heartily, thinking and thanking the sergeant for marking his cards in advance and telling him that Bridie was probably going to land it on him. He didn't mind anyway. He trusted Bridie to make the correct decision, and it was far from his area of expertise to talk about orphaned babies. He had more orphaned drunks to take care of and assign to their rightful owners after the week that was.

So it was that in the middle of October 1986 – as Halley's Comet bid its farewell to planet earth, saying adieu until another seventy-six years had elapsed – that the orphan boy now known as Sean entered the world of the Robinson family, meeting his new sister, Molly, and his older brother, Kevin, for the first time. He looked around him and gurgled as if he knew that this was his destiny, that here he would be cared for and loved – until faith decided he was ready to do what he was meant to do.

The first wise man.

Judge Conran looked down at the day's list of vagrants and vagabonds that were due to be presented to him in his court. It was always this busy for a couple of weeks following the end of the fair. This was a period when he earned the money the state paid him. His court consisted of him and his clerk – and whoever Sergeant Malachy brought before him.

There were two large tables and a number of chairs. Judge Conran had his own office at the back, and there were two adjoining rooms to hold the defendants or for people to use to discuss matters between themselves.

It was always the same misfits, the same people who were drink driving and driving without tax and insurance. There was also the usual list of the Finnerty tribe. The judge must have seen the entire family this past week as they were marched into his court. He saw that today he had the mother lode of the Finnerty clan coming in – none other than Joe Finnerty himself, the leader of the pack. He had been accused of causing bodily harm to an assortment of people, mostly travelers like themselves. Doubtless it would be impossible to have any witnesses because they'd be afraid for their lives testifying against any of the Finnertys. Anyway, the travelling community preferred to settle their own disputes. That was all very well, until they encroached on the local population.

'Bring in the first accused,' Judge Conran told his clerk.

Two hours skipped by as the judge issued decrees, sentences, and fines. He tended to turn a blind eye to most things if he thought that they were purely drink related, knowing that he probably wouldn't see the defendants for another year.

Next up was Joe Finnerty. Sergeant Malachy – as the judge referred to him, not by his full name of Malachy Brown – brought in a handcuffed Joe Finnerty and stood beside him as the clerk read the charges.

'On the night of October third, the accused was alleged to have caused the destruction of part of the premises known as Meaney's Public House in the main street. He was also involved in a public disorder fracas on the main street, where he was arrested.'

That was the first charge. The clerk took his seat. Judge Conran asked, 'Have you anything to say in your defense?'

'Naw-thin',' muttered Finnerty.

'Joe Finnerty, I see you also have two other charges against you on this sheet. Every year it's the same with you people. I've had all of your family before me this past week, and not one of you seems the slightest bit remorseful over your shocking behavior.'

Joe Finnerty gave a smirk and looked out the window, ignoring the proceedings.

'I'll tell you what I'm going to do with you,' continued the judge. 'I know there's no point in putting you into jail, as it's probably a lot more comfortable than what you're used to. So I'm giving you twenty-four hours to pack up your caravans or whatever you're transporting yourselves in nowadays and leave this town. Otherwise, I'll not only have you arrested for vagrancy, but I'll throw the whole lot of your wretched family in prison – and you will go to Mountjoy Prison up in Dublin. We'll see how you like it there. In addition, you'll pay a fine of twenty-thousand euros to cover court costs and damages. Failure to pay will result in your immediate incarceration.'

Joe Finnerty started to shout out obscenities, but the judge brought down his gavel and ordered the bailiff and the sergeant to escort him into a side room. The judge told his clerk he was taking a recess and would be back in a half hour.

Later that evening, the judge called into Dan's for his usual tipple before going home. He loved the atmosphere, and it was the only place where he could calm himself down. He made his way into his usual snug part of the lounge. Dan was already on his way with a glass of Paddy and a pint.

'Good evening, Judge. How was your day?'

'Terrible day altogether, Dan,' he said as he took a slurp of the pint, licked his lips, and raised his whiskey glass. 'Slainte, Dan.'

'Slainte, Judge. Tell me what happened.'

'It's like every year, as you know – the same faces, the same lowlifes, and of course the usual drunks with their stupid, but sometimes funny, shenanigans. Except this year I had more than enough Finnertys to keep me busy. They're a bad lot. They bring the rest of the travelling community down with them. I never have too much trouble with the others, always the Finnertys.'

'I believe that fella Joe Finnerty was causing all sorts of trouble throughout the town all week'

'He was to be sure,' replied the judge. 'How come they never come near your place, Dan?'

'They did one year, but I ran them. Let's say I had to use a little bit of brute force to explain my reasoning. I also enlisted a little help.'

'I'd love to see the back of them for good. I've ordered them to leave the town by this time tomorrow, but I know they'll just ignore me, forcing my hand. They know I don't have the power to move them along that quickly, as I'd have to get the authorities to approve, file procedural papers, and a ton of other stuff. In addition, if I can't get any witnesses to any of their crimes, it could drag on for months, if not years. They need to be taught a lesson – a damn good lesson.' The judge knocked back his whiskey and breathed a sigh.

'I might be able to help out there, Judge. There's somebody – not a million miles from where you sit – who has no love for the Finnerty tribe. I could have a word and see if he can talk to them on the town's behalf.'

'I can't be a party to any wrongdoing, Dan. You know that.'

'This wouldn't go anywhere, Judge. A little persuasion might be all that's needed,' assured Dan.

'I'll be off, Dan. Thanks for listening to my woes.'

'Any time, Judge.'

Dan waited until the judge was out of sight. He walked into the bar and called Boxer. The big man in the corner was playing cards with three others. He looked up at the sound of his name, saw that it was Dan, and made his way over to the counter.

'What's up, Dan?'

'Your old friends the Finnertys are encamped out the road and have been causing a lot of trouble. Have you heard anything?'

'They'll be no friends of mine, and well you know it. I know they're at old Willie's farm, about six or seven trucks. I hear they're thinking of maybe settling there.'

'We can't let that happen. I hear the judge has ordered them to be gone by tomorrow night. Perhaps a few words in Joe Finnerty's ear might push them along.'

'I hear what you're saying, Dan. Let me see what I can do.'

Dan had known Boxer, as he was affectionately called, for the past twenty years. He had been a decent professional boxer in his day. He was burly, about six feet two, and had a right hook that could floor any man to this day. It was Boxer whom Dan used to help rid him of the Finnertys using his bar as their local. Dan's was known as the headquarters of Boxer and his men, and Dan had no problem with that. Dan was the only one who had stood up to Boxer, and he felt he had Boxer's respect. He knew Boxer lived a life of petty crime, but he never abused his position with Dan's place. As a result, Dan never had anything stolen from his property. He would also wipe his slate clean every now and again for the sake of good public relations.

Bridie had come home early from work. She wanted to spend time with her children and baby Sean. It had been three weeks since she had found Sean.

Sergeant Malachy said there was still no word whatsoever about anybody looking for an abandoned child. Malachy had managed to keep it out of the public domain, a result being that none of the local or national newspapers or media had picked up on it. Ireland was a small country, and something like this would have been big news. Malachy had told Bridie that he couldn't conceal the story for much longer, that she had better start preparing herself for having the baby taken by the authorities.

She looked into baby Sean's blue eyes. She reckoned that his eyes were going to remain blue, even though most babies' eyes changed color. He gurgled and smiled at her, without a care in his tiny world. *What will become of him?* she thought. She was still cradling him when Dan came home.

'Huh, Bridie, you're home early!'

'I know, Dan. I wanted to see the children since I haven't been a good mother for the past few weeks.'

Dan bent down and kissed her. 'Nonsense. You're a great mother. You've been run off your feet with the new baby and the hospital and all the other stuff.' He looked at her and saw she was in another world looking at the new baby. 'Bridie, don't be getting yourself too attached to that little critter. You know it's only temporary. Have they found out anyone yet?'

'Not a thing, Dan.' She looked at Dan, then at the baby.

'What's on your mind, girl?' asked Dan, knowing that he was about to be ambushed again.

'Sergeant Malachy told me that he has to make it public over the coming days. I wanted to ask you something. Now, before you say anything, hear me out.' Bridie laid the baby down in Molly's crib, pulled up a chair beside Dan, and took his hand.

'This looks serious,' he said as he puckered one eyebrow.

'Dan, I love you. You know that. When I see what someone has done to this baby, my heart cries out for them, especially the mother. There's not a woman born who would abandon her child unless there was something terribly, terribly wrong. I feel it's a gift from God that made me be there to look after this child. You know that we can't have any more children after the complications with having Molly. We're both more than happy to have been blessed with two beautiful children when a lot of people cannot have any. Now this little creature has landed at our doorstep. It's as if we were meant to look after him. I can't explain it. I love him, Dan, as much as I love Kevin and wee Molly. I want to look after him, but I know it's practically impossible. Can you help me?. Can we find out if we can adopt him?'

Dan crumpled the tablecloth he was fiddling with. He stared out the window. After what seemed like an hour to Bridie, he said, 'Bridie, my answer is no. It's a totally foolish mission to be giving yourself. You have to get this notion from your head. I know you. I know that me saying this will tear you apart until you hound me into submission. But my answer is still no.'

Bridie went to say something, but Dan raised his hand, demanding quiet and saying, 'Before you say anything else, I want you to seriously think about what I'm saying. It's a stupid thought to be entertaining. At the same time, you asked me if I would help you, and my answer to that question is yes, of course I'll help any way I can. I love you, and I don't want you getting all hot and bothered over this. I'll make enquiries, but remember, as soon as I reach a dead end, it's a dead end for both of us – understood?'

'Dan Robinson, I adore you,' said Bridie as she jumped across his lap and planted kisses all over his face.

'Enough.' He smiled as he gently pushed her away. 'You need to tell me everything you know about the adoption process and what we can expect.'

'You're right, Dan; it's not going to be easy. It can take years to get approval, and before that you have to go through the mill. There will be the applications, the interviews, cross-checking, references, medicals, God knows what else. The main thing is to try to get a stay of execution for baby Sean, to somehow try to have the authorities approve us as his guardians, at least until the adoption process is completed. At least if we could be his official guardians, then we could prove to the authorities what good parents we were while we were minding him. Then who knows? They might grant us approval to adopt him. Wouldn't that be great?'

'Don't go running ahead of yourself, Bridie. That's a long way down the line. I think I'll have a word with the judge next time I see him. Now, what's for dinner?'

It was around midnight when four vans pulled into Willie O'Brien's farm. They screeched to a halt once they'd reached the first of the caravans that was parked in the field. Four men jumped out of each van, each holding some sort of weapon. There were no guns, just iron bars, hurleys, and chains.

Boxer came to the front of the group, shouting, 'Get out here, Finnerty! Don't keep me waiting or I'll come in there and wreck your place!'

The doors of two of the caravans burst open as each member of the Finnerty clan came running. They stopped when they saw that they were outnumbered. Joe Finnerty made his way up front.

'What do you want?'

'We're here to make sure that you leave Ballinasloe and never come back. Now, you can drive out of here with your miserable bodies in one piece, or we can ship the body parts to you.' Some of Boxer's men laughed.

'We're not going anywhere. You'd better do what you came to do.'

'I see you're still hiding behind women and children. Why can't we settle this like real men? How about you and me fight until the death? If I'm dead, my men will leave without bothering you again. If I kill you, then your lot will move out of here and never come back. Does that make any sense to you, you stupid, pathetic excuse for a man?'

Joe Finnerty was incensed. Nobody ever talked to him like that. He was the leader of his clan. He would deal with it and nobody else.

'If that's the way you want to see your maker, then don't let me stop you.' Finnerty turned to his brothers. 'You hear what I'm telling you? This is a fight to the death. We'll be staying here for good once I get rid of him.'

'And you'll be leaving here for good when I win!' shouted Boxer at the Finnertys.

Joe ran at Boxer, toppling him over, and landed a number of heavy punches as they rolled along the muddy ground. Boxer needed to get both of them on their feet; that way he could use his boxing knowledge to fight him. As long as they were on the ground, he was at a disadvantage. Finnerty was smaller but built like a house. He was wiry, and he knew how to fight.

Boxer managed to get upright. He dodged another of Finnerty's swings and landed a punch to his lower belly. It wasn't taut, and Finnerty felt it. Boxer dodged Finnerty's first kick but got caught with his second, which landed on his shin. It hurt, but he ignored the pain as he saw Finnerty pick up a shovel. He charged at Boxer, crashing the shovel over his back.

Boxer, with all of the strength he could muster, swung around and was fortunate to land a left hook on Finnerty's jaw. He followed through with his favorite right hook, and Finnerty went down. Boxer had always noticed that Joe Finnerty had a glass jaw. He could see it as sure as he'd notice a bad pint of Guinness just by looking at it. Finnerty was not going to get up. He was down and out. Boxer had no intention of killing anybody. That was not the way he did business.

'Now, pack your stuff and get out of here; otherwise, I'll finish him off. Do you hear me?'

The rest of the family moved back into their homes.

'My men will escort you out of the town, and you'd better not be seen around here again!' Boxer shouted again and instructed his men to make sure they left.

Dan checked the invoices from the breweries. He had gone through some stock. Guinness was always the front-runner in these parts, although Smithwick's was putting in a good run nowadays as well as the lagers. The younger people seemed to have more of a taste for the European lagers. He didn't care, as long as they continued drinking in his bar. He was writing out checks when Boxer walked over to him.

'You won't be having any more trouble from the Finnertys. We had words.'

'Did you get hurt, or did you hurt people?' asked Dan as he perused Boxer's face, which seemed pretty much intact.

'A bit of both. Let's say Joe Finnerty came out the worst of it. I'd say his pride is probably more hurt. He won't be living down the embarrassment of it all for a very long time.'

'Thanks for that, Boxer. I'll send over a tray of drinks for your lads – on the house, of course.'

A few hours later, the judge walked in for his usual. Dan told Jimmy to look after things while he spoke with the judge. Dan reminded him to give Boxer and the boys whatever they wanted on the house. Dan pulled a pint and measured out a Paddy, the judge's favorite tipple.

'I might have a bit of news for you, Judge.'

'What sort of news?'

'Just that you'll be having no more trouble from those Finnerty boys for now and for the future.'

'Holy God, that's great news, Dan. Should I be worried about any reprisals?'

'Not a bit of it. Let's say there was a meeting of heads, and all was resolved without any bloodshed.'

'I can't tell you what a relief that is to hear. I've been worried sick all day as the deadline approached. I can't thank you enough, Dan.'

Dan watched as the judge, obviously very relieved, knocked back the remainder of his stout. Picking his moment, Dan continued, 'Can I bounce something off you, Judge?'

'Of course. Fire away.'

'Have you heard about the abandoned baby at the hospital?'

The judge put his empty glass back down, glanced up at Dan, which was the signal to start pouring a replacement. 'Sergeant Malachy told me something about it all right. Why? What's the problem?'

Dan explained everything to the judge, how Bridie had found the baby, nursed him, and looked after him. He also explained how Bridie had become very attached to him and that, from what they knew, there were very strict laws about adoption. However, he wondered if there was any way that he and Bridie could be assigned as legal guardians before the authorities dragged everything through their rules and regulations. That way, he and Bridie could make a formal application to become the adoptive parents in the future.

'I see,' said the judge as Jimmy brought in his replacement pint. He scratched his balding head as he went into thoughtful mode, as if he had just been presented with a murder case that would make Agatha Christie proud. 'Sounds to me like you have a religious and a political problem there, Dan.'

'What do you mean?'

'I mean; I can very easily assign both of you as legal guardians. That might hold off the authorities for a year or so. You're going to need to pull a lot of religious and political strings to shortcut the adoptive process.'

'I know the parish priest very well,' interjected Dan.

'We're going to need a bigger piece for this game of chess,' said the judge. 'We're going to need a bishop.'

Then there were three.

Bishop O'Malley looked out through his large bay window, down the driveway, and over the fields. It always looked so beautiful at this time of the year. The cattle looked well fed, and the colors along the rolling hills were simply breathtaking. He wondered where it had all gone awry. Years ago, there had never been a question of any impropriety by a member of the clergy. Now it appeared to be happening on a weekly basis somewhere in the world throughout the Catholic church. He was disgusted that it was happening, but more disgusted that it had recently become a part of Irish society. Was there nobody keeping a check on these scoundrels who had invaded the church? Were there no checks and balances on clergymen who had the people's trust? Now he had one of his parish priests in his waiting room, probably going to tell him of some scandal or other that he should have known about. Parish priests, clergymen, bishops! They were all involved.

There was a knock on the door. The secretary announced the arrival of Father Crowe.

'Send him in,' said the bishop.

'Good morning, Your Grace,' said a meek Father Crowe.

'Good morning, Jim. A great morning it is. We are indeed blessed. Tell me, what it is that concerns you that you couldn't tell me over the phone?

'Your Grace, I don't know where to start. I'm being subjected to the most horrible ridicule by someone in my congregation. I want to assure you that I am wholly innocent of these very false accusations.'

Bishop O'Malley turned towards the window. *Here we are, then. A scandal of the highest order. My own parish priest involved in some pedophile act, and I'm supposed to deal with this perversion,* he thought to himself.

'What are you trying to tell me, Jim?'

'My housekeeper is suing the parish, accusing me of raping her.' Father Crowe looked pleadingly at the bishop.

Holy God, it's only a rape case with another adult, he thought. Then he checked himself. *What am I thinking? I'm saying to myself that it's 'only' a rape. I'm happy because it's not a case involving children!*

'Tell me exactly what happened,' said the bishop.

'My housekeeper has threatened me with disclosure to the press, alleging that I raped her.' Father Crowe looked down at the floor, unable to look the bishop in the eyes.

'Just a moment. Isn't Mrs. McKenna your housekeeper?'

'She is – and was. Unfortunately, she was taken ill a couple of months ago, and I needed a replacement. I ended up with Martha Maguire. I swear on my mother's grave that I did nothing she purports, Your Grace.' This time he looked pleadingly into the bishop's eyes.

'Calm down, Jim. Give me the sordid details.'

'There's nothing sordid to report, Your Grace. She quite literally came into my office and told me she would be seeing a solicitor unless I paid her to keep quiet. She accused me of raping her. I'm at my wit's end, Your Grace. Tell me what I should do.'

At that moment, a car pulled into the driveway. Bishop O'Malley turned to the noise. He saw Judge Conran alight from his car. *What does he want?* thought the bishop. Father Crowe waited for the bishop to speak.

'Wait here a moment, Father. I need to speak to somebody. I won't be long.'

The bishop stepped out into the hallway just as the judge was being led in by the secretary. 'Judge Conran, what are you doing this far from town?'

'Bishop, I'm sorry to come unannounced, but I have some pressing business I need to discuss with you.'

'Well, come into my study. We might be able to help each other.'

Judge Conran and Bishop O'Malley sorted out their seating arrangements. 'Who goes first?' asked the judge.

Bishop O'Malley thought about Father Crowe in the other room. He felt that he had gotten himself into this mess; he could wait.

'You go first,' said the bishop.

'I have a very dear friend in Dan Robinson, who owns Dan's Bar in the town.'

'I know of Dan. He's a good man, does a lot for the community.'

'Indeed. He has a problem not of his own choosing. There was an abandoned baby left on the doorstep of the hospital a few weeks back. Dan's wife, Bridie, has taken care of the infant boy ever since. They have two other young children. Dan tells me his wife wants to look after the child as guardian in the hope that she might be able to adopt it in the future. Is there any way you can assist, Your Grace?'

'Adoption rules are very strict. I hadn't heard anything about this child. Have the police done their work?'

'Yes, Sergeant Malachy has investigated and concluded that nobody is looking for the child. He says that it is a bone fide adoption case.'

'You do know that I'm on the adoption board? Of course you do; otherwise, you wouldn't be here,' the bishop asked and answered himself.

'It's a terrible sad thing to see a baby abandoned like this. I've issued the guardianship document, assigning the child under the Robinsons' care,' said the judge.

'I don't have a problem with that,' said the bishop. 'It would certainly help their adoptive case if they were seen to have looked after the child while the process went through. Let me see what I can do. But tell the Robinson family that it's not a certainty at all that they could railroad themselves to the top of the queue.'

'They realize that, Your Grace. They are under no illusions whatsoever. I do want to help them if at all possible. I'd appreciate it if you could help in any way. Now how can I help you?'

The bishop stood up and rounded his desk alongside the judge. Looking seriously at the judge, he continued, 'I have one of my parish priests in the next room who has been accused of rape by his temporary housekeeper. Can you guide me?'

'Who is the priest, and who is the housekeeper?'

'He's a Father Crowe, and the housekeeper is a certain Mrs. or Miss – I'm not sure which – Martha Maguire.'

'Martha Maguire! I know her well. She's been before me on at least a couple of occasions. A poisoned chalice – excuse me, Your Eminence – if ever there was one. I'll be able to deal with her.'

'Do you think we'll have any problem with her?'

'Not a bit of it. She'd try anything, that one, to wangle money out of a stone. You'll hear no more from that one, I assure you; otherwise, she'll be in jail somewhere far away, or my name is not Judge Conran.'

'Thank you, Judge, and I promise I will give the Robinsons' case my own personal attention. Bear in mind that even if I am successful in getting the adoption board to agree with me about letting the Robinsons be the adoptive parents, the road to final adoption will need the assistance of someone in the political field. These things have a way of getting into the public domain.'

'Already on to it,' nodded the judge.

The meeting coming to its conclusion, both men rose from their chairs and made for the main hall door. Bishop O'Malley bid the judge farewell and entered the other room to see Father Crowe still in a state of distress.

'Your problem is sorted, Jim. Arrangements are being made to have this woman – Maguire – ostracized from the community. Make sure this sort of thing never happens again. You know the unwritten rules – hire them old and nonfrisky.'

'It won't happen again, Your Grace; you can be sure of that. Thank you.'

'Was there anything else?'

'No, Your Grace, that was it. I'll be off now.'

Judge Conran walked into Dan's Bar the following night. He motioned to Dan to come over. Dan pulled a pint and let it settle.

'Good evening, Judge. How can I help you?'

'It's not me who's needing help, Dan. I have some news for you. I was with the bishop yesterday, and he's going to work on your case. Here's the official document assigning the young baby over to both of you as guardians. Have you got a half hour to spare?' enquired the judge.

'Why?'

'Frank O'Connor, the Fianna Fail TD, is at his constituency office up the way. I thought it would be an opportune moment to put our baby case forward.'

'Jimmy, use that pint that's settled. I'll be back in a half hour,' Dan said as he grabbed his jacket and followed the judge out the door.

Frank O'Connor represented the Fianna Fail Party in County Galway and had done so for the past two elections. His rival, Mark Donovan, represented the party currently in power, known as Fine Gael. Dan and the judge made their way to Frank's office, which was situated in the main street. They saw him at his desk, knocked, and walked in.

'Judge Conran and Dan Robinson, as I live and breathe,' said Frank enthusiastically.

Dan was always amazed at every politician's ability to remember names and faces. Frank's face was easy to remember because he was constantly publicizing himself. He made sure to have his picture in either the national newspapers or at least the local one whenever and wherever possible.

'To what do I owe this pleasure?' Frank said.

'Dan and I have a request to make of you,' said the judge.

'I am your humble servant.'

'Humility is not one of the characteristics I would attribute to your good self, Frank!' retorted the judge.

'Is business good with you, Dan? And how is your lovely wife, Bridie?'

'All good, Mr. O'Connor.'

'Please, call me Frank, and take a seat.'

'You probably heard that Bridie is looking after a wee abandoned orphan boy,' said Dan.

'Aye, I did hear something or other about that.'

'Dan's Bridie has been doing a wonderful job of nursing the wee thing, so much so that I've granted the Robinsons legal guardianship and custody of the boy until such time as adoption procedures can be finalized. I'll cut straight to the chase. Bridie and Dan would like to legally adopt the boy.' Frank went to say something, but the judge raised his hand and continued talking. 'Before you say anything, let me finish. I have spoken to the bishop. He has said he will do whatever he can to investigate the possibility of making the Robinsons the adoptive parents, providing it doesn't interfere with their regulations. Meanwhile, we need you to see what you can do to cover any legal or political loose ends. Is that something you can help us with?'

'I see now. An interesting dilemma indeed,' Frank mused. 'While I consider your problem, could I ask Dan something on my behalf?'

'Of course. Fire away,' said the judge.

'You know that the Fine Gael Party is just about still in power. That eejit Mark Donovan is barely hanging onto his seat in these parts.'

'I'd say he has a good hold on the votes in these parts regardless of how Fine Gael is doing in the rest of the country,' corrected Dan.

'Whatever. Anyways, I was going to ask you if you had ideas about how I could amass an additional two to three percent of the votes in Ballinasloe and surrounding areas. If you could help me in this regard, it should just about swing the forthcoming election my way,' O'Connor concluded.

'While we consider your problem, could you get back to ours?' interrupted the judge, winking over at Dan.

'Surely, surely. Now, let me see. I'd say – depending on the results of the next election' – he looked straight at Dan – 'that I might be able to do something. Considering you'd have the bishop on your side, that should be enough influence to swing any naysayers in our direction. But it's going to take some time – at least until after the next election,' he emphasized.

'Okay, then,' said the judge. 'Let's put out some soundings. We'll get back to you about your problem as soon as we come up with something worthwhile.'

'Aye, and I'll put the wheels in motion on my end. Is there anything else I can do for you?'

'No, that's fine, Frank. Good luck in the election anyway,' said Dan as both he and the judge made their exit.

Walking back to the bar, Dan asked the judge how in Dickens' name he could possibly help that idiot get reelected.

'I'm sure you and God will come up with some solution. I put my faith in you; you put yours in God. Good night, Dan.'

'Good night, Judge, and thanks for everything.'

With that, the judge waved, and Dan went back to work.

They followed the star.

The next few months went by quickly. Bridie divided her time between the hospital and home, changing her hours so that she started work earlier and got home earlier. That way, she was able to help Kevin with his homework, play with Molly, and cuddle little Sean – all with Rosie's help, of course.

Bridie never stopped appreciating Rosie. She too had been an orphan, having known two sets of parents. Bridie had never known Rosie to be angry or to lose her head in any way. She was a terrific cook. Bridie hoped that she did well at college because she knew she'd love to be a nurse herself one day. Bridie thought that she'd have no hesitation in hiring Rosie at the hospital. She had known her all of her life, and she found it hard to believe that she was going to reach twenty-one in the next week or so.

'What are your plans for your big birthday, Rosie?'

'Nothing much, Bridie. A few of the girls and meself are going out for a meal, probably over to Galway, then a few drinks and maybe a nightclub somewhere.'

'Is there anything special you'd like? I don't know what to get for you.'

'I don't need anything, Bridie. I'm more than happy here.'

'Aw, come on, Rosie, that's not fair. I want to get you something nice, something that you'll use.'

'Let me think about it,' said Rosie as she took young Mollie up the stairs to her bed.

'Fair enough,' said Bridie, all the time thinking, *what would I do without Rosie?*

Dan was getting ready for the five o'clock rush hour. He was stocking the shelves with Jimmy's help. He stood up to be greeted by, 'How are you, Dan?'

Turning around, Dan saw the Liddy brothers standing side by side.

'And to what do I owe the dubious pleasure of having my two favorite auditors visiting me on this cold night?' asked Dan as he put the empty beer case to one side.

'Dan, we have a proposition to put to you. Is there anywhere we can talk?' asked Paraic, the older of the two.

The brothers had a small auditing firm in the town. They were local lads, both in their mid-thirties. Their father had started the accountancy firm when he had qualified. He was now retired, leaving the business to his two sons.

'Sure. Come into the snug,' offered Dan. He poured a Club Orange soda for Mark Liddy and a cup of coffee for Paraic. 'Now, what's this proposition you have for me?' asked Dan as they all sat down beside the flaming fire in the snug.

'We've managed to identify a two-hundred-acre plot of land on the outskirts of the town,' said Paraic.

'We were wondering if you'd like to join us in our venture, Dan,' said Mark Liddy enthusiastically.

'What are you planning to do with it?' asked Dan.

'That's the great thing about it. We're not planning anything at all – in the short term. Longer term, we see a great future for a housing development,' remarked Paraic.

'You see,' Paraic continued, 'we figure that the land is only going to go up in value as the population increases, especially with how popular the annual fair is. There's something like twenty thousand people a year visiting from all over the world.'

'And this number is only going to increase,' interrupted his brother, Mark, excitedly.

'And how much is this venture costing?' asked Dan.

'We estimate that if all three of us contribute fifty thousand euros apiece, that should secure it,' said Paraic.

'Not only that Dan,' added Mark, 'if we manage to get planning permission for a housing development, the value will soar.'

'Which is why we came to see you in the first place, Dan,' said Paraic.

'I thought there was a catch, all right,' said Dan.

'No catch at all, Dan,' said Mark. 'You see; we know that you have the political contacts to see through the approval. You should see a doubling of your money in next to no time.'

Dan pondered his auditors' move. He had always respected their judgment since they had steered his business and tax affairs wisely over the years. They seemed keen enough, and doubtless they had done their homework on the suitability of the venture for housing. *It just might kill two birds with one stone,* thought Dan.

'I'll tell you what I'll do,' said Dan.

The two Liddys propped up in their seats with their ears pricked. 'What's that, Dan?' said Paraic.

'If I'm to come on board with this project – and bearing in mind that I'd have the important work of trying to get planning permission – I feel that the split as it currently stands is very much in your favor.'

'What would you have in mind, Dan?'

'I was thinking more like a thirty-thousand-euro investment on my part and a sixty-thousand investment by each of you, seeing that my work brings in the added value.'

'You're using very complicated words there, Dan,' said Mark.

'I've been reading a lot lately,' retorted a smiling Dan. 'If I don't bring in the planning approval, then I'll pay my equal share – how's that?'

The two Liddy brothers had a discussion amongst themselves. 'Agreed' said Paraic.

'Let me see what I can do. Now, give me the details of the site and where exactly you are in the negotiations,' said Dan as he grabbed a sheet of paper from the bar and started to write.

Today was Rosie's birthday. Bridie made sure she was there to greet Rosie as she arrived.

'Aw, Bridie, you shouldn't have,' smiled Rosie when she saw the birthday card and the gift-wrapped package on the table. They hugged each other.

'Happy birthday, Rosie girl. We love you and hope you have a wonderful twenty-first.'

'Thanks, Bridie. I'm really looking forward to my day.' Rosie ripped the wrapping paper to reveal a new gym outfit. 'Oh, Bridie, I badly needed this. Thank you so much.'

'I know you love working out, and I heard you discussing the other day how badly you needed a new outfit.'

Bridie made them both a cup of tea. As Rosie sipped on hers, Bridie said, 'Rosie, I've been doing a lot of thinking. You know I said that I wanted to give you something special for your twenty-first?'

'Bridie, I don't want anything – really. This is wonderful, and you do more than enough for me as it is.' Rosie smiled.

'No, listen to me. I know you don't earn that much working for us, and at the same time it must be difficult enough trying to pay your rent and run your car – so – we would love if you could live here with us rent free. That way you have some extra money in your pocket. Of course, we'd still pay you what we're paying you now. How does that sound?'

Rosie looked shocked. Then a big smile came over her face, and she jumped up and hugged Bridie.

'Oh, thank you, Bridie. There's nothing I'd like better. I promise I'll do extra work around the house and everything,' she said excitedly.

'You'll do the exact same as you're doing. You do a brilliant job.'

'What about Dan? He doesn't mind, does he?'

'In Dan's world, he thinks you're already living here. You don't have to concern yourself.'

They both laughed and thought they'd better get the children ready.

'Frank O'Connor speaking. How can I help you?'

'Frank, it's Dan Robinson.'

'Good man Dan. What can I do for you?'

'I may have a little bit of good news for you.'

Dan outlined his plan. He told Frank about his investment with the Liddy brothers and how they were proposing to build a huge housing development on the outskirts of town. The little matter of planning permission for their venture needed to be sorted out. It didn't take much for Frank to see the benefits for his side, especially when Dan told him that he would send all of the publicity his way, which would be perfect timing for the forthcoming election. Dan said that the *Connaught Tribune* would splash his photo all over the West of Ireland as being the 'man who saved the West,' not only for all of the new construction it would create but also for the hundreds of jobs it would bring into the community alongside the additional business.

'Holy God, Dan, that would be just the thing I'd need to put that Fine Gael Donovan fella back in his box.' *He'd never get reelected again,* Frank thought to himself.

'I hear what you're saying, Dan. I'll get working on the planning right away. The election looks like it's going to happen in March. The whole party is all primed up and ready for action. The coalition of Fine Gael and the Labor Party looks like it's going to end in divorce, so every elected representative is vital. If I can bring in my side of the vote, I'll be a hero to the party. Holy God, I might even get a cabinet position!' said Frank enthusiastically.

'I'm sure you will,' agreed Dan. 'Now, don't be forgetting your side of our little baby bargain, if you get my meaning?'

'Mum's the word, Dan. Rest assured, if this works out, then you won't be wanting from me.'

They hung up.

Frank wasted no time in putting the wheels into motion. He travelled to Dublin every week over the next few months. The party did everything they needed to do to make sure that the planning process was approved. Dan and the Liddys met with him on numerous occasions to agree on their plans. Frank might have suspected that his new partners had no intention of building anything because none of them had the financial backing to develop something this big, but he never mentioned anything. His only concern was in telling the electorate how wonderful he was working on their behalf in this way.

It was late January when Dan read about it as the *Tribune* blared:

O'Connor brings four hundred new jobs to Ballinasloe!

The article went on to exclaim that if only for Frank O'Connor, the Fianna Fail representative for the area, the new housing development would never have taken place. He had used all of his influence to bring the project to the town. The article expounded on his attributes in a way that a reader would think that he was the leader of the party. It quoted Frank's previous great works on behalf of the community. It signed off with the obligatory photo of the ribbon-cutting ceremony, showing a beaming Frank O'Connor side by side with the developers, local well-known publican Dan Robinson and the accountancy firm of Liddy and Liddy. Dan thought he should have worn a tie for the photograph as he put the paper down and finished his breakfast.

Six months later, it transpired that Frank O'Connor didn't need an extra two to three percent of the votes because his election was an easy victory, not only for him but for the entire party across the country. Fianna Fail pushed the sitting government aside in a landslide victory that put their leader, one Charles J. Haughey, into power, leaving the sitting party – Fine Gael, led by Garret Fitzgerald – in total disarray.

A couple of months had gone by when Dan arrived home to find Bridie and Rosie laughing and working busily in the kitchen as the children played and generally made a lot of noise.

'Could I have everybody's attention please?' said Dan in a loud voice, which seemed to shock-calm even the children so that everybody was looking in Dan's direction.

'What are you doing home so early, Dan?' asked Bridie with a concerned look on her face.

'I have a bit of news for you all. Take a seat, Bridie.' Dan made a place for himself at the head of the table.

'I'm busy, Dan. Say what it is you want to say so I can get the dinner ready.'

'I think you'll be needing a seat – you too, Rosie.'

Bridie and Rosie looked at each other, took their seats, and looked up at Dan.

'Is something wrong, Dan?' asked Bridie with a deep look of concern on her face.

'Quite the contrary,' said Dan. 'As they say on the TV, have I got news for you!' Dan continued, 'Remember you asked me to see if I could get help with the adoption process?'

'Yes,' said Bridie, nodding.

'Well, not only have I managed to get help, but I've got three gentlemen outside who have a little something for you. Now, stay where you are.'

Dan turned and walked out the door. Bridie turned to Rosie with a confused shrug of her shoulders. Dan reappeared within a minute or two followed by the judge, Frank O'Connor, and the bishop.

'Oh my God!' said Bridie, holding her hands to her lips. She stood and curtsied towards the bishop.

Dan beamed as if he were going to explode. 'Bridie, all of these fine gentlemen have . . .' – he paused, looked at the three men, and continued – 'assisted in seeing that we are now the legal parents of little Sean.'

Bridie screamed, ran towards Dan, and hugged him for all she was worth.

'I can't believe it. Is it true, Your Excellency?' Bridie asked, staring at the bishop.

'It most certainly is, Bridie. I'm delighted to say that the adoption board had no hesitation in seconding my proposal that a God-fearing, law-abiding, pillar-of-the-community-type family like the Robinsons would be more than suitable candidates to be the recommended adoptive parents for little orphan Sean. Where is the little fellow?'

Bridie turned to Sean, who was oblivious to all that was going on around him, dedicating his total attention instead to a hanging toy attached to the playpen.

'Here's the man of the hour,' Bridie said as she took the baby in her arms and presented him to the bishop.

'Bless him. He's a gorgeous child. I can understand why you were so determined to have him as your own.'

The judge made his way over to take Sean's little hand in his.

Then the bishop turned to Frank, saying, 'Hand me my bag over there by the mirror, Frank. Give me the phial of holy water and a little tin of incense.' He then turned to Bridie. 'Has the child been baptized?'

'No. I didn't want to presuppose that the mother was Catholic in the event that she materialized.'

'Quite right,' added the judge.

'Good, good. I want to bless the house and then baptize the child,' said the bishop as he took out a wafer of charcoal, lit it, and poured the incense over it, creating a plume of smoke. He then walked through the house blessing it and saying some prayers.

Bridie smiled a radiant smile at Dan. 'Dan Robinson, you never cease to amaze me, you know that?'

'I do, I do, Bridie girl. I suppose some dumplings would be out of the question?'

'You'll be eating dumplings until you explode.'

The judge felt through his pockets and produced a small golden necklace with a crucifix hanging from the weighted end. 'This is something my mother gave me. I found it before I left the house, and I thought it would be a nice keepsake for the infant.'

'Why, thank you so much, Judge. How sweet of you,' said Bridie as she took it and put it around Sean's neck.

'It's a bit too big for him just yet, but it's gorgeous,' enthused Bridie and Rosie at the same time.

Frank shuffled. 'I'm afraid I didn't bring anything, Bridie. I'll make sure to send something up during the week.'

'Not a bit of it, Mr. O'Connor. Don't be silly. I'm so elated about it all being legal. I don't need anything else, for sure.'

The bishop returned and took command of proceedings. 'I think we should all say a decade of the rosary, and then I'll start the baptism rite. Who'll be the godparents?'

Bridie looked around the room. 'I'd be never as proud if Rosie would be the godmother, and perhaps you, Judge, would be the godfather?'

'I'd be honored to do so,' said the judge.

Bridie looked at Rosie, who was wiping her tears. She sniffled a 'thank you' towards Bridie.

The bishop put on his vestments and started. 'Our Father, who art in heaven. . .. Hail Mary, full of grace, the Lord is with thee. . .. Glory be to the Father, the Son, and the Holy Spirit, as. . .. Amen.'

He then turned towards Dan and Bridie. 'What name do you give your child?'

'Sean James Robinson,' said Bridie.

Dan looked at her and smiled, knowing that his second name would be the new baby's too.

'What do you ask of God's church for Sean?'

'Baptism,' Bridie and Dan responded together.

'You have asked to have your child baptized. In doing so, you are accepting the responsibility of training him in the practice of the faith. It will be your duty to bring him up to keep God's commandments as Christ taught us, by loving God and our neighbor. Do you clearly understand what you are undertaking?'

'We do.'

The bishop turned towards the child. 'Sean, the Christian community welcomes you with great joy. In its name, I claim you for Christ, our Savior, by the sign of his cross. I now trace the cross on your forehead and invite your parents and godparents to do the same.'

The bishop concluded the ceremony with the anointing of baby Sean. Everybody stood in silence, and after a short prayer, the bishop said, 'I'd better be off. Congratulations, Dan and Bridie. I'm very happy for both of you.'

'Will you not stay for a quick one, Your Grace?' asked Dan.

'No time, Dan. Maybe some other time. Oh, by the way, I'd appreciate it if you kept my doing the ceremony under your hats. If the rest of the town hears I did your baptism, I'll be inundated with requests.'

They all smiled, assuring the bishop that mum was the word for all time.

'What about you, Judge, and you, Frank? What's your poison?'

'No, I have to be going too,' said Frank. 'Judge, you're driving me, remember! I have so much work to do. Did you hear I've been offered Agriculture, Dan?'

'Agriculture, by God. That's a huge promotion for you, Frank. Will you be based up in Dublin?' enquired Dan.

'Aye. I'll be up in the Department of Agriculture all the time from now on. I'm looking forward to it.'

With that, Frank led the judge, and both bid their fond farewells and best wishes.

'Oh, Dan, pour me a double whiskey, will you? I could do with it,' said Bridie as she sat down, totally drained and exhausted. Rosie said she'd get the children ready for bed as soon as she finished feeding them. 'Thanks, Rosie. I don't think I'd be able to do anything,' said Bridie as she knocked back a mouthful of whiskey, choked, and coughed.

'That seems to have hit the spot,' joked Dan as he reached over to Bridie, hugging her and whispering, 'Are you happy, girl?'

'Oh, Dan, I couldn't be happier.' She leaned on Sean's cot and smiled at him, saying, 'You are really ours, little fella. You are a gift from God.' Then she looked up at Dan. 'Are you sure it's all legal, Dan?'

He laughed, saying, 'When you have the triumvirate of the bishop, the judge, and the local minister for agriculture, I think you could safely assume that it's all pretty legal.' He raised his glass to

Sean, saying, 'You're one lucky boy to have a mother like Bridie.' He downed the last of his drink to the sounds of a gurgling, happy baby.

In the Temple.

It was a beautiful summer's day in July as Grandma Robinson gently lullabied baby Sean in her arms. *He'll be walking in next to no time,* she thought to herself.

'Dolores, you'll crush the living daylights out of little Sean. Let him breathe,' mused Bridie as she drew up a chair beside her mother-in-law.

'Dan tells me that you named him after my Sean. Is it true?'

'Of course. Granddad Robinson is looking down at him from heaven at this very moment.'

'Oh, Bridie, the child is truly a gift from God,' Dolores said, looking into his striking blue eyes.

'He surely is, Dolores; he surely is. Come on, I see me Mam and Dad arriving. Let's get this party under way.'

With that, everybody joined in the festivities. Bridie's parents showed their obvious delight at the new addition to the family. Judge Conran and Frank O'Connor turned up, the latter bearing gifts for every one of the Robinson family, including all of the other children and even the grandparents. *Never one to miss a trick,* thought Dan.

Frank made his way over to Dan and the judge. 'I'm sorry I'm so late bringing these, Dan. I hope you don't mind.'

'Not a bit of it, Frank. There was no need – really.'

Kevin and Molly screamed with delight at their new toys.

'Tell me, did you get any grief over the fact that we never developed the site?' asked Dan.

'Never a bit of it,' enthused Frank. 'In fact, rumor has it that we might be doubling the size of the site. I don't know where that rumor came from,' he said, winking.

'It's amazing how rumors spread, huh?' said Dan as he poured the judge another large one.

'Right. It's time to get these steaks on the barbeque. Give me a hand with these, lads,' said Dan as the judge and Frank tried to make themselves useful.

The nineties were as normal for the Robinsons as they were for everybody else growing up in those times. Everybody was simply trying to earn a living. Ireland was seeing the benefits of previous governments' investments in the technology sectors as companies from all over the world, especially the United States, set up their headquarters all over Ireland. There was Intel, Microsoft, Dell, Digital, and Apple, as well as the pharmaceutical giants such as Allergan, Pfizer, and Merck, all benefiting from the availability of highly educated personnel and in no small part to the huge taxation benefits of establishing their enterprises in Ireland.

Ireland had made a claim to their taxation uniqueness and had seen it through the European legislative bodies. The results were there for everybody to see. Unemployment went down, and immigration – instead of emigration – became the norm in the new Ireland. Tourism also increased, and the Ballinasloe horse fair reaped the benefits like everybody else. Dan was happy knowing that he could support his newly enlarged family. Visitors liked the coziness of his bar and lounge. It was always a family-oriented public house, serving good beer and wholesome foods.

Sean went from kindergarten to junior school with little effort and no drama, while Molly and Kevin were in their second and third years of secondary school respectively. All of them had celebrated their first Holy Communion, and Sean had his confirmation when he turned eleven. All of the children got on well together. There was nothing out of the ordinary. They had their fights and tantrums like every other kid.

Bridie had managed to shuffle her work schedule to enable her to do her duties as Matron and still manage to cater to all of her children. Rosie had gone on to nursing school, leaving Bridie to manage as best she could, shunting one child after another through school runs, child-minding, and what not. She always achieved what she needed to achieve regardless of the difficulties.

The Robinsons shared their good times and bad times equally – in their own personal lives when the children passed their school exams or won a medal in some sports event, in general terms when Ireland's footballers qualified for a major trophy like Italia '90, or when Nelson Mandela was released from prison that same year. They shared the sad and the bad times when Grandma Robinson passed away at the relatively young age of seventy-nine or when world events disclosed atrocities such as the genocide in Rwanda or when the world learned of the death of Princess Diana in 1997. Women, especially, shared shock and sadness watching the massive funeral that beamed across the world's televisions.

It was when Sean turned twelve that Bridie began to notice how different he was compared to both of her other children. It was around this time that she began to think back to that night when she found him outside of the hospital and nursing him through infancy to where he was today.

Sean had excelled in junior school. All of the teachers had great time for him, and all commented on how bright and accommodating he was. They all used the same adjective to describe him – *serene*. One day, as Bridie was waiting outside the school to collect Sean and Molly (Kevin was too old to be collected by his mum), one of the teachers surprised her as he knocked on her car window. She rolled down the passenger window.

'Mr. Sullivan. How are you?' she said, surprised since she rarely had any need to speak with him.

'Bridie, have you got a minute?' he asked as he opened the door and climbed in.

She smiled at his audacity in taking such a liberty before she had given him permission. She liked that aspect of Irish people's personality.

'I won't keep you long,' said Mr. Sullivan. 'I don't suppose you're aware of what happened during the week at school?'

Bridie displayed an anxious look. 'Did one of the children do something wrong?'

'No, nothing like that. In fact, quite the opposite. Extraordinary, I'd say. You see, as an exercise in religious doctrine, I had asked all of the children in your Sean's class to do an exercise on why they believe in God. I also asked them to ask their older brothers and sisters the same question and to write down their answers. If they didn't have any older siblings, they were to simply ask their parents. It's an exercise I give to all of the children every year. I was passing the senior class the following morning before school time began when I looked in because it was very quiet. I couldn't believe my eyes or my ears. There was your young Sean lecturing to the final-year students!'

Bridie looked at the teacher with wide eyes and amazement. 'What do you mean, lecturing?' she asked in mock surprise.

The teacher continued, 'Apparently, he had asked his older brother Kevin, who's in the senior class, if he could ask all of his classmates the question I had given him. Kevin had led him to the top of the class, and Sean was literally holding court. Some of his answers were way beyond anything a twelve-year-old could possibly have any knowledge about. The older lads were mesmerized, I tell you! They were so mesmerized that they asked him to come back and talk to them some more. That's exactly what he's doing now. I wanted you to see this for yourself.'

The teacher opened the car door and Bridie grabbed his shoulder. 'But I don't understand. What do you mean he's lecturing? And where's Molly?'

Mr. Sullivan smiled assuringly. 'Molly is doing her homework in one of the other classrooms. Come on, Mrs. Robinson. This is your son. You've got to see this.'

Bridie stepped from the car and followed the teacher through the main doors and down the hallway. After turning left, she stopped in her tracks. There, before her very eyes, was a logjam of adults and children, all peering through the windows of the classroom.

Mr. Sullivan cleared a route for them through the crowd. 'Make way, there. This is the boy's mother.'

The assembled crowd scattered somewhat, allowing Bridie to peer through the clear window of the classroom. Her mouth opened as she saw her young boy standing atop of the class expressing himself, using his hands and arms in obvious discussion about some important matter. The classroom was packed with one student crowded beside another, trying to get the best position. Questions and hands shot up, interrupting Sean. He wasn't the slightest bit flummoxed or perturbed as he appeared to explain the answers to some algebraic question that had baffled the world.

'What's he saying to them?' she appealed to Mr. Sullivan. 'I can't hear anything.'

'Bridie, I'm sorry we cannot interrupt the class, but all I can tell you is that . . .' He paused, searching for somebody in the room. He spotted somebody and turned to Bridie. 'Him, that man over there.' Bridie looked in the direction he pointed. 'That man there, Mrs. Robinson, is none other than Father Reginald Rice, a Jesuit theologian. He was invited by the man behind him, who is our principal. When our principal heard that Sean was reinvited to speak – or should I say preach – he immediately contacted Father Rice. I was going to ring you to tell you about your son but then I realized you'd be here today to collect them from school.'

'But what is Sean saying to them?'

'The discussion has been going on for over an hour and a half. They have covered a number of topics ranging from the beginning of time, the Gospels, Jesus's time on earth, his resurrection, and as far as I'm aware, they are currently discussing the Second Coming!'

Bridie began to feel faint. 'Oh, dear Jesus, he's going to get expelled or get put into some loony bin,' she gasped.

People around her smiled, as Mr. Sullivan said, 'Quite the contrary, Bridie. I would say that people are beyond being impressed, despite the stern look on Father Rice's face.'

'Could I have a glass of water, and could you let me see Molly?' asked Bridie as she found a shelf like bench to rest upon. Mr. Sullivan handed her a plastic cup of water. Bridie gulped it down and then found Molly in another room, completely oblivious to what was going on with her younger brother.

'What's Sean doing, Mum?' she asked as she folded her books into her bag.

'I wish I knew, Molly girl. The teachers seem impressed, though.'

It was another hour before the principal decided that they should send everybody home before it got too late. Sean appeared in Molly's classroom and found his mother sipping a cup of tea.

'Are you okay, Mum?' he enquired.

'Sean, what have you been up to? You'll get us all into trouble.' Bridie stood up and folded her arms around him. 'Are you all right, Sean?'

'It was really interesting, Mum. We talked about a lot of things, and I felt I was able to explain myself to the students very clearly.' He said this as if it were as natural as playing football was to another twelve-year-old.

The two men she had seen in the room with Sean were talking amongst themselves outside. They motioned to Mr. Sullivan to join them.

'Sean, you and Molly wait for me in the car. I'll be out in a minute,' said Bridie, looking nervously at the group of men outside the door. Sean and Molly grabbed their things and went on their way.

Bridie gingerly made her way out of the classroom, and as she was about to pass the three men, the non-stern one said, 'Mrs. Robinson, I'm Gerry O'Brien, the principal here at St. Andrews. Could we have a few words?'

Bridie felt her legs wanting to fold beneath her. 'Of course,' she managed to reply.

'This is Father Reginald Rice. He's the chief theologian at the Jesuit college in Maynooth.'

Father Rice turned to Bridie. 'I must say–' – he interrupted himself – 'Bridie, isn't it?'

'Yes, call me Bridie, please,' she responded, wondering what was to befall her.

Father Rice took up the conversation. 'Bridie, your young boy has flabbergasted me. It's as simple as that. His awareness, understanding, knowledge, and delivery defy his age. In fact, I would hazard to say that he could debate with success with any of his peers. I'm not talking about student peers; I'm talking about most theologians I know.'

Bridie looked for somewhere to lean. Not finding anything, she said, 'Are you saying he knows what he's talking about?'

They all laughed in unison.

'Mrs. Robinson – eh, Bridie,' the principal said, 'your son is beyond being gifted. What's really appealing about him is his total lack of arrogance during his delivery.' The other two men nodded in agreement.

'Extraordinary,' said Mr. O'Brien.

'What do you want me to do?' asked Bridie.

'Absolutely nothing, Mrs. Robinson. We want to congratulate you on producing a boy like Sean, who obviously comes from a home where parenting goes beyond the norm of Christian living. You and your husband deserve all of the congratulations in the world for raising such a unique child. It is our pleasure, and our reward, that we have come to know him. We look forward to educating him in the best possible way. We will keep a careful eye on him to ensure that he gets the best of all attentions,' added the principal.

'Can I go now?' stuttered Bridie.

The three men smiled. 'Of course. Thank you for your time,' said Mr. Sullivan.

Bridie walked outside, took a deep breath of air, and tried to gather herself together. She walked towards the car and looked at Molly in the back seat while Sean sat in the passenger seat looking like a young lad without a care in the world.

'Who are you, Sean Robinson?' she whispered.

Sean's young teenage years blossomed, as did Kevin's and Molly's. Kevin's schoolmate and best friend – Gabriel, or Gabby – as he was known – always included Sean in whatever games they played despite the age difference. Gabby treated Sean as an equal to Kevin, and they all enjoyed each other's company. It didn't matter whether they decided to go fishing or play football; they were attached to each other like bosom brothers.

Bridie appreciated Gabby being there. He was a strong-looking seventeen-year-old young man. She felt that both Kevin and Sean were being looked after. She knew Gabby's family. They were well-respected farming people in the town. Gabby would not lead them astray, which was more than could be said for that fella Harry Devlin. Bridie didn't like him. Whenever there was trouble, Harry Devlin was sure to be close by.

When she came home from the hospital and found the boys playing in the yard, she took no notice unless Harry Devlin was around. She would await the opportunity to break them up and send Harry on his way. She told Gabby not to encourage Harry by inviting him along with Kevin and especially Sean. Gabby said he would deal with it – and deal with it he did, so much so that Harry seemed to disappear from Sean's life and started to mingle with a group of no-good boys in the town. *Good riddance,* thought Bridie.

While Bridie always encouraged the children to say their prayers before they went to bed – teenagers being teenagers, she found she was barking up the wrong tree where Kevin was concerned. Sean, on the other hand, never had to be reminded. She often found him in a contemplative mood. Sometimes he would go missing. She would find him sitting on a wall or by the river, staring into space. She would never disturb him or embarrass him when she found him doing this. Bridie often got the impression that he knew she was looking at him.

The event at the school seemed to be consigned to history as far as everybody at the school was concerned, although every now and again she would run into the principal, and he would remind her of that week when Sean held the school enchanted. He would always bring her up to date on his development. He advised her that he thought that he should be moved up a year. He was plainly well ahead of the other students in his class.

She asked Sean about it, and he said he didn't mind in the least. The new boys in the senior class took to him just as everybody else had done.

The Calling.

The new century arrived with all the fanfare one would expect as the whole world wondered in their excitement what the new millennium was going to bring.

Kevin finished his secondary school and obtained his Leaving Certificate with enough honors to enable him to get a position working for Intel in County Kildare, a drive of only an hour or so away. Gabby decided to stay on his father's farm and go to agricultural college at the same time to learn about modernizing the family farm for today's world, which his father had let drift on by.

Dan's pub business blossomed as the fair grew stronger and stronger. The annual crowds numbered forty thousand. All of the public houses thrived under the newfound wealth of the Irish population and its welcomed tourists. New businesses sprung from nowhere. The hospitals, Garda stations, fire brigade, and other infrastructure grew exponentially. Ballinasloe prospered as all the towns and cities of Ireland languished in this unforeseen bonanza.

Bridie was kept unusually busy when the board decided that they needed to expand the hospital, both physically and in the services they provided. More and more patients were being referred their way. The board decided to build a new extension and upgrade the old building to meet the new demands. They secured a government grant and, with additional European funding, managed to set about the new construction with a tentative completion date of 2006. Bridie found herself in new surroundings, dealing with architects, engineers, planners, and bankers, something she knew precious little about, thereby exhausting her limited available time. Luckily for her, Kevin had flown the coop, and Molly was doing her final Leaving Certificate examinations that year so that her sole responsibility rested with Sean, and he was no problem whatsoever.

Bridie had been relieved to see that Linda McDowell had taken a keen interest in her Sean. Linda was from a good family in the town. Her father was one of the most popular local doctors. She was from a large family. She had taken a shine to Sean, as they shared the same class at school. Bridie encouraged the bonding whenever she could. Sean also developed a more than friendly bond with Linda. They were both aged fifteen, but that didn't stop them from being more than a little close.

On a September day in 2001, Bridie was at home going through the household bills while Sean was studying at the kitchen table. The telephone rang, and when Bridie hung up, she turned on the television without saying a word. She gasped as she watched the pictures showing the city of New York and the headline reading, 'Breaking News: The Twin Towers are on fire.'

'Sean, oh my God, look at this!'

Sean turned to see that indeed the famous Twin Towers of New York were ablaze. They both stood as they watched in complete silence.

'Oh, Sean, why is this happening?'

Sean put his arm around his mother's shoulder and said, 'Perhaps we should kneel and say a prayer.'

Bridie turned to him, nodded, and knelt down on the carpet.

'Heavenly Father,' Sean began the prayer, 'help the world to understand why these things happen. Give our leaders the wisdom to be calm in the face of such turmoil. Let the people see that man's bitterness towards his fellow man will not go unpunished on the Day of Judgment. We pray for the innocent souls who have lost their lives in this terrible tragedy in New York. Let their souls and the souls of all the faithfully departed rest in peace. Amen.'

Bridie repeated the 'amen.' She looked at Sean, who seemed to be in tears at the pictures he was witnessing. She tried to rewind the last few moments as he had recited his prayer. *Where did he learn to pray like that? How could he be so knowledgeable for a fifteen-year-old boy?*

Before she could think any more about it, the phone rang. It was Dan asking her if she had seen the news. Before long, any thoughts of what she had just heard from her young son dissolved in the drama that was unfolding before the world.

Linda McDowell fell in love with Sean the moment she first set eyes on him. After that, she had no other thought about any other boy other than Sean. She watched him at school. She saw him as he played football. She loved his smile and his laugh, and how all of the other boys liked him too. He wasn't rough in any way. He was gentle and smart. She had heard about the day he had stood up in front of the senior lads' class and spoke to them about things they didn't understand themselves.

Linda had thought that Sean liked her too. Whenever she had the chance, she made sure that she was in his way. If he volunteered to help with the school play or any such event, then she also volunteered. He didn't seem to notice at first, but eventually he began to, and she radiated in his attention. It wasn't long before the tables turned and Sean began to follow her, just as she had dreamed. They became a pair. They would share everything and help each other with their schoolwork. Pretty soon they became inseparable.

Bridie always welcomed Linda whenever she appeared at their house, which was frequently. Linda helped Bridie with the housework while she waited for Sean to arrive home from wherever he was. Little did she know that Bridie was helping cement the union any way she could.

'Sean, what are you going to be when you leave school?' asked Linda one day when they were walking down by the river.

'I don't really know. I know I don't want to do a whole lot of things. I know I don't want to work in my dad's business or join Kevin in the technology field. I don't want to be a farmer, and I know I'd be no good at a load of things. What about you, Linda?'

'I suppose I'll know better the older I get. For now, I'm just happy being who I am. I like being with you. I do know that.' She smiled at him, and he returned the smile in a shy way.

'And I like being with you too, Linda. Do you think you'll ever want to leave Ireland?'

'No, I don't suppose I will. I mean, it's great here. I like living here. It's all I've ever known, really. I want the simple life. I don't want to be anything or anyone I know I cannot be. I want to be myself. Do you understand?'

Sean looked distant, thinking deeply. Then he said, 'I understand perfectly. I guess I've always known that I'd be different from everybody else. I mean, I know I'm adopted, and I don't know who my real parents were. It's a strange kind of feeling not knowing who or why you are, who you are. Sometimes I feel my mother looks at me as if I'm from outer space. I love her more than anything – and my dad. I just feel confused sometimes.'

'Don't feel confused, Sean. I understand you,' said Linda as she reached out and took his hand in hers. He responded by holding her hand tightly.

The next two years flew by. Sean and Linda both completed their Leaving Certificate Examinations with honors. Linda was unsure what she wanted to do with her life, so she decided to do nothing. She took some temporary jobs in the town, making some money to keep herself. As far as she was concerned, her only ambition was Sean. If she didn't have a life that included him, then she had no inclination to do anything.

It was a summer's day in mid-July. Bridie was sorting through clothes, wondering what she should throw out and what she should donate to the local charities, when Sean wandered into the living room.

'Mum, can I have a word?' He looked pensive.

'Sure, boy, what's on your mind?'

Sean got a bottle of water from the fridge, grabbed a chair, and sidled on up beside Bridie. 'I need to talk to you. I've been thinking for a long time about what the future holds for me. The school career advisor has been at me for the past year or so to get myself involved in engineering. I know I did well in math and physics for the exams, but . . .' – he paused as he looked for words – 'it doesn't feel right to follow a career I don't care much about.'

'What do you mean, son? What do you care about?'

'You know, Mum, I've always been inclined towards God. My every waking moment has been about Him. My feelings, desires, and inclinations have always been about God. I don't think there has been a moment in these past few years when I haven't felt absolutely certain that my destiny is mapped out for me.'

Bridie looked into her son's eyes and could have told him there and then that she knew it also. She let him speak.

'I don't know whether I told you, but I have been contemplating becoming a priest.'

Bridie opened her eyes wide. 'But Sean, I thought that you had feelings for Linda. Even bigger than feelings, I thought you were beginning a relationship.'

Sean took a sip of water. 'I have got deep feelings for Linda. We've spoken about it, but we are still too young to be getting any way serious. I'm not saying that I don't want to be with her, but I need to be sure. I have to find out if becoming a priest is right for me. Do you understand?'

Bridie looked at her son, then out the window as the birds flew by. 'Of course I do. How do you go about it? What's involved?' she asked helpfully, not wanting to interfere with her son's thoughts. She knew he was more than capable of working it out himself. He needed her as a sounding board.

'I've been talking to a Father Rice – he's a Jesuit priest.'

Bridie sat up. 'Wait a minute. Isn't he the priest who was at your school when you were talking to the senior students many years ago?'

'Yes, he was. I've seen him every week while I was at school. He always had great time for me. In the past year, we've been talking a lot about my becoming a priest. He told me that he has no doubts that I have a vocation. He says he was never more certain of anything in his life. He has already spoken to the bishop and got his approval for me to enter the novitiate. He brought me up to the Jesuit college in Maynooth and showed me around. It's only an hour's drive from here.'

'Is he forcing you to do something you're not sure of?'

'Not a bit. You know me, Mum; I'm not the sort of person to be coerced into anything I'm not sure about.'

Bridie nodded her agreement.

'He's a high-ranking Jesuit theologian. He said I could attend the college in Maynooth. I would be considered a novice. Novices spend four months to see if they have a vocation. Then there's a forty-day retreat, followed by two years preparing for the priesthood. There's a further four years of study in philosophy and apostolic work. Finally, I would do an undergraduate degree while being ordained. That's the agenda. Whether or not it's for me is for me to find out. I want to do this, Mum. What do you think?'

Bridie scratched her head. 'Have you spoken to your father about it?'

'I've only had a basic conversation with Dad. He said that he would go along with whatever you decided.'

'That's typical of your father. It's not up to me, Sean. You don't need my permission. My advice is to do whatever your heart is telling you to do. Don't be forced into anything. Perhaps after spending the four months, you may find out that you don't have a vocation. If the opposite is true, then proceed to the next phase, taking stock at that time. It's no different when somebody wants to become a nurse. They may feel it's something they want to do, but a lot of them drop out after a few months. Some drop out a lot later than that. The ones who do make it realized early on that their vocation was genuine.'

'Thanks, Mum. I will go along and find out if I have the vocation. It's only four months. Then I'll take it one step at a time.'

Sean stood up and hugged his mother. Bridie started to cry.

'Hey, Mum, this is meant to be a happy time for me.'

'I know, Sean. I am happy for you, son. Your dad and I love you more than anything in this world. Kevin and Molly too. I guess I've always known that one day you would become involved in something different. It's incredible to think that day is already here.'

'I'll be back and forth as much as I can, so don't be worried about me. I'll keep you both informed as to the way I'm thinking.'

They hugged each other again.

'When will you be going?'

'Probably next week. I have to see Linda and sort out a few things before I go.'

Linda was looking into Sean's big blue eyes and not hearing a word he spoke.

'Linda, are you listening to me?'

She heard his words but couldn't comprehend them. She shook herself back to reality saying, 'Sorry, Sean. I'm sad that I won't see you for such a long time. I'm already feeling very lonely. What were you saying? I'm listening.'

'I'll be back before you know it. It's six months at most. Then I'll be taking time out to consider whether to continue or not. You are an important part of my life, Linda. I want us to be sure about everything. If I decide to become a priest, then I can't be with you. I need to examine my whole life. I need to think about my life with you and my life serving God. It's a huge decision. I've got to get it right.'

'Does it mean you can't kiss me?' added Linda.

Sean smiled. 'I've made no decisions on anything yet, but this is an easy one.' He leaned forward, and they kissed.

Split decision.

St. Patrick's College in Maynooth is an imposing building. Its architecture envelops the visitor with its majesty. Anybody would feel reverent in its shadows, and Sean was no different.

Father Rice showed him around, pointing out the history: the famous Stoyte House dating back to 1780, the magnificent Russell and John Paul II Libraries, the halls, the museum, and of course the chapels. The libraries were stocked with over fifty thousand books, half of them from before the mid-nineteenth century, collected by various professors and eminent churchmen through the centuries.

Father Rice showed Sean his living quarters. The room was small but adequate. Creature comforts were modest.

'Remember, Sean, that the next four months are your time for reflection. I will act as your vocations director. It will be my responsibility to ensure that all of your questions are discussed at length to both of our satisfactions. Discerning whether or not you have the call to priesthood cannot be done alone. I am trained to facilitate you at this initial stage. You should be viewing this time as creating space for yourself where you can explore and reflect on your sense of being called. By the end of the four months, you should have a good grasp of the demands of priestly life and of the training involved in studying for the priesthood. Usually this process takes about a year to complete. In your case, I've discussed with the bishop about letting you go back home after the forty-day retreat so that you can make further reflections about your priestly celibacy and on what commitments you may have. After that period of time, we can then discuss whether you want to continue on your journey of discernment. We can then plan ahead for the rest of the course once you have reached that place in your life.'

Sean looked around him. He looked out at the beautiful lawns and age-old trees.

'I'm aware, Father Rice, about my commitment. I fully understand my position here, and I thank you for giving me this great opportunity. I'm wanting to do this.'

'That's very important, Sean. I look forward to helping you on your journey. Let us pray.'

Both men knelt down on the floor as Father Rice recited some prayers and Sean responded. His novitiate had begun.

Linda contemplated her life as the months went by. Sean had always been very honest with her. She knew she could trust him implicitly. Whatever he decided would be done with her in mind – she had no doubt about that. Thank God it would be only four or five months of waiting for him to reach a decision. Now they both had only another month or so to wait. Linda knew she had no doubts about her love for Sean. She also knew that he loved her but understood that she could have no part in his life should he decide to become a priest. He was due to make a decision for both of them.

These were the thoughts that went through Linda's head each and every day while they were separated. She was now working in her father's surgery as his secretary. She liked the distractions of organizing his patients, making appointments, and keeping his accounts up to date. She had never realized how much work was involved. She got to appreciate how much her father was respected throughout the town. He was more than good at his job, and they worked well together. Sometimes he asked for her help if he had to examine a nervous patient or he needed an extra pair of hands.

Linda got to know her father a lot better than she ever had. Sometimes, whenever time allowed, they had lunch together. She confided in him about her feelings for Sean. He had a good shoulder to cry on, and he seemed to understand how she felt. He advised her to keep an open mind. It could go either way. He said that he had no experience with what they were both going through since it was an unusual situation, but he also assured her that he knew Sean was a decent young man and that he would not knowingly do anything to hurt her. These were the exact words she needed to hear, and it made the waiting that much easier for her.

Linda had bought herself one of the new mobile phones. Everybody seemed to be buying them these days. They could do everything including giving you everything you needed to know without having to use a computer. While she found the convenience was terrific, she still couldn't contact Sean. He was incommunicado, especially as the forty-day retreat was due to start that coming weekend. She understood that he needed to be with his own thoughts. She also found the feeling of being an outcast infuriating.

Sean stepped out of the car and looked once more at the home he grew up in. He thanked Father Rice for the lift. They shook hands, having agreed on their next steps during the drive from Maynooth. He was happy to be home again. He watched Father Rice disappear down the lane.

Sean turned to see Bridie running towards him.

'Oh, Sean, you never said that you'd be home today,' his mother said as she ran to him with outstretched arms. They hugged each other.

'I'm sorry, Mum. Things happened a little faster than I thought. I don't suppose you have a potato in the pot for me? I'm starving.'

'Some things never change, Sean Robinson. Of course I have, and I can always rummage up your favorite dessert too. Now come inside and tell me all about it.'

They walked hand in hand into the house. Sean was full of questions. 'How is Dad and Kevin and Molly?'

'They're all doing great. Your dad is super busy, as usual, doing this and that and generally running the town, totally oblivious to the fact that he has a wife and three children.' She laughed. 'Kevin got promoted with Intel and loves his job. He should be home for his holidays within a couple of weeks, so you'll see him then. As for Molly, every young buck in the county is trying to get her attention. She has just blossomed into a gorgeous young woman. I think she has her eyes on that chap who runs the pharmacy.'

'Michael Twomey?'

'Yes, that's him.'

'Good for her. Michael's a very nice guy. She could do an awful lot worse.'

'Have you been in touch with Linda?' Bridie eyed him carefully.

'God, Mother, it didn't take you long to put on your reporter's hat, now, did it?'

'Well, I'm only asking. I know she misses you a lot. She's been around the house a good number of times. She and I are getting along great. She's asked me everything I know about you. I think she might be writing a book.' Bridie smiled and took her son's arm in hers. 'Come on, let's go for a wee stroll down the lane while we're waiting for the spuds to cook.'

'All right, Mum. First let me plug in this new mobile phone I bought.'

Bridie looked at him and saw how much he had muscled out. He appeared taller to her, and now he had the makings of a beard.

'Those things. They'll be taking over the world next!' she enthused.

Sean put on a sweater. It was a nice, fresh day for April. They walked arm in arm down the lane, turned right at the end, and headed up towards O'Malley's fields.

'Tell me, have you reached a decision about what you are going to do?'

'Straight from the hip and to the point. Our ace reporter doesn't mess around, does she?' Sean smiled as they both chose a dry spot under a tree to sit down.

'Aw, come on, son. The suspense is killing me and everybody around me.'

Sean looked towards the sky. He took some deep breaths and stared in silence with his mum for about a minute or so.

'It's just not easy, Mum. I thoroughly enjoyed my time at Maynooth. I was enlightened. The clergy couldn't have been more helpful towards me. I felt they nearly singled me out at times for extra attention. I don't know why. At one stage I felt a bit embarrassed for the other novices because I seemed to be getting more attention than them. I actually had to ask Father Rice to pull back a bit. Apart from that, I'm still in a state of reflection. Not so much confusion anymore – although I never really felt confused about my faith or my destiny. The forty-day retreat was truly inspirational. You are literally left alone to your thoughts. All you have to accompany you is the Bible and the Holy Spirit. I fasted and felt good about it. I have experienced things I never thought possible.'

'What do you mean?' interrupted Bridie.

'It's hard to explain. I felt a nearness to God like I never had before. It was as if He was physically there beside me. I could literally hear His voice. At first it was scary, then totally calming. I have never felt a peace like it before. I don't suppose it'll ever happen again. When I had my final discussion with my spiritual director before I left the college, they told me that there was no hurry, that God will send his spirit to guide me in the direction that He wants. I related very much to that thought.

'So, you ask me what are my plans? My answer is, Mum, I don't know yet. I'm going to take whatever time is necessary to get my mind one hundred percent clear and focused. It might take another few months or maybe another year. Then again, it might never happen. But it won't be for want of trying on my part.'

'Fair enough, son. You are fully capable of working it out yourself. So I have you for the present and a little bit into the future?'

'That's right, Mum. I do want to see Linda, though. I haven't been in touch with her since I left.'

'Okay. Let's head back and have some dinner. I'm sure she's dying to see you.'

Linda was busy at the surgery. Her father said it was always busy at this time of the year because people get excited when spring arrives, that they stop wearing warm clothes, and as a result, they come down with colds.

Linda's phone rang. Not recognizing the number, she sent it to voice mail. It was only after she got home later that evening that she noticed a number of missed calls. She checked her voice mail and started to cry when she heard Sean's message. He was home. She dialed his number and, like a little girl, jumped for joy upon hearing his voice.

'Sean, I can't believe it! When did you get back?'

'I've been trying to reach you all day. I got back this morning. When can I see you?'

'Now. Collect me, and we'll go somewhere.'

As soon as Linda hung up, her delight turned to trepidation. 'What if he's going to tell me he's joining the priesthood?' she said aloud to herself.

Her mood was glum as she heard Sean talking to her father downstairs. When she saw him, her heart jumped again, and her gloom quickly left her.

'Oh, Sean, you're back.' They embraced and kissed and said their goodbyes to Linda's parents as they made their way to Flanagan's Restaurant downtown.

They spoke wildly about every subject. Neither approached the subject that each knew was on the other's mind. It was only after they had finished their meal and relaxed with a cup of coffee that Sean started.

'Linda, I know you're waiting to hear my decision. I have to tell you what I've already told my mum. I'm still undecided. The four months away were amazing. I got to know things about myself I never knew existed. I love God – there's no doubt in my mind about that. I want to follow Him. I want to do His will. At the same time' – he looked into Linda's eyes, who looked at him and waited for the cannon fire – 'I also know that I missed you. I know that I want to be near you too. So I want us to spend as much time together over the coming months, and let's see where it takes us, if indeed it takes us anywhere.'

Linda's face lit up with a radiant smile. 'Oh, Sean, I couldn't be happier. I'm glad you missed me. I'm thrilled that we can be so honest with each other. I have feelings for you that go deep too. We are still young. We have lots of time. Let's enjoy each other.'

Kevin came home for his holidays the following month and immediately teamed up with his friend Gabby. Gabby was now engaged to Angela, a girl he met while he was at agricultural college. She was a breezy girl, full of life and great craic.

Molly came up with the suggestion of taking a cruise on Ireland's longest river, the River Shannon. They decided to spend Kevin's vacation cruising the river. For two glorious weeks in May, they hired a boat, and all eight of them took off from Ballinasloe on the River Suck, a Shannon tributary, and headed north to the historic towns of Athlone and Killaloe.

Kevin had a new girlfriend named Emma. Gabby took charge of the boat's maneuverings while the rest of them did his beckoning. They visited the sixth-century monastery at Clonmacnoise and visited loads of pubs and some great restaurants. Because the weather was kind, the guys went swimming and fishing while the girls did what girls do best – have fun. They even spotted a white-tailed eagle, which is rare enough. Sean and Linda talked and walked down the twisting country lanes whenever they moored, which was often. The two weeks flew by. They all agreed that it was great fun and that they should do it again next year.

They all got to know one another very well. Gabby and Angela were a perfect match. Gabby was a big, strong man who could pick Angela up with one arm, as he did many times and then jump into the river. She was a farmer's daughter too and loved the fact that they both shared each other's interests. Molly was definitely attached to Michael. It was plain for everybody to see, as they became inseparable on the trip. As for Kevin and Emma, the general consensus was that Kevin would be moving on; some people click, others don't. Nobody quizzed Sean or Linda about their plans, deciding that it wasn't appropriate.

For the rest of the summer, Sean, Linda, Angela, and Gabby became an item, doing everything together. Sean spent a lot of time on Gabby's family farm, helping out wherever he could and learning a lot. Gabby had obviously chosen the right path for himself, having obtained his degree at the first attempt. His father gave him a free hand in running the farm his way and supported the project financially. Angela spent most of her time there too, and the family considered her part of their family.

It wasn't long before the summer had gone, and autumn was preparing for winter. Linda still didn't know what Sean's plans were. They had become even closer over the past number of months, which was going to make their parting even more painful. She decided she had to know.

Linda arrived out at the Robinsons around five o'clock one evening. She let herself in. Bridie was in the sitting room.

'Hi, Bridie. I was looking for Sean.'

Bridie was fixing some clothes. 'How are you, girl? I saw him leaving about an hour ago with Gabby. I think they've gone down by O'Malley's fields. You should catch him there. Be sure to bring a jacket; it's getting cold.'

'Thanks, Bridie. I'll do that. See you later.'

Linda walked down the lane, and as she turned into O'Malley's, she saw Gabby walking down the hill towards her.

'Gabby, is Sean around?'

He smiled at her, saying, 'He's up by that tree on the hill. He's expecting you.'

Linda was puzzled. How did he know she was coming? She made her way up the short hill and saw Sean leaning against a tree.

'Sean, is that you?' cried Linda as she saw Sean turn towards her.

'Come on up.'

She made her way up the hill, and they embraced warmly and kissed. She sat down beside him.

Sean looked into her eyes and said, 'I've come to my decision, Linda.'

Linda stared at him wide eyed. 'Oh, Sean, I'm glad. It's why I came here to see you today. I don't think I can take the suspense any longer.'

Sean smiled and took her hand in his. Linda closed her eyes, waiting for the moment when he was going to say it was over between them. A tear came to her eyes, and she looked away so he wouldn't notice she was about to cry.

'I'm sorry, Linda. I know it must have been horrible for you – all of this waiting, never knowing. It finally came to me last night. You probably passed Gabby on your way up here?' Linda nodded. 'Gabby is a man you can always trust, Linda. He's a good Catholic, a great Christian, and a true friend. We've been seeing a lot of each other over the summer months. I found his contribution to my dilemma enlightening. Anyway, I've decided I do want to become a priest.'

Linda closed her eyes tightly, and her head became light. 'I see,' was all she could say.

'Hear me out. I've decided I want to become a priest, but I've also decided that I can't live my life without you!'

Linda looked up, confused. 'But you cannot do both, Sean. The Catholic church won't allow their priests to have a relationship.'

'I know that. That's why I'm going to become an Anglican priest. That way I can marry you and Jesus Christ at the same time!'

Linda was speechless. She tried to get the words out, but none came.

'I love you, Linda. I always have, and I always will. I'm going to marry you someday – if you'll have me?'

Linda swallowed drily. She tried to take in everything that Sean was saying. It felt as if all of his words were in slow motion, that they were drifting over her head.

'Oh, Sean, of course I love you, but I'm totally confused. I don't know anything about being an Anglican. I don't know anything about married priests. I'm still getting used to hearing you say you want to marry me. I'm shocked! I'm thrilled – but I'm totally shocked!'

'Let me explain. When I was in Maynooth College, I was left totally alone with my thoughts. Father Rice and other directors were always available to me. I asked them question after question, and they were able to satisfy my thoughts and problems at every turn. But

Father Rice, especially, always knew that I was very much in doubt because of my relationship with you. That's why I was allowed to take a break after the four months. Normally they don't allow that. I'm glad that they did. It was only after we spent so much time together during the summer that I realized that I couldn't live my life without you. I've since spoken a number of times with Father Rice, and he's agreed that the Catholic church would not be able to accommodate me. He wished me well, but he was glad that I had found my true self.

'However, I couldn't stop wrestling with myself. I know I have a vocation. The feeling inside me is too strong. I have a calling, Linda – and you are a part of that calling. I knew about the Anglican Church. In Ireland, they are known as the Church of Ireland. In America, they are called the Episcopalians. The Anglican Catholic Church is the exact same as the Roman Catholic Church in every way except for one major difference. They are effectively cousins in the same family. The Roman Catholic Church is under the auspices of the Vatican and the pope; they uphold the infallibility of the pope. The Anglicans think that is wrong, and that's where their major differences start and end. There are minor arguments about revering the Blessed Virgin Mary, but that's not so much of a problem because the Anglican Church acknowledges Mary's role in humanity and celebrates her feast days in the same way as Roman Catholics do.'

'But you don't know anybody in that church. They won't let you in, will they?'

'That is a problem, but I feel that things will work themselves out. I do need the blessing and approval of an Anglican bishop in order for me to proceed. But let's not worry about any of that for now. The important thing is that I've made up my mind. We know we love each other and that we want to spend the rest of our lives together.'

Linda finally let out a sigh of relief. 'I couldn't be happier, Sean. You know I'll support you in whatever you decide to do.'

They then kissed for a long time.

'I'm so delighted for the pair of you,' Bridie exclaimed upon hearing the news. 'Have you decided on a date?'

'Holy God, Mother. We just said that someday we'd get married. We're not even engaged yet, and already you have grandchildren coming down the stairs!' They all laughed.

'I know. I'm sorry. I'm so happy. Tell me, Linda, what are you going to do?'

Linda looked over at Sean, then back at Bridie. 'I don't know Bridie. Everything is spinning at the moment. I won't be able to work at my dad's surgery because the regular girl is due back from her maternity leave next week. I guess I'm redundant for now.'

'Well, how about this for a suggestion? You could come and work for me at the hospital. You are great with the figures and the accounts. I'm hopeless, and besides, I'm up to my neck with this new building extension and trying to run the hospital. I've decided I need help. Tell me you'll come and work for me.'

Linda smiled and looked at Sean, who hunched up in an *It's not my decision*–type of look.

'I'd love to, Bridie. I need to be trained, though. Someone needs to show me the ropes.'

'Done and dusted.'

Bridie got on her phone to the hospital. 'Can you start on Monday?' she asked Linda as she covered the mouthpiece.

Linda nodded elatedly.

Wheeling and dealing.

Dan sat pensively, studying the documents that Paraic Liddy had handed him.

'What's the long and the short of it, Paraic?'

'Well, Dan, for the year ended March 2006, the figures show that you had another great year. Your accounts show that your revenues are up over twenty percent on last year, your costs were down, and with some financial wizardry on my part, your tax bill will be the same as last year. You ought to be delighted.'

Dan turned the pages from the profit and loss account to the balance sheet. He never understood these blasted balance sheets. The only thing he ever wanted to know was (a) how much tax do I have to pay? and (b) how much did I make? He knew how much he had in the bank. He always knew that.

'I suppose so. Tell me, what are we doing with the housing site we own?'

'I wanted to talk to you about that, Dan. You see, with the country booming and unemployment way down on previous bad times, my brother, Mark, and I feel that the time is right to put the plan into motion now. Our accountancy practice has also been doing really well, attracting new business as the town has grown. We were thinking about breaking ground later this year.'

Dan shuffled his legs, crossed them, and putting the accounts on the table in front of him, said, 'How much will this entire venture cost me?'

'That's just it. We've formed a limited company, which means we will be liable only up to the amounts we invested. I've done my figures, and I feel that an investment of around two-hundred-fifty thousand euros each will be more than adequate to build the first five houses. We can then sell them and use that money to build another five, and so on. That way, our borrowings should be kept to our initial investment. Once we get past the fourth tranche of houses, say twenty houses, we'll be able to take our profits, reduce our borrowings, and make real money.'

'How long do you think it'll take to complete the first five houses?'

'I'd say if we laid the foundations by the end of September this year, then come March or April 2007, we should be ready to put the houses on the market.'

'Two-hundred-fifty thousand euros is an awful lot of money for me, Paraic. First, I don't know if the banks will loan me that kind of cash, and second, I'd surely have to put up my pub as security. Jasus, if this goes belly up, I'd be screwed,' commented Dan.

'That's not the way to look at it, Dan. Every venture has risk. But if you're not in, you can't win,' added Paraic.

'Yes, and you can't lose, either' said Dan.

Dan looked more scared than unconvinced, so Paraic continued, 'Besides, I know the Bank of Ireland manager very well. We continue to do a lot of business together. I'm sure you won't have a problem getting the loan you need. I'll make sure to put in a good word for you.'

Dan looked up at Paraic. He thought about how it was pretty rare for any opportunity, businesswise, to come his way. It was a good site, and the more he thought about it, what could possibly go wrong

'I might as well pop in and see him now while the iron is hot,' said Dan. 'There's no point in discussing it any further if I can't raise the money.' With that, he rose from his chair and bid his farewell to Paraic.

'True enough. Let me know how you get on. I'll ring Cronin, the manager, now,' said Paraic as he shut the door behind himself.

Dan had an aversion to borrowing. His father had run into trouble with the banks in his day, and they had hounded him for their money when things went bad. It took him most of his life to pay it off. In fact, it probably helped to shorten his life, having died at the young age of fifty-five. Because of that experience, Dan made sure that he would never spend unless he had the cash. He had no borrowings for the business and a one-hundred-thousand-euro mortgage on his house, which was manageable enough.

Driving to the bank that day, Dan was tempted to turn around and forget the whole thing. Surely he had already doubled his original investment of thirty-thousand euros; wouldn't that be enough? he thought. Then again, his mind wandered to the temptations of finally making a truckload of money for the first time in his life. He'd be able to give Bridie her dream house that he had always promised her; he could help the kids with a down payment on their first houses; they could finally take that trip abroad, maybe even travel in luxury across the States. There were so many things he could do! He knew he could never do any of that from the money he earned running the pub. Sure, it was a steady provider of income and paid for all of their day-to-day costs, but it was never going to be like one of the Dublin mega pubs that were sprouting up all over the country.

'Blast it,' he said to nobody in particular. 'I'm going to do it.'

Seamus Cronin was a surly old bank manager. He must have been close to retirement age. Dan had never heard a good word from anyone in the town about him. He made his way into the bank and asked the secretary if the manager was available. She went into his office, and within seconds, surly Seamus came rushing through his door.

'Dan Robinson, if it isn't yourself. How have you been?'

Dan was more than a little taken aback. He put out his hand, and Cronin nearly shook it out of its socket.

'Come into my office; take a seat. Miss McNulty, make sure I'm not disturbed while I'm at meeting, and no phone calls,' he barked.

'Yes sir,' replied his secretary as Cronin shut his door.

Dan made himself comfortable, not knowing what to expect.

'Now, Dan, what brings you into my neck of the woods?' Cronin clasped his bony hands together and gave Dan an insincere grin.

'You're probably aware that the Liddy brothers and me have owned a chunk of land on the Dublin side of town.'

'I am. I financed Paraic Liddy when he first bought the site. Paraic had done his homework, that's for sure, as otherwise I wouldn't have financed him.'

'I'd believe that all right. We want to start developing houses on the site, this year if possible. I'd need a loan of somewhere in the region of two-hundred-fifty thousand as my part in the investment,' said Dan, moving uneasily in his chair.

Cronin shuffled himself, raising his eyebrows. 'That's a lot of money, Dan. I'm delighted that the town will finally see some of the prosperous development that the rest of the country is bathing in. I don't know whether you are aware, but I'm due to retire from the bank in the not-too-distant future. You know, I wouldn't mind getting into your investment myself. I see it as a big opportunity. I respect you and the Liddy brothers, as I know all of your judgments would be sound.'

Dan raised his eyebrows skyward in surprise. Was old man Cronin seriously thinking about investing? If that was the case, then it would put Dan's mind at ease knowing that the wily Cronin was putting his money into the venture.

Dan pursed his lips, not wanting to appear enthusiastic about Cronin's request. 'I'm not sure we'd be able to accommodate you. We weren't looking for any new investors at this stage.' Dan brushed an imaginary hair from his trouser leg, then crossed his legs, awaiting Cronin's response.

'Of course not, Dan. I appreciate that you guys have a nice investment there. I'm just saying that if you were to look kindly in my direction, then I'd say you won't have any trouble borrowing any money from my bank. In addition, my lips would be sealed.'

Dan knew that they had each other by the short and curlies, but he was damned if he was going to let Cronin have the upper hand. Dan tossed some numbers about in his head.

'Well, if we're investing a quarter of a million each, and bearing in mind that you'd be coming in after we had already delivered the planning permission . . .' Dan trailed off, looked out the window at the crowded bank, and turned back to look at eagle-eyed Cronin, who looked like he had his tongue hanging out from the side of his mouth. 'I'd say three-hundred-fifty-thousand on your side would give you a twenty-five-percent stake like the rest of us.'

Cronin's eyes bulged. A smile crossed his face. 'I'd go along with that. Will you be able to swing the Liddy boys to your way of thinking?'

'That depends on whether or not I get the loan from you,' said Dan poker-eyed, staring Cronin down. If there was one thing that was certain, nobody got the upper hand on Dan Robinson when it came to wheeling and dealing.

'If you get me in on this, you won't have any problem obtaining your loan,' said Cronin.

Dan stood up immediately before Cronin changed his mind. 'I'll have Paraic Liddy call you later on today.' Dan made for the exit. He turned to Cronin. 'Who is going to take your place at the bank?'

'Oh, that young pup Mick Mullaly. I've also got that Christy fellow who just started as a trainee.'

Dan looked out the glass dividing wall and saw the young Christy he was referring to. 'Why, I know that chap. He's friendly with my son Sean.'

They shook hands, and two happy men parted. Before he left the bank, Dan walked over to where young Christy was seated.

'How are you, Christy? So this is where you're hiding nowadays,' said Dan, noticing the tabloid newspaper spread open on his desk at the horse racing section.

Christy turned to Dan's voice, smiling. 'Hello, Mr. Robinson. Yes, my father got me in here. It's grand. How is Sean?'

'I hope you're not putting the bank's money on the horses,' said Dan jokingly.

Christy closed the newspaper. 'This paper was left here by one of the customers,' he said shyly. 'I'll call around during the week to see Sean,' he said to Dan as the elder Robinson left by the front door.

Dan explained the new situation to Paraic Liddy on the phone.

'That's fantastic, Dan. With him in on the deal, it means we can fast-forward our plans. We can now build ten houses immediately instead of doing it in chunks of five houses at a time. I'll sign him up before he changes his mind, and I'll make sure that your loan is approved before I let him in.'

They both hung up.

Over the next few months, all stages of the development got under way. Dan juggled his pub business with his new developer's one. He handed over the pub deeds as security on his loan.

They appointed the architects from Athlone, the biggest firm in the Midlands, who appointed the engineer. Dan was insistent on using local builders and tradesmen. He got his wish when the Parker brothers got the contract having tendered the second-lowest price but winning it on Dan's say-so. Everything was all set. Photographers from the local papers as well as the *Galway Tribune* took lots of photographs, and Frank O'Connor captured prime position again on all of the front pages.

The development got under way in late August of that year. Dan and the Liddy brothers, together with Seamus Cronin, were all mightily relieved to see the heavy equipment move in.

Bishop O'Malley was happy that the number of new entrants for the priesthood was up on the previous year. He didn't know if all of the bad publicity the Church had been getting of late was going to have a negative impact on their recruiting drive. Thankfully it hadn't. He wasn't at all sure if future years would be as lucky.

While the bishop was thinking, his assistant knocked and announced, 'A Mrs. Bridie Robinson is outside and wants to know if Your Grace would give her a few moments of your time. She has no appointment.'

'Send her in.'

Bridie came into the bishop's office looking nervous. She curtsied. 'Your Grace, thank you so much for seeing me at such short notice. I don't know if you remember me.'

'I certainly do, Bridie. How could I ever forget the baptism night for your beautiful son? How is Sean now? He must be well grown up at this stage.'

'He's turning twenty this year, Your Grace. He is the reason I wanted to speak to you.'

'Please go on,' insisted the bishop.

'Sean is truly a special young man. He recently attended Maynooth College in the hope that he might find his vocation. He had intended on becoming a priest.'

The bishop looked surprised and delighted. 'I didn't know anything about this. How wonderful for him and for the entire family.'

Bridie moved nervously in her seat. 'I know, Your Grace. We are – were – delighted.'

The bishop raised his eyebrows, curious.

'What I mean, Your Grace, is – unfortunately, Sean has other feelings too. He's in love with his childhood sweetheart. He knows he cannot become a Catholic priest.'

'I'm sorry to hear that, Bridie. Has he sought any guidance?'

'Yes, he was speaking to a . . .' – Bridie consulted her written notes – 'a Father Rice. He's a Jesuit priest.'

'I know Father Rice very well. If he's on your son's case, then he couldn't be in more capable hands.'

'The reason I'm here today, Your Grace, is that my son still wants to be a priest. He tells me that he can become an Anglican priest. That way, he can marry his girlfriend and complete his vocation. He doesn't know I'm here with you asking for your help. I was wondering if you could make an approach to the Anglican bishop by way of a reference for my son.'

Bishop O'Malley smiled, turned to look out the window, and said, 'You know, Mrs. Robinson, this is not like asking a politician to get you something to ensure that he gets your vote. The Anglicans are very much a part of the overall Catholic family. Some people refer to them as our distant cousins. I can understand why your son is thinking that way. I wish – between you and me, you understand – that my church allowed marriage. It would solve a lot of problems and more than likely increase the number of candidates for the priesthood.' The bishop savored his last words, nodding his head to his own approval. 'I do happen to know the Anglican Archbishop of Dublin rather well. I've never met the Archbishop of Armagh, but I hear he's a regular fellow. Let me think about your problem, and I'll get back to you.'

'Oh, thank you so much, Your Grace. I can't thank you enough. It's a load off my mind.'

'I haven't done anything for you, and I can't promise anything, either. I will do my best.'

Bridie was relieved. She didn't know how Sean would take her interference on his behalf.

The Ministry Begins.

Sean took a job at his father's pub, helping him out while he waited for an answer to his application to join the Anglican priesthood. He had made the regular application in the hope that the Holy Spirit would work on his behalf. He didn't know any of the Anglican community, let alone any of the clergy. All he could do was hope and pray.

Dan appreciated having Sean around because the building project was taking up a lot more of his time than he'd figured. It was also getting close to the October fair time again. This year promised to be the biggest yet. Some forty thousand extra visitors were planned for by the town council. Dan was on that board too. The work occupied Sean's mind and stopped him from wondering whether he was going to be accepted.

Linda was extra busy too. She loved working with Bridie. She met Rosie, who used to work for Bridie raising Sean when he was only a baby. She had qualified as a nurse, and she told Linda all about looking after little Sean and how excited they all were when he became part of the family. The new hospital extension was going well, and Linda barely saw Bridie until she was needed to sign the checks or purchase orders.

Linda found she was good at her job. She managed her time so that she could meet up with Sean after work. They had their meals at the local restaurants and sometimes at the pub. Dan had taken on a new chef, and business was booming.

It was while they were having their dinner one evening that Sean took a call. The caller announced himself on behalf of the Archbishop of Armagh – His Grace, Dr. Boland – and wondered if Sean would accept the call. Sean stood up nervously and went outside so that there was little noise. 'Yes, of course. Please put the archbishop through.'

'Sean, this is Archbishop Boland of the Anglican church in Armagh. I'm not sure if you are aware of me.'

'Yes, Your Grace. I'm honored.'

'Sean, we have been busy looking at your application. I see you have friends in very high places.'

Sean made a nervous sound in response, not knowing what the archbishop was referring to.

'Normally speaking, any applicant for the priesthood has to be recommended by a bishop. I know your background, and one could say that you have qualified in that regard – although it might be construed as being the wrong bishop!'

Sean was even more confused but decided to say nothing.

'The applicant should also have been an active member of his community. We've done our homework, and our local pastor has given you the thumbs-up in that department. I understand your family is highly regarded, not just in Ballinasloe but throughout the county. I have also had long conversations with a Father Reginald Rice, with whom I know you are well acquainted. Even though he is of the Jesuit persuasion, he is also a much respected figure. He has also spoken in your favor. With all of this in mind and following our other background checks, I'm going to issue the approval for your application. I trust you will not disappoint us. I believe you are a man of integrity; otherwise, I wouldn't have approved you personally.'

Sean dropped his jaw, flabbergasted. It took him a moment to realize what was happening.

'I won't let you down, Your Grace. You've made me very happy.'

'I am sure you are aware that we have two ways of completing your studies. Have you decided which one suits you?'

'Yes. I'll be taking the one-year distance learning, followed by the three-year residential degree.'

'I think that's a great idea. It's our most popular method. It means you could be ordained in four years. I wish you God's grace and speed, Sean. I hope we will meet some day. I have heard great things about you.'

'Thank you, Your Grace.'

Both men hung up their phones.

Sean ran back into the pub and grabbed Linda. They danced around the floor as the regulars looked on in amazement.

'Drinks are on me!' shouted Sean, and a mini-stampede took place to the bar.

The foundation course meant that Sean could study from home during his first year. It also meant that he could be with Linda and help his dad out at the same time. Bridie never mentioned her visit to the bishop, although she had a sneaking suspicion that Sean knew something about it. Anyway, he seemed more than happy, she thought, so better to leave well enough alone.

The year 2007 saw the completion of one new wing to the hospital. It created an additional seventy beds. They also had a new children's ward and better staff facilities. The opening was performed by the minister for health, with Frank O'Connor not a stone's throw away at all times. Bridie had recruited two new medical staff and three extra trainees. She was delighted to have both Linda and Rosie close by her; they gave her great solace and encouragement. Bridie was now in her early fifties and was beginning to feel more easily exhausted the older she got. She was looking forward to it all being completed in the not-too-distant future.

Sean and Linda decided to celebrate their twenty-first birthdays at the same time, knowing that Sean would soon have to leave for college. He would be based in Nottingham in England, and he didn't know when he would be able to return on vacations. Neither of them minded too much, knowing that they had an inseparable bond.

Gabby's father decided to retire, leaving the farm entirely in Gabby's capable hands. Gabby and Angela got married that same year, and the celebrations went on for a week in true Irish tradition. Kevin still came up to see them whenever he got the chance, always with a new female friend in tow.

Molly and Michael split up after coming to some major disagreement with his mother. Michael's mother was one of those people who liked to control her son and didn't take to Molly from the outset. The fact that Michael's family was Protestant probably had something to do with the animosity that his mother felt towards the Robinson clan. Molly was devastated at first but seemed to be getting over it gradually. Molly and Linda became closer, and that helped matters a lot. Molly decided to become a teacher and was studying for her degree, which helped in healing her wounds.

The fair that year was the biggest the town had ever seen. Visitors came from all around the world to see this unique event. The fair could be described as being tribal. Travelling families from all over the United Kingdom and Ireland made their way to Ballinasloe for the gaiety, laughter, festivities, and business that the fair offered.

Make no mistake – the Ballinasloe Fair is first and foremost about money. A sea of horses is on display, of all shapes and sizes, both for racing and show-jumping. They are bought and sold for many thousands of euros. Up to fifty thousand cattle and ten thousand sheep could be sold at the short event. Bartering is done traditionally, with a spit on both hands and slapped with the buyer's or seller's hands, or done in a businesslike manner – in one of the many pubs, naturally. There are tug-of-war competitions, dog shows, and art and cultural events, as well as parades and beauty competitions. There is never a dull moment as the entire population drinks, eats, sings, and dances for twenty-four hours a day for each of the nine days.

In 2007, nobody knew that they were celebrating the last big event for many years to come. Anybody would have said you were mad if you had told them that a certain something was about to occur in America that would have repercussions the world over, that even this far east, the little country of Ireland would be shaken asunder by the utter incapability of everybody in the banking and regulation sector as the banking system imploded, causing financial ruin and mayhem in every corner of the globe.

There was a big going-away party organized at the house for Sean. It was more a happy occasion than one of sadness. Everybody seemed relieved that it was happening. Those who had muttered in a disparaging way about one of 'their own' becoming an Anglican seemed to have come around to thinking, what harm was there?

Bridie cried at seeing her last child leaving the house. The next time she would see him, he would probably be a full-fledged priest. She felt many emotions, but the overall one was that he was doing the right thing. Bridie, more than anyone, had witnessed firsthand how different her son was from anybody else she had ever seen. From the moment she had found him to adopting, rearing him, and watching him grow up as a boy far more mature for his years than anybody she had ever known, she knew he had a destiny. What that destiny was, she had no clue.

Bad times – Good times.

The winter of 2007 was the worst in living memory. The rain was relentless and extended itself into most of the spring of 2008. The ground became waterlogged, and the construction was delayed for months. The heavy machinery was getting bogged down. They had to lay the men off, then rehire them, if they were lucky enough to get the same workers. The Parker brothers did their best to maintain their staff, but they too became very frustrated at the interminable delays.

Dan was working away in the bar on another wet afternoon. He looked up and found the Liddy brothers standing there looking worried. He put away the glass he was cleaning.

'What's the problem, men?' asked Dan, hoping it wasn't as serious as they looked. They positioned themselves near the snug, near enough that Dan could watch anybody entering or leaving the pub, as Jimmy was on his day off.

Paraic started the conversation. 'Dan, we have a major problem. You might have seen on the news recently that the banks are no longer lending the money the way they used to. Bank of Ireland is no different. Because of the weather delays, we've used up most of our available capital. Now they've stopped our line of credit. They say it's only temporary, but they are looking for –'

'I would say demanding,' interjected Mark.

'– more security, or for us to make more payments to reduce our debt.'

'But they must know that there's not a damn thing we can do about the weather, that we're doing everything we can to rectify things. It might mean we could be four to five months behind schedule, but we'll still have great properties to sell at the end of it!' insisted Dan, becoming upset and annoyed.

'I hear what you're saying, Dan. The problem is exacerbated because of the downturn in the economy. People are not buying properties the way they had been. The general public are afraid for their futures with all of the uncertainty that's going on. They are sitting on the fence, and the banks know that. It's not just us; they're giving every developer a hard time,' concluded Paraic.

'So where does that leave us?' asked Dan, now getting worried.

'Up the creek without a paddle,' said Mark unhelpfully.

'We have to finish what houses we can, sell them, and take it one step at a time,' said Paraic.

'Is Cronin aware of what's going on?' asked Dan.

'I'm sure he is. He hasn't been asking too many questions. I guess he's hoping and praying that we can get everybody out of this mess.'

'So what are we supposed to do now if the banks won't give us any money?' asked Dan.

'We have just about enough cash to finish off three houses right away. If we can sell those pretty quickly, we might just be able to dig ourselves out of trouble,' added Paraic.

'That's providing the weather holds and gets better,' said Mark.

'Jasus, you're a bundle of absolute joy,' said Dan, staring at Mark.

'He's always negative, Dan. Don't be minding him. I'm saying for the present, let's all keep calm heads. If the builder gets wind that we have any cash problems, he'll leave the site, and then we're all screwed.'

The Liddy brothers walked meekly to the door, letting themselves out. Dan sat in the snug for twenty minutes contemplating the problem. His whole business was being used as security against the development. If it failed, then he would have nothing. His savings were meagre, to say the least. What would he do? The thought sent shivers up and down his spine. The idea that he could be kicked out on the street was the most frightening feeling he'd ever had. What could he say to Bridie and the kids?

The next three months were a nervous time for everybody. The banks were reducing their mortgage lending. Every day Dan turned on the television, an announcer was telling the viewer about some imminent doom or another. Dan tried to put the dark thoughts to the back of his mind. He needed to put on a brave face for everybody. Nobody could know what was really going on. The three houses had been complete for over a month, yet nobody was buying. Not only was nobody buying, but it appeared that nobody was interested in buying.

Then as September broke, all of their worst fears were realized when the news broke that a firm called Lehman Brothers had gone into receivership, or chapter eleven, as it was referred to in the States, the newsreader explained. Thousands of people had lost their jobs. Worse than that, all of the lending institutions were running for cover. The next thing Dan knew, there was a run on the banks. A bank in northern England called Northern Rock went bust and had to be bailed out by the British government. The lenders were falling like dominoes across the globe. Just when it appeared it couldn't get any worse, it hit home, very close to home, in the form of the largest Irish lending institution called Anglo Irish Bank. It hit the wall with a crash that reverberated all over Europe. It had gone down the toilet, and nobody, especially the government, knew what to do about it.

Dan stared down at the table in the living room and was disconsolate. The builders would close down shop. They had no hope of ever selling any of their houses. As for the future, it looked worse than bleak.

The phone rang. It was Gerry Parker, the owner of the building company. He wanted to know what was happening. There was no point in trying to bluff his way out of it. Dan told Gerry that it was over. There was no point continuing, at least until the market came back again. He had been paid up to date, but Dan explained that they could no longer continue to hire his team. Gerry reminded Dan that they had a legal contract, but Dan scoffed at his remark and reminded Gerry that he could have conned him if he had the will. Gerry acknowledged it, saying he was sorry for Dan's troubles. His company would move on, and hopefully they would all see better days ahead.

Next up was Cronin. He arrived up at Dan's house in the middle of the night, obviously the worse for wear having downed a lot of whiskey. Dan told him that he should have known, more than anybody else, the risks that were involved. God knows he would have said the same thing to many a person during his time as a bank manager. Dan had no sympathy for him whatsoever and sent him packing.

Dan and the Liddy brothers sat down for their daily meetings, trying to decide what to do. It was obvious that the whole country was going down the drain. All they could do now was sit tight and hope that the banks wouldn't come calling. Paraic explained that their business would be doomed if they had to pay back their loans. There was no way that they had that sort of money. Dan admitted he was in the same boat. The only hope he had depended on his pub business remaining buoyant. That way, he could at least keep up with the interest payments. Until he heard from someone to the contrary, all he could do was keep the business going.

That's the way they broke up. They arranged for Boxer to look after security at the site. Boxer wouldn't charge very much as long as his beer slate was kept to a minimum. Boxer assured Dan that he needn't worry about anybody running off with anything from the houses; otherwise, they wouldn't be able to walk again.

Bridie knew there was something wrong with Dan, but the more she prodded him about it, the more he clammed up. She could see the strain on his face getting worse with each passing day. Dan was the type who kept his problems to himself. He was a man's man, not in a chauvinistic type of way, but more like a 'protecting my family' sort of way. He didn't want her worrying; he could do all the worrying for both of them. Anytime she asked him if the finances were okay, he retorted by saying, 'Of course they are. Isn't there always enough money in the hole in the wall whenever you go to withdraw money?'

Bridie accepted his answers rather than causing him any more stress. She understood why he was so irritable but felt frustrated that she couldn't do anything to help him. She was able to save a little rainy-day money whenever she could for those incidental things that always seemed to crop up whenever she least expected them. God, what she wouldn't do to win the lottery at that very moment. She'd give it all to Dan, and he'd be back to being his beautiful self again.

Bridie was worried about his health. Dan wasn't the type of man to be going down to the only gym in the town. As for taking a walk, he'd say, 'Aren't I always walking?!' No, Dan wasn't the type of man who bothered with that sort of stuff. That was more for the younger set. After all, he was in his mid-fifties, and the time for getting in shape was long gone. He was happy to eat and drink what he wanted, when he wanted, and damn the begrudgers!

Sean had contacted Linda to tell her that everything was going great. He had finished his first year with exception, according to the director of religious instruction. He told her that he missed her more than anything he could have imagined. Her heart raced when he said that. She told him over and over that she loved him. She said she couldn't wait to see him but that she understood that she needed to be patient. Linda relayed the information to Bridie, who told all and sundry who wanted to hear.

Bridie was shocked and thrilled to get a call from Bishop O'Malley one day, asking her how Sean was doing. Seemingly Father Rice had been telling him how Sean was such an extraordinary man, the likes of which he had never encountered before. The bishop asked Bridie to make sure to have Sean pay him a visit whenever he was next back in Ireland. Bridie assured him that he would be only too delighted to see the bishop.

Evil Lurks.

'Come on, Lulu! Come on, number four!' shouted Christy as he jumped up and down with other gamblers at the dog track who also had their money on Lulu. Lulu was in fourth position as they turned the second bend; she was two lengths behind the leader. As the dogs tried to capture the artificial hare, the lead dog started to pull away from the pack. Lulu managed to push herself into third position and was neck and neck with the second dog as they approached the final bend. Then the lead dog slipped; it was barely noticeable, but it was enough to allow Lulu to take the lead, and in a mad dash to the finishing line, she just managed to win by a nose.

Christy was jubilant, as were the other punters, while all those who lost threw their tickets on the ground. It was a larger crowd than usual for a Saturday night at the track. Christy liked the atmosphere and assumed the larger crowds were due to the stalling economy. During a recession, people always bought more lottery tickets in the never-ending hope that they would be the lucky one. He'd seen it at the bank too. There was a large increase in withdrawals as people took their cash out of the banks to pay off their debts or simply stash it under the mattress. Others, like Christy, took to gambling. He had a routine that included horse racing, the greyhounds, and his twice-weekly poker game. He reckoned he was smarter than the rest. He had an infallible system, which was how he knew that Lulu was a certain winner.

Christy stood in line waiting to collect his winnings when he felt a pat on his shoulder, which made him jump slightly. 'Christy Welch, what are you doing here?'

Christy turned around. 'Holy God, Harry Devlin. I didn't know you went to the dogs.'

'I went to the dogs a long time ago,' Harry said with a big grin on his face. 'You look like you're winning.' Harry looked at the teller count out a wad of twenty-euro notes.

'Havin' a bit of luck tonight, all right. I'm breaking even so far. I had better luck earlier today with the gee-gees.'

'Were you at the horse racing as well?' asked Harry, seemingly surprised.

'Sure was. It was great. I backed three winners.'

'Then you'll be good to play in our little card game later on tonight?' Harry looked at Christy to see if he was interested.

'Card game? What do you play?'

'Usually five-card straight or stud – depends.'

Christy brushed his face with his hand, thinking earnestly. 'I just might do that. Where and at what time?'

'Anytime after the pubs close tonight, over at Boxer's.'

'Boxer's,' Christy said, surprised.

'Sure. We have a regular game over at his place or mine every Saturday. You can earn quite a bit of money.'

'Let me think about it. Who else will be playing?'

'There's Dino and Fonsie. Sometimes Hugh John might play. A good crowd.'

Christy stuffed the cash into his pocket.

'Come on, you can buy me a few drinks with your winnings,' said Harry as he led Christy off in the direction of the bar.

'Your dinner's ready, Gabby,' Angela called to Gabby, who was busy trying to lift the main axle off the harvester.

Angela marveled as she gazed at her man, seeing his muscles strain with the effort. He was six-feet-four and looked the same in width, except he was all muscle. He was her protector, and that was for sure. How she had managed to appeal to this handsome young man when every girl in college fancied him she'd never understand. Yet he preferred this diminutive blonde-haired girl, all five-feet-nothing of her, when he had the pickings of every girl in the county. But it was Angela who took his fancy, and she thanked God every day that she did. She adored him and would do anything for him.

'What's that you're doing there, Gabby?'

He rested the axle on a supporting bench. 'This machine is knackered, like the rest of the equipment we have around here.' He wiped his oily hands in the cloth, throwing it aside. 'Come on. Let's eat.'

They sat down at the dinner table, and Angela put a plate of lamb and four large flowery potatoes with his favorite marrowfat peas in front of Gabby. She poured him a pint of milk, and he dived in. She sat watching him enjoying her cooking while she picked at hers.

'You seem to be miles away, Gabby. What's bothering you?'

'You know, girl,' – she smiled every time he called her 'girl'; it was his nickname for her, and she liked it – 'I've been doing a lot of thinking. I had a good report from the brewery in Athlone. They're saying that the barley I produced was the best they had seen. They want to buy all I can give them.'

Angela looked surprised. 'You never told me anything about this.'

'I was keeping it as a surprise. You see, I've been researching based on their requirements, and it just so happens that the chemical balance in the outer fields has the perfect ratio for producing what they call tannin barley. I never knew anything about this until I started experimenting. The ordinary barley they can get anywhere, but the tannin gives it a certain individual taste that's unique. It could mean that the money the barley crop could create would more than match everything we earn from the cattle, the creamery milk, and the wheat. What's more, I wouldn't have half the workload or the need for a lot of the equipment.'

'What's the catch, then?' asked Angela.

'I'd need to invest in new harvesting equipment. That machine we have is on its last legs. It probably won't see another winter. But if I sold all the animals, I should earn enough to meet most of the cost myself without resorting to bank borrowings.' Gabby swallowed the last of his milk. He wiped his lips on his sleeve. 'Anyway, it's certainly worth considering, especially since the annual fair is only two weeks away. It's a golden opportunity to sell the lot.'

Angela looked at him pensively, then said, 'Let's sleep on it. We'll make the decision over the next couple of days. We need to do our sums because we'll only get one shot at this. Has the distillery given you anything in writing?'

'Not yet. I know one of the directors very well. Rest assured, girl, they won't be pulling the wool over Gabby's eyes that easily. They are due to send me the contract of supply during the week.'

'Let's wait and see,' said Angela.

'Who have we got here?' joked Boxer as Harry accompanied Christy into the kitchen.

'Christy reckons he can take our money away from us,' laughed Harry. Both of them had just arrived back from Athlone. Christy had won over seven hundred euros and was beaming.

'Of course, if you don't want me to play, then I'll walk away,' added Christy.

'Nonsense,' said Harry. 'Take a seat there, now, and I'll get us a couple of bottles.'

Boxer introduced Dino and Fonsie, who both nodded with all of the personality of dead rats. Then there was a loud noise as the door burst open.

'My name is Hugh John O'Kane, and poker is me game,' he said with a great big grin as he shoved himself into a chair.

'Mr. O'Kane, you were my English teacher in secondary school,' said Christy.

Hugh John looked at him with one eye open and said, 'Tonight, my boy, you'll be able to put all of the nouns, pronouns, adjectives, and verbs to good use because I'm about to get my retribution for all of the grief you obviously gave me as I threw my pearls before all of you swine. Now, are we playing cards or what?'

Boxer announced that they would be playing five-card stud followed by five-card draw every other round. Each player put in five euros, and the maximum raise was half the pot. IOUs were accepted, but they had to be paid off within the week; otherwise, a price would be paid. Boxer didn't elaborate on what that price might be, which concerned Christy. All concerns went out of the window as the money was thrown into the pot.

Christy had a system for poker too. It was simple, really. Poker was primarily a game of bluff. His method involved betting heavily on the first couple of hands. That way, he was able to expose his playing method. If he was dealt a bad hand to start; then he bet wildly. If somebody saw him, then he exposed that he had been bluffing. The opposite was also the case. If he happened to be dealt some good cards, he would again bet heavily. If somebody went to the end with him, everyone would see that he was a player who liked to have good cards before he bet. That way, they never knew if he was bluffing or not.

Christy looked at his hand. He had been dealt two kings in the hole. He bet a fiver. All followed with their money. His third card was a ten of diamonds. He bet half the pot. Fonsie backed out while the other four followed with their money. Christy's fourth card was another king. Again he went with half the pot. This time Harry and Hugh John threw in their cards. The last card up was a two of spades. Boxer was showing a pair of queens face up. Christy was showing nothing. Christy checked. Boxer went with half the pot, knowing that he had the upper hand. Christy went back with seeing him and raising him again – half the pot. Harry and the other boys looked on with eyes wide open. They had never seen this much money in the pot, especially for a first hand.

Boxer stared down Christy. Christy never blinked. 'I'll check and see you,' said Boxer as he pushed in the last of his pile of money.

'Three kings,' said Christy.

Boxer threw his cards face up on the table. 'Damn it! Three queens.'

Christy drew in the pile of money. It looked as if he had cleaned Boxer out, as well as a good portion of everybody else's money.

'What did you bring him here for?' cried Boxer to Harry.

'It's pure luck, isn't it, Christy?' asked Harry, appealing to Christy to say something before Boxer got mad.

'Pure beginner's luck,' agreed Christy.

'Is it my deal?' asked Christy innocently.

The game continued for another three hours before Boxer announced the game was over for now. He demanded that Christy come back the next week to give everybody a chance to win their money back. Christy assured him that he would as he folded the big euro notes into his pockets. He reckoned he had cleared over thirteen hundred euros that night, which, together with his win on the dogs and the horses, gave him a nice little nest egg of over two grand.

'I'll give you a lift, Christy,' said Harry as he got up to leave.

As they drove towards the town, Harry turned to Christy. 'How is your job going at the bank?'

'Fine. It's kind of boring, but the salary and the perks are pretty good.'

'Is that old codger Cronin still in charge?'

'Yep, but he won't be there much longer. He's due to retire soon.'

Harry pursed his lips in surprise. 'Retiring, is he? I'd say there's an awful lot of people in this town who won't be sorry to see the back of him. He should get a tidy sum for his retirement, would you say?'

'Well, he certainly won't have to worry about money, that's for sure, although I believe he'll be taking a good chunk of his pension by way of a lump sum. I heard he lost a lot of money in the Dan Robinson investment.'

Harry let Christy speak. Christy told Harry all about the housing development that went sour.

'I didn't know Cronin was involved,' said Harry.

'Yeah, he wanted to keep it quiet because the bank might have looked down on it as some sort of insider knowledge thing. He had me sign the documents as a witness because he wanted to keep it quiet.'

'How much do you think he'll be pulling out in cash?'

Christy turned towards Harry, who was pulling up outside of Christy's house. 'I'm not sure I should be telling you all about this. It's meant to be confidential.'

Harry shut off the engine.

'I'm just curious. I mean, if he lost a quarter of a million, like you said, then I'd say he's going to need a lot of cash to pay off any borrowings.'

'Yeah, whatever. What do you work at, Harry?'

Harry didn't want to make Christy nervous, so he decided to back away from his questions about Cronin. 'A little bit of this and that, as they say. Me and Boxer have a scrap metal business. We do all right. We also do some security work.' Harry lit a cigarette and offered one to Christy, who declined.

'I don't smoke. What do you mean by security work?'

'Boxer, as you can see, is a well-built fella. His services are in demand from time to time, and I help organize the business. For example, he's doing security work for Dan Robinson over at that site in case someone tries to steal anything.'

'Where do you live?' asked Christy.

'I live up on Old Angel Road, about ten miles east of the town. My father used to have a farm, but I had no interest in farming or farm animals. After he died, I sold all the stock and went into the scrap metal business. Anyway, you had a great win tonight, Christy. Will I put your name down for next Saturday?'

'Yeah, sure.' Christy stepped out of the car and saluted Harry, who drove back the way he came.

'Did he fall for it?' asked Boxer as Harry pulled up a chair and drank from a bottle of beer.

'Hook, line, and sinker, just like I said he would.'

'You were dead right about his style of play. It's not a bad system he uses, but when you know how he plays, it's easy to give him a win – although having Fonsie as the dealer makes it like taking candy from a baby.'

'Fonsie is very deft with those hands of his,' said Harry. 'I could never spot him dealing from the bottom or wherever he deals them from. Even though I know he's cheating, what chance would Christy have?'

'So you're saying that we'll draw him in over the next number of months, and then we do a number on him. Is that still the plan?' asked Boxer.

'We might have to do a number on him sooner than we expected. It appears that old man Cronin is retiring from the bank at the end of October, and he's due to have a wad of cash. I'm thinking that we should let Christy win about five hundred next week; then we'll let him break even for two weeks and skin his hide in two sessions about a week before the end of October. If we have him owing you about ten grand, that should be enough to frighten him. That way, I'll get him to tell us when Cronin withdraws his cash. We'll send Dino and Fonsie over there and relieve him of it. Then we'll sweeten Christy by wiping the slate clean for him.'

'Sounds like a plan,' said Boxer as he gulped down the last of his beer.

Gabby had been to the annual fair with his dad every year since he was a boy. He learned by watching his father make deals the traditional way, with spits and slapping of the hands. He also saw how the professionals did it, with contracts and documentation. He had never actually sold anything himself. He watched how things worked for a few hours to see who was offering the best prices. He knew to avoid the con men and to deal directly with the principals, not their stoolies.

When he was ready, Gabby backed in his truck with the animals he wanted to sell. He approached the main cattle merchants, and within minutes, he had off-loaded all of his animals. He took a check when he saw other sellers accepting them. He wanted cash if he thought there was anything shady about the buyer. The second and third days, he sold his sheep and the few pigs he had. He also managed to sell the harvester even though he informed the buyer that it was giving a spot of bother. The buyer said he'd be using it for spare parts. Gabby was happy with the deal. Each day he transacted, he deposited the money in the night safe if the bank was shut. He didn't want to be carrying any cash around with him.

All in all, Gabby was more than happy with his trading. He could definitely follow through with his new plan for the farm. Angela and he had agreed on what they needed in equipment and how much they should spend. Gabby thought how lucky he was to have somebody as smart and level-headed as Angela in his corner. She controlled the purse strings, and he was glad to let her do it. He would spend the winter getting the fields ready for sowing come the spring. He had estimated that the distillery should get some of his crop next summer. Angela was more than happy when she read the contract, especially after she had the Dublin solicitors review it.

Gabby was excited about their new future.

Harry leaned across the bar and picked up the two pints of Guinness from the counter. The heads of the pints were perfect. He went back to Boxer's corner, as it was known in Dan's Pub. Nobody sat in Boxer's corner.

Fonsie was giving Boxer the news about his work around town. It was the last day of the fair. Fonsie was the best pickpocket there was. Every day of the fair was a bonanza for him, and of course for Harry and Boxer. With the massive crowds shuffling around every street eating, drinking, and reveling until all hours, it made for easy pickings.

Fonsie took a rolled bundle of euros, held together with an elastic band, from his pocket. He handed it to Boxer.

'Keep it under the table,' said Boxer, annoyed. 'How much did you clear?'

'I managed to sell the jewelry pretty easily. I think there's around five grand there.' Fonsie took one of the pints that Harry handed him and slurped the big creamy head, leaving only half of the pint in the glass.

'That's pretty good,' said Harry. 'You've had a great week.'

'The best week ever,' agreed Fonsie.

'How much did we clear for the week?' Boxer asked Harry.

Harry was the manager of this enterprise. Even though he knew he could be flattened by Boxer anytime the big man wished, Boxer needed Harry just as much because he was illiterate when it came to reading, writing, or counting.

'That will make it a cool twenty-five grand in all,' said Harry as Boxer handed the roll of money to him under the table. 'I'll bring your shares over to your house tomorrow night. Be at Boxer's around eight o'clock.' Harry turned to Fonsie. 'Tell Dino as well. We have a job for the two of you coming up fairly soon.'

'Will do, boss,' said Fonsie, polishing off the rest of his pint in one pour down his throat.

'Okay, wheel in some more drink. I feel like celebrating,' said Boxer as Fonsie rubbed his hands together with joy.

Harry turned to go back to the bar. He thought he noticed somebody familiar looking at him. When he turned to see who it was, the bloke stood up and walked out of the bar. Harry couldn't put a name to the face.

Dan was happy with the business he had done that year. The pub had been packed every night, as people seemed not to be bothered by the pandemonium that was going on between the government and the banks.

Unlike his patrons, Dan hadn't been able to sleep at all, only managing to grab a few hours each night before he'd shoot up in the bed in a cold sweat, thinking about his financial situation. It was a week like this that made him forget his problems, but he knew his problems would still be there when the fair was all over and everybody would be long gone. He had to be very careful with his money from now on. There would be no spending unless it was absolutely necessary. He still hadn't told Bridie because he felt there was no point in the two of them not sleeping. He had lost some weight too since he had lost his appetite. It was no harm, he thought, losing a few pounds.

'Will I pull in another round of drinks?' asked Fonsie.

'No, we've had enough. Come on, Boxer. I'll get you home,' said Harry, helping Boxer to his feet. They had lashed back a lot of drink, and both of them were the worse for wear. Fonsie seemed to be able to manage.

'Let's go out the back door,' said Harry as they made their way through the crowd. As they pushed open the door that led to the dark lane at the back of the pub, Boxer wobbled and nearly fell down as the air hit him.

'The great Boxer can't stand up' said a voice behind them. The owner of the voice stepped forward. Harry and Fonsie looked at the face of Joe Finnerty as he led another six of the Finnerty clan armed with hurleys and bats. Harry then realized it was one of the Finnerty boys he had seen in the bar.

'What do you want?' asked Harry.

'Payback is what we'll be wantin', and payback is what we'll be gettin'.'

A hurley came crashing down on Boxer's head from behind, sending him to the floor. Two others grabbed Harry and pinned him up against the wall as they crashed blow after blow into his belly and his face. Fonsie ran for his life as Joe Finnerty grabbed Boxer's jacket and pulled him up, only to send his fist in a right upper cut smashing into his face, knocking out one of his teeth and breaking his nose. Boxer collapsed onto the ground as two others landed kicks into his ribs and arms.

'That's enough!' said a voice from behind.

Joe Finnerty looked to where the voice came from. All he could see was the silhouette of a large man at the end of the lane against the backdrop of the streetlights. The man moved forward, and when he was about six paces away, the Finnertys recognized the figure of Gabby Doyle.

'What do you want?' asked Joe Finnerty.

'I'm telling you to leave them alone. You've done enough.'

With that, one of the brothers rushed towards Gabby, wielding a stick. Gabby grabbed the stick in midair, at the same time crashing the back of his left fist into the brother's face, sending him clattering into the wall and collapsing in a heap. The other brothers gasped at how quickly Gabby had knocked out their brother.

Joe Finnerty stared at Gabby, then down at his prostrate brother, then back at Gabby again, who seemed like an immovable force.

'Right, lads, we'll leave it at that. You shouldn't be interfering into things that don't concern you,' Joe said at Gabby. He then reached down to Boxer's jacket, and putting his hand into the unconscious man's pocket, he took out the wad of cash.

'You'll be leaving that where it is,' said Gabby, standing straight up, making him appear even more formidable than he was.

Finnerty threw the roll of cash down on top of Boxer. 'Come on, boys, let's go. Pick him up.' He pointed at the comatose brother. Finnerty brushed past Gabby, who waited until they had reached the street and disappeared.

Gabby looked down at Boxer and saw that he was still unconscious. He was badly bruised but still breathing. He then turned his attention towards Harry and saw that one of his eyes was bloodied and closed, as was his nose. Gabby reached out his hand to Harry. 'Here, I'll help you up.'

Harry peered upwards and focused to see it was his archenemy, Gabby Doyle. 'I'll not be needing any help from you,' he said as he grunted in pain.

'I seem to remember offering you help one other time, and you refused that too – and regretted it,' said Gabby, staring into Harry's face.

'I regret nothing. I don't need your help and never will.'

Gabby stood tall and said, 'Even my greatest enemy I can forgive, but you will never beg for forgiveness.' Gabby turned and walked towards the street.

The Bad Thief.

Seamus Cronin read the document in front of him. It set out in clear and concise terms the details of his retirement pension. One clause after another stipulated how he was to conduct his association with the bank after he had retired. It stated that he was never to discuss or divulge any information, financial or otherwise, about any of the bank's clients. It implied that there would be penalties for any breach of confidentiality attributed to the retiree that could be proven in a court of law. The fact that he had requested a lump-sum settlement instead of a monthly pension brought additional constraints.

Seamus had read the document many times, and his fears were not abated. He knew he should not have gotten involved with a client of the bank in any business deal. He would be held liable by the bank if it ever went public. They could easily say that he had abused his position as a bank manager using insider information to profit personally. It made no difference that he had lost his shirt on the deal. He had abused client confidentiality, plain and simple.

He didn't know what effect that would have on his pension. That was why he needed the lump sum and not a monthly stipend. The only thing to do was to pay off the loan and get it off the books before anybody started asking questions. That meant finding €350,000, which wasn't going to be easy. The lump-sum pension yielded €270,000 immediately and a further €70,000 after one year. He had savings of €170,000. His savings had been carefully put away over his forty years working with the bank. He had denied himself during his working life because he wanted to be able to do all of those things when he had officially retired. Now it was all for nothing. After paying off the loan and outstanding interest, he would have nothing to live on, and he would have to wait another year to collect the €70,000.

What a disaster, he said to himself as his hand shook, accepting the terms and conditions while scrawling his shaky signature on the last page.

Christy couldn't figure out what had gone wrong with his system. He had used it again the following two weeks but had only barely broken even. Boxer seemed to be able to second-guess his every move. If Christy raised, Boxer saw him. When he folded, Boxer did too. Christy had lost a packet the previous Saturday, around €1,200. He felt that tonight his luck was in. He had had a couple of winners on the horses that day at Leopardstown. He needed a win because he didn't have very much cash.

Boxer and Harry seemed delighted to see him. Their bruises seemed to have healed. Harry had explained that a number of people had tried to steal equipment from the building site, and Harry and Boxer had had to do a lot of fighting.

'You'd want to see the other guys,' Harry laughed.

Even Fonsie and Dino were in a good mood tonight, which was surprising because they rarely spoke a word about anything.

'Are you gonna clean us out tonight, Christy?' said Fonsie.

'I need to,' answered Christy as he nervously sat in his usual chair.

The game started off slowly with little or no money being won or lost. It was after an hour or so that Boxer started to up the stake. Pretty soon there was four to five hundred in the pot. Christy had a good hand – two aces and two sevens showing. Boxer had a seven, nine, and ten. Boxer kept raising as Fonsie dropped out, followed by Harry. Hugh John didn't show tonight. Christy got his final card. He had two pair, which was a strong hand, as Boxer only showed the possible run. Boxer bet half the pot.

'How much is it?' asked Christy.

'You'd need to be putting in fifteen hundred to see me,' said Boxer.

Christy looked at his money. He had nowhere near enough.

'Of course, if you want to sign an IOU, that'd be fine too,' added Harry.

'Okay, I'll sign an IOU.'

'For how much?' asked Boxer.

'Make it for five grand.'

Boxer and Fonsie whistled. They hadn't expected Christy to ask for that much.

'Give it to him,' said Boxer.

Christy signed the chit. He saw Boxer's bet, raised him half the pot again, and threw in the chit.

Boxer looked over at Harry, smiled, and said, 'I'll see you. What have you got?'

Christy turned up his hidden cards, showing two pairs – aces over sevens.

'I've got a straight,' said Boxer as the blood drained from Christy's face.

'Great win there, Boxer,' said Dino, looking with a sneer at Christy, who seemed to be in a trance.

'Don't worry about the IOU. You can pay me back by the end of the week,' said Boxer, dragging the money from the center of the table.

'I'd better be going,' said Christy as he slowly stood up, wondering to himself what he had just done. He felt dizzy.

'Here, I'll give you a lift into town,' added Harry, standing up and grabbing his jacket.

'See you during the week!' shouted Boxer as Harry led Christy to his car.

They drove in silence. As they approached the main street, Harry said, 'Are you going to be all right?'

Christy stared out the front window. 'Yeah, I'll be fine. Was Boxer serious about me having to pay him back by Friday?'

'Oh, Boxer never jokes about money. I would say he was dead serious.'

Christy began to feel cold. Harry let the moment fester and then said, 'There is a very easy way out of your debt.'

'What do you mean?' asked Christy with a look of desperation.

'Remember you were telling me about old Cronin retiring from the bank?'

'Yes, he's retiring next week. Why? What has that got to do with my debt?'

Harry parked the car, turned off the engine, and turned to face Christy. He continued, 'You were saying that he will have a lot of cash coming to him. If you were to find out when he might have that cash, I think I can persuade Boxer to tear up your IOU. Let's say it could be for services rendered!' Harry looked into Christy's eyes, looking for any sign of consent.

'I can't do that. I could be arrested!'

Harry smiled and patted Christy's shoulder. 'Nonsense. Who is going to find out that it was you? You'd be telling only me, and sure who would I be telling?'

Christy thought some more. Opening the car door, he turned and said, 'I'll have to think about it.'

'Sure, take all the time you want. If I don't hear anything from you by Friday, I'll let Boxer know. Look after yourself.'

Christy banged the door closed and made his way to his house. Harry looked at him in his rearview mirror and smiled to himself.

Mick Mullaly closed the door of his new office. He had just completed the handover giving him full managerial responsibilities for the bank. Seamus Cronin went into the adjacent office and thought to himself that he was glad to be leaving. He was fed up having to deal with these bright young pups who were now all over the banking industry. It was no wonder that the banks had collapsed. If he and his ilk had been in charge, it would never have happened. *To hell with them,* he thought.

Cronin had received the lump sum and put it immediately against the loan. That, together with the transfer of €80,000 from his savings account, meant that the loan had disappeared. He had managed to follow the paper trail and tear up any of the documents associated with the loan. He now needed to withdraw his remaining cash from his savings. He couldn't be seen doing it himself. He was damned if he was going to let Mullaly sniff at his account. He picked up the phone and punched two numbers.

'Mr. Welch, come into my office.'

Two minutes later, Christy closed the door. Cronin handed him a slip of paper. 'I need you to get me this amount in cash. Don't go telling anybody about it or who it's for. Then put the debit against this account number here and close that account. Is that understood?'

'Yes sir, Mr. Cronin. How did you want the money?'

'In as large a denomination as possible. No five-hundreds but as many single hundreds as you can.'

Christy closed the door behind him. As he went to conduct the transaction, he couldn't help thinking that this was the only way out of his problem with Boxer and Harry. He had only tomorrow before Boxer would come looking for him. He had thought about skipping town altogether, but he reasoned that he had a good job, and besides, where would he go? He couldn't jeopardize his career.

He went into the bathroom, and taking out his two phones, he decided to opt for his gambling mobile phone. He rang Harry. He could destroy his gambling 'throwaway' phone immediately. Nobody would be any the wiser.

Seamus Cronin took the paintings down from his office wall. He stared at his favorite one, depicting a half-open blue door into a garden. The picture was aglow with bright blues and yellows. He often wondered what was behind that door. He had imagined he was about to finally step through it.

His thoughts were interrupted by a knock on the door. His secretary, Mary McNulty, told him that there was somebody outside demanding to speak with him. Seamus placed the painting on his desk and walked dejectedly outside to be met by all of his staff, dutifully looking in his direction behind a large cake aflame with candles. They all burst into applause.

Mullaly stepped forward, calming the noise, and said, 'Seamus, the staff and I want to wish you a very happy retirement. They have all contributed to your going-away present.'

Mullaly handed him an envelope and a gift-wrapped rectangular box. Seamus's secretary, Mary, encouraged him to open it. It revealed a two-part trout fishing rod.

Seamus forced a smile. 'This is so unexpected. Thank you, everybody, for this gift. I hope to be able to use it a lot, and I promise that I will think of each of you every time I cast.'

They all applauded again as Seamus cut the cake, and then they all dutifully dispersed back to their posts. Mullaly shook Seamus's hand once again, telling him that he should drop into the bank anytime he felt like it. He would be more than welcome. Seamus thought how insincere Mullaly's platitudes seemed to him, only confirming his views of the new bank manager.

Seamus went back into his office and opened his drawer to ensure his package containing his €90,000 was still in place. It was all he was going to live on until he received the balance of his pension. At least, he thought, he had his house, which was mortgage free, his mother having bequeathed it to him in her will. Thank God he had never married; at least he had only himself to worry about. Who knows? Maybe the property market might take off again in the near future, and he might recoup his investment.

Seamus brushed his thoughts aside as he focused on getting out of the building and home with his cash. He placed the package in his briefcase. He was amazed how heavy and bulky the money felt. All of his life he had handled money, yet never for himself.

He walked over to his secretary, handed Mary a card with a personal check, and thanked her for her services. She was embarrassed, and before she could properly address the situation, Seamus Cronin had already left the building, leaving only the swinging doors to announce his departure.

It had started to rain as Seamus fumbled for his car keys, getting wet in the process. *At least it fits my mood,* he thought as he finally got into his car and placed the briefcase on the passenger-side floor. He made his way down the street, never looking back at the building he had worked in all of his working life. It was as if it had never existed.

A fishing rod, he scoffed to himself. *I know what I'd like to do with their fishing rod!* he thought as he turned his car away from the main street and headed for home.

Twenty minutes later, he drove up the lane to his house. He looked at the house and thought how he had always liked it. He had grown up here. He had looked after his mother when his father died at the tender age of fifty-seven. Being an only child, he felt it was his duty to stay with his mother, and she appreciated having him around as she reached old age. He didn't deny that he liked his life, especially when he saw and heard how other men had miserable married lives. *Not for me,* he used to say to himself.

Seamus looked around to make sure there was nobody about, smiling to himself at how there was never anybody around these parts. He liked the isolation of where he lived. He closed the door and made his way to the bottle of Jameson he had yet to open. He felt he needed a good stiff drink.

'You can pour one for me too,' came a voice from the corner of the room, making Seamus turn around quickly. Dino was looking at him with a threatening smirk on his face. Dino was rough looking, unshaven, and shabbily dressed, matching his large frame.

'What are you doing here? Get out of here or I'll call the police. How did you get in here?'

With that, Fonsie came into the room from the kitchen. 'There's nobody else around. He's on his own.'

Seamus recognized them. He had seen them around town. They weren't customers of the bank. He knew them as wasters, always up to no good. He suddenly felt fear. A cold dart ran up his back as he glanced down at his briefcase.

'I take it that you might have something special in that briefcase of yours,' said Dino, his smirk becoming a fully grown grin.

Seamus reached into his pocket and took his phone out. He tried to dial 999 but only managed to get one of the numbers punched in before Dino was on him, forcing the phone to the floor and pushing Seamus back against the wall.

'There'll be none of that,' said Dino as he grabbed the briefcase. He opened it and tore the packaging, revealing a large wallet stuffed with hundred-euro notes.

'Yee-haw!' he beamed, showing the package of money to Fonsie.

'Holy Jasus! We've hit the jackpot!' added Fonsie.

Seamus now shook with fear. 'Take it! Take it! Get out of here!' he shouted, practically screaming.

'What are we going to do with him?' asked Fonsie.

Dino looked over at Seamus. 'How much is in here?'

Seamus blubbered out, 'Ninety thousand euros.'

'Great,' said Fonsie, urging Dino to pick it up and get the hell out of there.

'We can't leave a witness, Fonsie.'

Seamus stared blindly as tears started to flow. He shuffled towards Dino, blabbering, 'Leave me alone. Take my money. I don't care. I won't tell anyone.'

'Of course you'll be tellin' no one,' said Dino as he produced a steel wrench from his coat pocket and struck Seamus across the head. He struck him again in the same spot, sending the older man crashing back against the wall in a torrent of blood that streamed from his open wound.

'Jasus, Dino, stop! Don't go killin' him!' shouted Fonsie. It was obviously too late as Seamus Cronin took his last breath and folded on the floor. 'Aw, bloody hell, Dino, you've killed him.'

'I had to. We can't leave any witnesses. They'll think it was a robbery. Nobody will know it was us.'

The eerie silence was interrupted by a light that streamed across the living room wall.

'What's that?' said Fonsie, ducking down on the floor.

'I thought you said there was nobody else around,' said Dino as he and Fonsie crouched down away from the light.

Fonsie made his way towards the window. 'It's some woman, and she's coming to the front door.'

Mary McNulty rang the doorbell. She had been up to her boss's house on only one other occasion, and that was on the death of Mr. Cronin's mother. She had always referred to him by his second name, never calling him Seamus. She felt she had to come by and thank him personally for his gift. She had always felt sad for him, even though everybody else hated him. They said Mary was mad to have worked for him for so long. He reminded her of her own father, and she had loved her father.

Mary's thoughts dissipated when she suddenly saw two men running from the side of the house and jumping the fence into the field. She moved towards them, shouting, 'What's going on? What are you doing here?'

One of the men tripped, turned, and looked at her. She recognized him instantly. It was that no-good Fonsie fellow that was always in the pub.

'Wait for me, Dino!' he shouted as he ran into the darkness.

Mary immediately felt something was wrong and made her way around the back of the house and through the open back door. She saw Seamus lying in a pool of blood. She threw her hands to her mouth and reached down, calling out his name.

The Gardaí and an ambulance arrived ten minutes after Mary's 999 call. They took Mary's statement. She told the police that she recognized one of them as Fonsie. She never knew his second name. She also told them that he had called out 'Dino,' who was also one of the no-gooders in the town.

Within the hour, all stations had been notified to be on the lookout for Daniel Dempsey and Alphonsus Murphy, also known as Dino and Fonsie. They were wanted for questioning regarding a murder.

Mary McNulty wept as she saw her boss being carried away in a body bag, leaving behind his blood as the only evidence that he had been there.

Harry stirred his cup of tea and was about to take a sip when there was a bang on the door. 'Who the hell is that at this hour of the night?' He opened the door to see Dino and Fonsie run by him in a panic. 'What the hell are you doing here? Did you do the job?'

'We did the job, all right. Dino here did too much of a job. The bank guy is dead,' blurted Fonsie.

Harry opened his eyes to a stare. 'What are you telling me here?'

'Look, I couldn't leave any witnesses. I had to get rid of him,' said Dino, looking very afraid.

'I told you to steal the money when he was asleep, not kill him.'

'It couldn't be helped,' said Dino as Fonsie looked on in silence.

'Why are you here? Get out of my house, and you'd better not tie me into any of this or you'll be joining the bloke you just killed. The same goes for Boxer. When he hears about this, you can be sure he'll be mightily pissed off.'

'Where can we go?' asked Dino, now looking scared for the first time.

'I don't care where you go as long as it's far enough away from here, and take that money with you. It'll see you through whatever time you can stay on the run.'

Dino stared into Harry's eyes, looking for guidance. He looked over at Fonsie and said that they'd better get going, that the cops would be looking for them.

'How do they know it was you?' asked Harry.

Fonsie explained about the woman dropping by. Harry raised his eyes to the ceiling and told them to disappear.

As they ran out the door, Harry looked around to make sure that there was no evidence to say they had been there. He walked outside and saw them take off down the road heading northwards. Luckily the loose gravel path left no tire tracks. He looked around again to make sure there were no cigarette butts, but he realized they wouldn't have had time to smoke because they had been too scared.

Harry reckoned he had a decent enough alibi. He and Boxer had been at Dan's most of the night, and certainly during the time that the robbery took place. Except now it wasn't just a robbery; it was a murder hunt. He had better drop over to Boxer's place, he thought. They needed to go over their alibies.

Concern.

'Have you seen Sean?' asked Mark Holly, the administrator of Nottingham seminary.

'I think I saw him in chapel,' answered a running student.

Mark had been college administrator for over twenty years. In all of that time, he had never experienced anything like what he was presently undergoing. Every week, somebody from the archbishop's office made contact asking about Sean Robinson. They had been doing so for the past two years since Sean had arrived at the seminary. On three occasions, the archbishop had gotten in touch personally. They seemed to want to know his every movement. What was Sean Robinson writing about this week? Had Mark any copies of his papers he'd written? Had he spoken to anybody? What had he said? Mark shook his head in amazement. Sure, Sean Robinson was an impressive student, probably the most dynamic he had ever seen at the college. What he couldn't understand was how or why the archbishop himself had been taking such a keen interest. And now, the *pièce de résistance* – he had never heard of this latest instruction in his lifetime.

Mark entered the chapel to find Sean kneeling at the altar, obviously in deep thought. He took to a pew in the back row, blessed himself, and knelt to pray. As he finished praying, he opened his eyes to find Sean in front of him, smiling.

'Were you looking for me, Father?'

Mildly startled at first, Mark gathered himself and said, 'Yes, Sean. I need to speak to you of an urgent matter. Have I interrupted your prayers?'

Sean sat down in the pew in front of Mark. 'I was asking our heavenly Father for guidance. I have never been so happy here. I have found great solace within these walls.'

Mark looked at him, puzzled. It was as if he already knew what he was about to say. 'Have you spoken to anybody from the archbishop's office?' asked Mark, clutching the document that was now crumpled in his hand.

'No, I haven't.'

'As you know Sean, you are here to complete the three-year residential degree. You have completed the first two years with exception, so much so that the archbishop has asked me . . . eh, instructed me to inform you' – Mark opened and read from the document – 'that he has decided to forgo the discernment process and make you an intern without having to complete your final year. This is a most unusual step, but obviously the archbishop is so suitably impressed to waive your third year and have you interned as soon as possible.'

Sean looked towards the altar and turned back to Mark. 'I may have misled you somewhat by saying that I had not spoken to anybody from the archbishop's office. In fact, he asked me about a year ago to send him my doctrines on a number of matters. We have been corresponding regularly.'

Mark was enthralled at how calm and collected his young collegian appeared, even talking about his communications with the archbishop, no less.

'I understand that he was more than impressed with your dissertation on current trends within the church. Is that correct?' asked Mark.

Sean, looking towards the altar, said, 'Yes. I have written my thoughts on where I believe the church is at this time in our history. I have told him that I believe that we have lost the people to a large extent. While I do believe that our church – more than any other Christian church – has done a lot to spread the word of God by actions as well as words. I still believe that our people need strong leadership, and that has been lacking. So many Christian souls who used to believe have waned.

'When Jesus told Peter that he would be his rock in order to build his church, he also meant for that church to never stop working for its people. I believe that it has stopped. I believe that we need to do a lot more to bring our sheep back into the fold. What's the point of feeding only those who are already well fed? Why do we surround ourselves with those who already believe? We have lost so many of our people that we need to start again, correct our mistakes, and always change for the times we live in now. People need to reach out for the Holy Spirit, to feel its power, and because of it, they can learn to live in faith.'

Mark looked down at his crumpled papers, turned to Sean, and said, 'I am not privy to all that has been said between you and the archbishop. All I know is that he wants to assign you immediately to our church in Galway city. I believe it's near to your hometown of Ballinasloe.'

'Yes, Galway is a fine city from which to start my ministry. Did they say when I would be made a deacon?'

Mark thought it presumptuous of this young man to be so bold. He responded, 'After your first year there – that is, providing you have met all of the criteria.'

Sean smiled and said, 'I'll be able to see Linda and my family. That's great news. When do I leave?'

'I'm told that the Bishop of Galway at St. Nicholas's Collegiate Church is expecting you this coming weekend. I've already booked your flight. I'll leave it up to you to inform your family of your arrival.'

Mark stood up to leave as Sean said, 'I'd like to say my goodbyes to my fellow seminarians before I go.'

'Of course. If there's anything else you need, just ask.'

Sean smiled his disarming smile and said, 'Would you join me in prayer?'

Mark knelt down beside Sean and said aloud, 'Our Father, who art in heaven, hallowed be thy name . . .'

Archbishop Boland stared blankly down at his desk. Was he witnessing something unique, he wondered? Certainly this young man had intrigued him. He shook his head despairingly. The phone on his desk rang, announcing the arrival of a Father Reginald Rice. He brought himself together and asked his secretary to show his guest into his office.

'Father Rice. Thank you so much for coming at such short notice.' The archbishop extended his hand in greeting.

Father Rice kissed the archbishop's ring. 'My pleasure, Your Grace.'

Father Rice pulled up his chair, and the two men sat down facing each other.

'Father Rice, as I said to you on the phone, my relationship with our seminarian, Sean Robinson, has been troubling me, to say the least. Perhaps our conversation will help me in my task of understanding this young man a little better.'

'Anything I can do to help in that regard is an honor, Your Grace.'

The archbishop continued. 'You see, I've come to know the man only these past two years. As you know, he is on a three-year residential degree course at our Nottingham seminary. He had only barely arrived at the college before I was getting reports from my administrator telling me of some . . .' – the archbishop paused and looked out his window, then, gathering his thoughts, turned back to Father Rice and continued – 'astounding – I don't think I'd be exaggerating by using that word – incidences involving our young seminarian. When you take account of his age,' – he shuffled through some pages in his file – 'I believe he's just turned twenty-six years. It seems all the more extraordinary to me that any man would be capable of his level of understanding.

'I undertook to handle his case myself. I engaged in conversation with Sean on a number of matters including the nature of his beliefs, his understanding of the Trinity, and his knowledge of the Bible. Pretty soon we were engaging in all topics that were far ranging indeed, so much so that I had to confer with my own historians to let me have their opinion as to the knowledge that was being imparted to me by Sean.'

Father Rice smiled and stared at the open fire ablaze in the magnificent fireplace.

The archbishop continued, 'At times I became perplexed. I even asked Sean to write up his papers on various topics and send them to me alone. I instructed him not to disclose our communications to anyone because I was afraid that anybody would deem him to be a fool, a schizophrenic, or worse. He kept to his word. Then I heard from my administrator that Sean had been holding court with his fellow seminarians on a regular basis on all types of subjects. He reported to me that not only has Sean been well received, but he is extremely well liked, to the point that they await his arrival in classes with great expectations. Even my lecturers wait until he arrives before they commence their classes!'

The archbishop looked purposefully into Father Rice's eyes for effect. 'This man, Father, has more intelligence and understanding of anyone I have had the pleasure of meeting since I started my ministry – and that was not today or yesterday.'

Father Rice smiled broadly. He raised his hand gently, saying, 'Your Grace, I understand completely your perplexity and your exasperation. Perhaps if I tell you how I came to meet our prodigy, we can link our histories together into some meaningful essay.'

The archbishop sighed and sat back in his chair. 'Can I get you some tea?'

'That would be welcome, Your Grace.'

The secretary was summoned, and Father Rice took up a position at the glowing fire.

'I first came across Sean when he was at the tender age of twelve. He was in our local Catholic school in Ballinasloe. The principal and I go way back. He brought to my attention that one of his pupils had been "holding court" in religious class, and he thought I should see it for myself. Of course I was more than intrigued when I heard that the lad was so young and that not only had he enthralled his fellow pupils, but also his fellow senior students and teachers. I sat in the classroom totally mesmerized. I saw and heard a young boy unfazed in meting out doctrines that any ecclesiastic would be proud to be the author of. This was his second discourse, the first having been held a few days earlier to an equally surprised audience.

'I spoke with the principal immediately afterwards, and like you, I discussed my concerns that if this were to continue, that the young lad could be subject to ridicule from the rest of the school. The principal agreed with me. But I was also concerned that Sean's thoughts should not be curtailed. For that reason, I undertook to meet with Sean one day per week to discuss all matters that came into his mind. I met with him each and every week until he reached the age of seventeen. At that stage, he was more than wrapped up in his studies for his Leaving Certificate Examinations, which he passed with full honors. It was only then that we had serious discussions about the priesthood.

'I have to say that what I witnessed in the classroom that day was no accident. The boy is unique, that's a certainty. If you ask me – and I'm sure that this is the real reason you asked me to come here today – if he was divine in some regard, then my answer would have to be no. If you ask me if I think that Sean sees himself as divine, my answer would still be no. However, that takes me to the parting of my relationship with Sean. He attended Maynooth College under my auspices. After only about four months, it became obvious to me that he certainly did have a vocation. Unfortunately – for my church – he had also fallen in love with his childhood sweetheart. He felt that he would be unable to become a Roman Catholic priest. It was then that I sowed the seed of your church into his mind. He was, of course, fully aware of the Anglican tradition. I believe that after Bishop O'Malley intervened on his behalf at the behest of Sean's mother, that was about the same time you contacted me. I was only too happy to recommend Sean to your church.'

The archbishop crossed his legs, and pouring each of them another cup of tea, he said, 'My researchers came across your name. I knew your credentials, and with all due respect to my friend Bishop O'Malley, I needed to know a lot more about the candidate. You are aware that before we allow any member of the public to be considered as a candidate for the ministry, the candidate has to go through a rigorous assessment period – of sometimes years – in his or her local community before we can consider him or her for our seminary.'

'Yes, I'm fully aware of that, Your Grace.'

'It was only after our talk that I considered bending our rules to allow an unknown to pass our threshold, particularly one from another faith, albeit the faith of a cousin church. You have given me much to think about, and for that I thank you. Can I avail of your time some more in the future?'

'That's not a problem. I am at your service for as long as you need me.'

Both men stood up. As they approached the door, the archbishop said, 'Maybe our churches need some divinity. God knows we have been losing a lot of our parishioners over the past decades. The majority of the world's population still does not believe in God or the Christ. Maybe it is time for a miracle or two. We can only pray, I guess.'

Father Rice nodded in agreement, asking, 'Will you be making Sean a deacon?'

The archbishop stared at the carpet, raised his head, and said, 'I'm putting him under the watchful eye of Bishop O'Dwyer in my Galway church. I've apprised him of his new recruit and asked him to keep me updated on his progress. I've also asked my bishop to keep a rein on him. He must perform his seminarian duties like everybody else. I expect he'll be made a deacon within the year, which is still way ahead of all other seminarians.'

The archbishop looked out his window, and after a long thought, he said, 'Father Rice' – he paused, looking for the right words – 'I have something to say in absolute confidence to you. My understanding, from my discussions with the young man, gives me the impression that he won't be here for long. I cannot say for certain that I am correct in making that assumption. Maybe I'm wrong. I certainly hope that I am, but it has made me work with haste where he is concerned.'

Father Rice looked surprised. 'I will keep your confidences, Your Grace. Sean never struck me as a boy who would act in any depressed state. He always seemed well grounded to me. I'm sure that it is aberrational due to the nature of your conversations.'

'I hope you're right, Father. Thank you for your time. I will take you up on your offer of further help. I will also keep you apprised of our young man's development.'

'I would appreciate that, Your Grace.'

The Coin in the Fish.

It was 2012, four years after the recession hit. *Where did all of those years go?* Dan asked himself. Even the annual fair, his life's blood, had deteriorated by about fifty percent. Every business in the town had been affected. The profits from Dan's pub were barely covering the interest on the loan. Unless things improved dramatically, he would be forced to sell the business.

Dan didn't think he could live with the shame. What would he say to Bridie? Sure, he knew she would be supportive, but that wasn't the point. He had failed her – that was the truth. He had let her down. His children had been fantastic. Molly and Kevin were independent of his distress. Sean was away in college. Bridie was well respected in the hospital and, by all accounts, was doing a superb job. He was the one who had failed his family. What would his father say to him now?

It didn't look as if the government knew what they were doing. There had been so much in-fighting that the country seemed to be leaderless. What hope had the ordinary businessman for the future? Everything looked as if it was on a downward spiral. Dan's only gamble in life had been an abysmal failure. He knew – his instincts had told him – that he should never have gotten involved with such a mad-hatter scheme. But his greed had gotten the better of him. Looking for the easy way out, he had thought. How could things go wrong? Yes, they bloody well had gone wrong – by the truck load.

Dan had heard of how other people had taken their lives because of the downturn. He had read how their wives had left their children at school only to find, on their return, that their husbands were hanging from a tree in the front garden or had suffocated in their garage from carbon monoxide poisoning. Dan looked over at the dining room wall. The two-shot Beretta was hanging where it had always hung. He hadn't used it to hunt for many years. He stood up and took it down from its mounting. He cracked open the barrel, and taking a shell from the drawer, he loaded the gun. He sat down at the table and stared at the gun. His mind went numb. He sat there for a long while with his demon thoughts.

Then his mobile phone rang, shaking him out of his dilemma. He took the phone from his pocket and thought he saw a picture of a cross being displayed. Blinking his eyes, he looked again to see it was from Sean. 'Hello,' he whispered.

'Dad, it's me, Sean. Can you come and collect me at the station?'

Dan breathed out heavily. 'Sean, what are you doing back home?'

'I decided to surprise everybody. I'll tell you all about it when you get here. Will you hurry up? I'm freezing cold, and I've no coat.'

'Yes, son, I'll be there as quick as I can.'

Dan hung up, and for the first time in his life, he cried loudly.

Linda couldn't focus on her work at the hospital. Sean's phone call telling her he was home was so out of the blue. At last her Sean would be home tomorrow. How she had managed to get through these past two years was anybody's guess. She was just glad that it had finally come to an end. Now they could get on with their lives – together.

There was a knock on her door. 'Come in; it's open.'

Sean popped his head around. 'Is there anybody here who's crazy about anybody here?'

'Sean, Sean, you're home!' Linda jumped up and ran into his arms.

They kissed wildly, embracing each other as if for the first time. After minutes had passed, Linda finally calmed down and needed to sit. Sean held her hand.

'I decided to surprise everybody, especially you. I couldn't wait to see you. The bishop is expecting me tomorrow, but I managed to escape a day earlier. I had Dad give me a ride from the station. I wanted to see you first, before anyone.'

'You told me on the phone that you are being assigned to the church in Galway under the bishop. Is that correct?'

'Yes. A Bishop Benny. I don't know if that's his first or his second name. Seemingly I'm very lucky to be under the auspices of a bishop for my first assignment. It means I'm only a stone's throw away from you. I'll be able to come home to Ballinasloe every weekday evening, so we can spend lots of time together. Unfortunately, the weekends are the busiest for me and for the church.'

'That doesn't matter,' Linda interrupted. 'I don't care, knowing we can be together now.'

'Is Mum around?'

'She's at some meeting or other. She's going to be thrilled to see you.'

'Before that, how about showing me around the hospital? I haven't seen any of the new renovations.'

'Come on. I'm ordering you to hold my hand, though, if you want the personal tour.'

'I'm going to hold it forever.'

Bridie glanced around the table. It was hard to believe that in a few short years, her hospital had grown to the size it was today. She was half-listening to her new doctor, Ly Oluha, just arrived from Nigeria. He had brilliant credentials. She smiled thinking that the locals would be shocked to see their first black man strolling through the streets of Ballinasloe. Dr. Luke O'Reilly had recommended him. As far as Bridie was concerned, she didn't mind whom he employed; they were his responsibility.

She now had seven doctors, fifteen nurses, and four administrative staff, compared to the two doctors, nine nurses, and three admin staff she had had before. Bridie was now full-time administrator. She missed the nursing part but had found she had a good disposition towards being in charge. Everybody seemed to respect her, even one or two of the more pompous doctors. The money was also a lot better than it was before, which was no harm because every little extra helped to relieve the money tensions at home. She thought about Dan for the umpteenth time. He seemed to be more withdrawn than ever before.

'Bridie, what's your opinion?'

She blinked out of her thoughts and saw everybody looking in her direction. She had to rewind her mind and try to figure out what they had been discussing. 'Whatever the majority consensus is, I'll go along with that.'

'Done,' said Dr. Luke.

Dr. Oluha rose from his seat and extended his hand towards Bridie, saying, 'I want to thank you for your trust in me. I promise I won't let you down.'

'I know you won't. You are very welcome. Besides, I don't know how we coped up to this.'

'That's so very true, Bridie. We seem to be getting patients not only from Galway County, but also from the city and surrounding counties,' added Dr. Luke.

'We must be doing something right,' said Bridie.

'It's all down to your administration, Bridie,' added Dr. Luke.

Both she and Dr. Luke had become closer since the new construction had been completed. He seemed to have a lot more confidence in her ability. He confided in her, unlike when he first appeared on the scene. Bridie welcomed that. She much preferred having a happy management; it seemed to have a positive effect on her nursing and administrative staff too.

Bridie made her way back to her office. As she turned the corner, she screamed, 'Oh my God, Sean Robinson! You wee divil!' She ran towards him and gave him a massive hug.

'I'm sorry, Mum. I wanted to surprise everybody.'

'How did you get here? Have you a car?'

'I rang Dad. He picked me up at the station and drove me here.'

Bridie gave Linda a hug.

'Linda was showing me around,' said Sean. 'You've done superb work, Mum.'

'Thank you, son. It's all down to my brilliant staff,' Bridie said as she hugged Linda some more. 'Come on. I need a cup of tea. Then you can tell me all about your plans.'

Dan arrived at his pub to see Paraic Liddy waiting outside in his car. *What's he doing here?* he thought.

Paraic wound down his window. 'Dan, have you got a minute?'

Dan put one hand on the roof of his car. 'Only if it's good news.'

'It is, in a kind of a way.'

'You'd better come inside, then.'

Dan punched in the numbers to switch off the alarm. He clicked on the lights and put a match to the fire.

'That won't take too long to warm up. It's bloody freezing in here, but I have to cut costs wherever I can. There's no point in wasting the central heating for the few stragglers who appear here in the morning.'

They both extended their hands to get whatever warmth they could from the young fire.

'What I have to say might warm you up.'

'Go on,' said Dan as he looked at Paraic tentatively.

'Dan, I've been approached by some developers who are interested in buying our property.'

Dan looked wide-eyed. 'What do you mean?'

'I've been on the lookout for anybody who might be interested in taking the land off our hands. I don't know whether you're aware or not, but Mark and I had to break up the practice. Mark got a job with a Dublin accountancy firm. I managed to keep a number of my clients. I can just about put bread on the table. I suppose, like me, you've found the weight of the loan a pretty hefty burden?'

'You could say that,' said Dan, thinking back to two hours ago and how his thoughts had taken a hold of him, only to be broken by a phone call from Sean. A cold fear swept over his body, causing him to shudder.

'I've had two meetings with these people. What they are willing to pay is nothing near what we invested. They are offering us a thirty percent return, which means we'd recover about ninety to a hundred thousand euros each.'

'You mean the bank will recover it,' corrected Dan.

'Yes, of course. But at least our interest payments will drop, and the loan will be that much more manageable. I suppose, like me, that you've been hounded by the banks ever since the crash,' added Paraic.

'They never leave me alone. There's hardly a week goes by without somebody calling me from the local branch or from their head office in Dublin. I never know who I'm dealing with. They always ask the same questions. They couldn't care less about me or my family, or that I'm doing the best I can to pay down the loan.' Dan fumbled with the beer mats on the table. Looking up to Paraic, he asked, 'What happens to poor Cronin's part in all of this if we do this deal?'

'Oh, the proceeds will go into his estate, and no doubt the banks will take all of it. What a terrible thing to have happened to him. I still can't believe he's dead! At least they caught those two bastards who killed him,' Paraic said, gazing back into the fire, which had taken hold and was now ablaze. 'Didn't they drink here in your place?' he asked.

'They did, and they'll not be drinking here again now that they're locked up in Athlone Prison. They were part of Boxer's gang – or is it Harry Devlin's gang? I'm not sure who's in charge. Boxer and his friend Harry still have their usual spots over there, only because they had no involvement in the affair. The police checked them out, and they had solid alibis for the night in question. In actual fact, they were here most of the night. Anyway, I know Boxer from old; he'd never get involved in murder. Those two, Dino and Fonsie, were caught red-handed with the cash. Old man Cronin had taken the cash out of the bank that very same day. It's unbelievable that something like that could have happened in our quiet little town.'

Dan joined Paraic as they both gazed into the now roaring fire.

'They got life imprisonment for their troubles,' added Paraic.

'And rightly so. May they rot up in Athlone,' spat Dan, shaking his head and returning to the problem at hand. 'But I heard that the property market is improving. There must be some hope that things will improve.'

'There has been a minor improvement but only in Dublin. There are still so many ghost estates scattered throughout the country that it would take a miracle before the likes of Ballinasloe saw any recovery.'

'I've used up my quota for miracles already today,' said Dan, throwing another two logs on to the fire. Paraic looked at him, not understanding his comment. Dan stood up. 'Excuse me for a minute. I need to go into the back room. I'll be back shortly. Help yourself to something in the bar.'

'I'll just get myself a bottle of water.'

Dan closed the door behind him. He walked towards a chair and knelt down on both knees, resting his elbows on the seat. He blessed himself, saying in a quiet whisper, 'God, our Father, I know I've never spoken to you. I'm no good, and I'm ashamed to be asking of you now. Whether you answer me or not, this much I do promise. I'm a changed man. There will be no more feeling sorry for myself. I've raised a great family, one of whom will be working directly for you. I'll be doing the same from now on. All I'm asking is that you guide me on making the right decision this time. Do I sell or not? God, please help me. I know I don't deserve your sympathy, but I'm begging of you.'

After some minutes, Dan stood up, blessed himself, and opened the door to the bar.

Paraic was sitting up at the bar, sipping his water. 'Dan, that frame is just about to fall off your wall.'

Dan looked around and saw that the frame hanging on the wall that was once square was now diagonal. He smiled to himself.

'It just moved when you opened the door,' added Paraic.

'That frame holds my lucky coin,' Dan continued. 'When I was a lad, I found that coin in the belly of a large trout up by the lake. My mother told me to frame it because it was a lucky coin. It's been hanging on that wall ever since. It's time to put it to work.' Dan took the coin from the frame.

'What sort of a coin is it, Dan? It's tiny.'

'It's an Irish three-pence coin. We used to call it a "thrupenny bit." You see, it has a rabbit on one side for the "heads" and a harp on the other side for the "tails." It's tiny and silver; that's why the fish was attracted to it. I'll tell you what we'll do. I'll flick the coin. If it comes down heads, we'll sell; tails we don't.'

Paraic looked at Dan, then at the coin, and said, 'You know, I could give you all of the financial reasons in the world why we should sell or hold, but doing it your way is probably just as useful. Flick it.'

The Good Thief.

St. Nicholas's collegiate church in Galway city is an imposing building. Built in the fourteenth century, it still commands a prominent position in Galway city to this day. Christopher Columbus himself stopped and prayed there back in 1477. The centuries have kept its walls intact throughout all of its history, both bad and good. It was into this fountain of magnificence that one Sean Robinson found himself on a windy Saturday morning in the depths of winter.

'Sean, me boy!' came a shout from the altar. 'I've been expecting you.' Bishop Benny came bouncing up the aisle, arms outstretched.

Sean beamed a smile in his direction. 'Bishop Benny, I assume?'

'Indeed it is. I've heard so much about you. I can't wait for us to work together. Tell me, when did you get here?'

'I arrived only yesterday. I was with my family last night and got a lift here this morning. I'm looking forward to our working together, Your Grace.'

'Please, call me Benny – when we are in private. "Your Grace" is acceptable when anyone else is present.'

'Thank you, eh, Benny.' Sean stalled his wheelie case in the aisle.

'Come on, let me show you around this amazing piece of architecture.'

The bishop proceeded to name names of previous inhabitants throughout the centuries, never missing the famous, or the infamous, as he led Sean through every nook and cranny, of which there were many. Everything from the early-seventeenth-century baptismal font to the fifteenth-century vaulted south porch exuded a period in history that only this structure could portray with bold pride. The bishop explained that the church was dedicated to St. Nicholas of Myra, in Turkey, best known as the patron saint of children, or "Santa Claus," although during the Middle Ages, he was revered as the patron saint of sailors. The crosses and banners were memorials to all of those who had died during the First World War as well as those who gave their lives during Napoleonic times.

When they had finished their tour, Bishop Benny showed Sean his living quarters. It was a modest two-roomed bed-sit, with a comfortable living room and a separate bedroom.

'You don't have to bother about any cooking as the wonderful Mrs. Harte, our housekeeper, looks after all of us,' said the bishop. 'Now, let me introduce you to the person you'll be seeing a lot of – Peter Wilson. He should be in his room, as I told him to expect you.'

Benny led Sean to an adjacent room. He gently knocked, calling out, 'Peter, are you there?'

With that, the door flung open, and a broadly smiling Peter spoke loudly. 'Ah, you must be the great Sean Robinson! How wonderful to finally meet you,' he exclaimed as he shook Sean's hand excitedly.

Sean was taken aback by such a display of exuberance and returned Peter's smile with, 'Well, I don't know about my being "great," but I thank you all the same for such a warm greeting.'

'I think Peter has been wanting to meet someone of his own age and demeanor for a long time instead of hanging around with old fellows like me,' explained the bishop.

Peter never answered. Instead, continuing with his exuberance, he grabbed Sean's arm. 'Come with me, and I'll show you around the area.' He suddenly stopped in his tracks and turned to the bishop. 'That is, if your grace is finished?'

The bishop smiled, saying, 'Yes, of course. You two do what you have to do. Be back here in a few hours. We have a busy couple of days. You show Sean the ropes.'

Peter continued holding Sean's arm and led him outside.

'It appears to be very relaxed around here,' stated Sean as Peter pointed him in the direction of the door, leading out onto Shop Street.

'Oh, you couldn't wish for a better superior – indeed, bishop, for that matter – than to have Benny as your boss. I've been here a little short of two years. I'm hoping to be conferred in the not-too-distant future. I believe – and hope – that I'll then be transferred to our church in Tuam. You're going to really like it here. You must know Galway like the back of your hand being from Ballinasloe and all?'

'Galway would be like a second home to me,' Sean agreed as they made their way past McDonald's leading towards Eyre Square. 'So it's just the two of us, then, and the bishop?'

'That's about it. We have around three hundred parishioners, two Sunday masses, and a daily mass at ten o'clock. The bishop hears confessions once a month. Other than that, we have the usual things such as hospital visits, parishioner problems, baptisms and funerals, and the occasional marriage ceremony. We're kept reasonably busy, but it does leave a lot of time for studies, which is a good thing.'

They continued their walk up Shop Street, passing Brown Thomas and turning right on to Eyre Square.

'Where are you from originally?' asked Sean.

'I was born into an Anglican family in Leeds in England. My family immigrated to Ireland when my father became the Anglican pastor assigned to the parish in Cork. I was the youngest of three children. I decided to follow in my father's footsteps and enter the priesthood from an early age. I guess I was always destined to follow the missionary route seeing I knew nothing else all of my life – and I'm glad I did so, especially after both my parents passed away at such an early age.'

'I'm sorry to hear that,' added Sean.

'Thank you. I completed the two-year formation program and followed that with the three-year residential degree. Now here I am, happy as a little piggy.' Sean smiled. 'Tell me about yourself,' asked Peter as they made their way towards Forster Street. The crowds hustled and bustled their way while Sean and Peter dodged them as best they could. 'Come on, let's go in and have a cuppa. There's a café express back there on the corner; otherwise, we'll be trampled alive by the Saturday crowds.'

Finding a table and giving their orders to the waitress, Sean continued. 'I was adopted as a baby. My mother, Bridie, found me outside her hospital – she's the Matron there – and somehow or other, they managed to cajole some higher-up people to have me legally adopted. My father, Dan, owns a small public house in the town. I have an older brother, Kevin, and an older sister, Molly. I knew I was always destined to be with God, in spirit and in body and mind. I never had any other ambition. I've thoroughly enjoyed the journey thus far.'

Peter sipped his tea and asked, 'Did you ever find out who your biological parents are?'

Sean looked towards the window, watching everybody going to and fro. 'No, I never did. It was never important to me. I was an infant when my mum found me. They've been great parents. I could never have wished for better.'

Peter smiled, saying, 'Is there anybody special in your life – of the nondivine class?'

Sean smiled back at him. 'Yes, I have someone I love deeply. Her name is Linda. I hope to marry her someday. What about yourself?'

'I've been engaged a year now. Her name is Shirley. We met a couple of years back. We got engaged earlier this year.'

'Congratulations. Who knows? Maybe I'll be able to officiate at your wedding someday,' added Sean. 'You were saying that Bishop Benny is great to work for – in what way?'

Peter poured himself another cup of tea. 'Bishop Benny O'Dwyer – known simply as Benny to all of the parishioners – came here about twenty years ago. He used to serve as bishop in one of the Dublin churches and got promoted to Galway at that time. He's married to Martha.' Peter paused to take another sip of tea. 'Unfortunately, she's unwell. Poor Benny is perplexed not knowing what he can do for her. He's had all of the doctors and specialists examine her. They don't know what's wrong with her. She's wasting away. It doesn't look good, I'm afraid.'

'I'm sorry to hear that. Is she old?'

'Benny is in his late fifties. I'd put Martha around the early fifties mark. He keeps her situation to himself most of the time. The odd time I've passed his rooms, I've heard him weeping to himself. He's a good man, Sean.'

'I believe that,' agreed Sean.

'Come on, we'd better be getting back. We have to prepare the church, and there's a ton of printing to be done. You'd also better meet the great Mrs. Harte. I hope you're not hungry!' he laughed as Sean let the unexplained comment pass.

'Lock up. Get your bony asses back in your boxes where ye belong,' cracked the officer to all and sundry inmates who were akin to nothing as far as he was concerned. 'You lousy bag of worms need to crawl back to where you came from.'

Fonsie was used to the insults. What he could never get used to was the never-ending fear he had that one day he wouldn't wake up – he'd be dead! Athlone Prison was unlike any other prison for those who had wandered in that direction. It was soulless. It had been used primarily to house all of the IRA scumbags who had killed, maimed, and degenerated normal human beings during a period of Irish history termed 'the Troubles.' The IRA had never had a forethought, let alone an afterthought, for the innocents who got in their way for the sake of a so-called 'freedom' that nobody in Ireland had signed up for. Now that these troubled times had passed, these reprobates had been admonished of their sins by the governments of the time, both Irish and English, and Athlone Prison returned to what it had been devised for – a concrete dwelling for those who had committed the gravest crimes against society.

Fonsie looked around. There was no sign of Dino. He made his way into his cell, a cell he shared with Mick O'Connell, another degenerate from Waterford who liked to con people out of their rightful inheritances. He was damned good at it too. The cell bars banged shut. Fonsie breathed another daily sigh of relief that he had managed to avoid Dino, all the time making it appear to everybody that he would do whatever Dino wanted whenever it was required.

Ever since that fateful night when Dino had killed old man Cronin, his life had been ruined. There had been no need to do it. Fonsie had never hurt a single individual in his life. He was a thief. A damned good thief, for that matter – what would he know about killing? Then again, he was also a cowardly thief. There was no way he was going to stand up in any court of law and testify against anybody, especially when Boxer and Harry were in the background making sure that nobody squealed. *Why can't I be doing what I'm best at?* he thought to himself.

Fonsie also knew that he needed Dino more than Dino needed his silence. Dino gave protection against all of the squalid behaviors that were rampant in this prison as in every other prison across the land. There was no way that Fonsie was going to lose that protection anytime soon, which was why he knuckled down in his cell every night, subliminally knowing that his guardian angel, known as one Dino, was there protecting him against anything untoward that might befall him, as long as he remained quiet. There was no way that Fonsie would have gotten himself involved in any murder. Stealing was fine. As far as he was concerned, if people decided to be loose with their belongings, that was their problem, and Fonsie was there to relieve them of their indiscretions or stupidities. Murder – never – it was too much like trouble.

Dino had found a niche in this prison. Even though he had never been inside, he was nevertheless admired. He was more than strong, well able to look after himself. He had proven it a number of times as one prisoner after another tried to make claim to his jurisdiction. Dino was well able to dispel any thoughts they might have had about gaining new territory. Blood and bile soon put an end to their aspirations. That didn't stop Dino from making sure that Fonsie kept onside. There wasn't a day went by when Dino didn't pay a visit or send a message to Fonsie via one of his stoolies, making sure he was fully aware of their predicament. Dino didn't have to explain anything about who was king of this castle. Fonsie did what he was told, make no mistake.

It was more than bad luck that that woman had appeared out of nowhere. Why the hell had she picked that night of all nights to pay a visit to the old man? Only for her, they would have gotten away with it. Then, after leaving Harry's, they were on the road to nowhere, as the song goes. Dino hadn't a clue where he was going, and then they ran into a roadblock, from which there was no escape. Dino had warned Fonsie that if he went down, then they both went down. The fact that they happened to have the money on them signed and sealed the case against them. The bank already had the serial numbers of the banknotes; therefore, they could say or do nothing.

Twenty-five years minimum, the judge had said. Even though Fonsie had told his solicitors that he had nothing to do with the murder, even though they had pleaded with him to tell the truth and to hell with Dino, Fonsie couldn't rat on his partner. Besides, Harry was always in the background, not to mention Boxer. There was nothing for it other than to go along with the lie that both he and Dino had committed the murder between them, Fonsie having invented a story that betrayed the two of them. They were both guilty as charged. Now he was to spend the rest of his life living – existing – for something he never did. Nobody was to know or ever give a damn.

Archbishop Boland hung up the phone. He had just been speaking with Bishop Benny, getting updated on their prodigy. Nine months had elapsed since Sean had arrived in Galway. During that time, he had dutifully followed the bishop's counselling, performed all of his duties methodically, warmed himself to the community, and made a name for himself, thankfully, in a quiet way.

The archbishop had given his instruction to his bishop that he was to arrange for Sean's deaconship. He felt there was no point in delaying matters any longer. He wanted Sean to be a fully fledged priest as soon as possible; making him a deacon now fast-tracked that plan. Archbishop Boland prayed that he was doing the right thing; he prayed for guidance.

Sean and Linda had gotten closer over the past year. They saw one another a few times every week. She half-expected Sean to propose to her every time they met, but it didn't happen. She didn't like to be pushy. She knew they loved each other. She also knew that this was the most important time for Sean in his career. They were also young enough to wait. She had heard of many Anglican priests who got married after they were ordained. She could wait, no matter how long it took. Besides, the new year was approaching. The big event of Sean being made a deacon was about to happen. Everything could wait until after that.

Linda took her seat alongside Bridie and Dan in the front row, accompanied by Molly and Kevin. The church was filled to half of its capacity by friends of the family, members of the congregation, and curious onlookers. Peter assisted the bishop while Sean knelt in front of the bishop at the head of the altar. Bishop Benny read aloud:

Every Christian is called to follow Jesus Christ, serving God the Father, through the power of the Holy Spirit. God now calls you to a special ministry of servant hood directly under your bishop. In the name of Jesus Christ, you are to serve all people, particularly the poor, the weak, the sick, and the lonely.

As a deacon in the Church, you are to study the Holy Scriptures, to seek nourishment from them, and to model your life upon them. You are to make Christ and his redemptive love known, by your word and example, to those among whom you live, and work, and worship. You are to interpret to the Church the needs, concerns, and hopes of the world. You are to assist the bishop and priests in public worship and in the ministration of God's Word and Sacraments, and you are to carry out other duties assigned to you from time to time. At all times, your life and teaching are to show Christ's people that in serving the helpless they are serving Christ himself.

'My brother, do you believe that you are truly called by God and his church to the life and work of a deacon?'

Sean replied, 'I believe I am so called.'

The ordination was followed by a full mass, after which everybody gathered outside on the church grounds. Bridie and Dan couldn't have been more proud. Sean and Linda looked so happy together, which made Bridie smile all the more. Bishop Benny greeted all of the guests and was interrupted to take a phone call.

Judge Conran made his way up to shake Sean's hand. Turning to Dan, he said, 'It's hard to believe where all those years went Dan, what?'

'Indeed,' answered Dan. ''Tis a proud day for the Robinson clan,' he continued.

Bishop Benny came back holding his phone and handed it to Sean. He said, 'There's somebody on the other end who wants to speak with you, Sean.' Sean took the phone, smiling.

'I want to offer you my heartfelt congratulations, Sean. It's Bishop O'Malley, from the other side. I don't know if you remember me?'

'Of course I remember you, Bishop. How nice of you to ring me.'

'How are your parents?'

'They're both fine. Thank you, Bishop.'

'You know, if it wasn't for the pair of them, God only knows where you might be today.'

'I'm fully aware of that, Your Grace. It's so good of you to remember me.'

'It's a very special day for you, Sean. I couldn't let it go by without giving you my blessing. I look forward to meeting with you someday.'

'The honor will be all mine, Your Grace.' Sean hung up and handed the phone back to Bishop Benny. 'I can't believe that Bishop O'Malley rang me. How did he know?'

Bridie smiled and said, 'I think it's time we all had something to eat. Let's go.'

The Disciple.

Vinnie lay in his bed. He had been awake for hours, as he had been every morning since he had heard the news from his doctor.

'Parkinson's,' he whispered to himself. Specifically, they called it 'young-onset Parkinson's.' 'Young is right,' whispered Vinnie again. 'I'm only twenty-bloody-seven, for God's sake!'

He jumped up in the bed and threw his legs over the side, staring at the floor. He raised his left hand. He had noticed it shaking every now and then. His father had had it when he was a young age, except they didn't know at that time what it was. He ended up in a wheelchair at the age of forty. He was dead at forty-seven.

'Jasus,' Vinnie said aloud, dragging himself into the bathroom.

In fairness, if not for the local doctor having treated his father, he would never have found out about the disease until it was too late. Vinnie had told his doctor about how he was having trouble standing up straight but had put that down to arthritis since all of his family had suffered from it. The doctor performed tests and came to his conclusion only last week. It was definitely Parkinson's.

Vinnie hadn't told anyone, especially his employers. He knew that a small engineering firm such as the one he worked for in Galway wouldn't be too considerate of having their chief engineer suffering from a debilitating disease. As far as they would be concerned, it would be time to look for a replacement. As if things weren't bad enough. His firm was just about managing to tick over. The year 2015 didn't look as if it would be any better than the previous seven years. Thank God he lived with his mother and hadn't to support a family. He decided he wouldn't worry his mother, as she knew only too well the pain his father had gone through.

'Vinnie, Vinnie, get up. There's someone down here to see you,' shouted his mother from downstairs.

Who the hell is looking for me at this hour of the morning? he thought. 'Give me a minute!' he bellowed back.

Ten minutes later, he made his way downstairs to the kitchen to find Sean sitting down to a cup of tea. 'Sean, what the divil are you doing over here?'

'How are you, Vinnie? I couldn't resist calling over to sample your mother's heavenly soda bread, knowing its fame is widespread.'

'Oh, you are a charmer all right, Sean Robinson, and always was. I remember you coming over here as a little boy begging me for my jam cakes. You have a wee devil of a sweet tooth, make no mistake. You're very welcome here anytime at all,' insisted Mrs. Baker. 'I'll leave you two boys to discuss whatever it is needs discussing. I have loads to do,' she said as she made her way from the kitchen.

'So, what brings you over to this neck of the woods?'

'First, tell me, how are you feeling health wise?'

Vinnie looked at Sean in a curious way, letting his curiosity dwell on his face. 'What do you mean?'

'I like to know that my friends are all well. That's all.'

Vinnie wanted to tell Sean so badly about his recent news but thought that it was better not to say anything to anybody. 'I'm grand. Couldn't be better. What can I do for you, now? Do I call you 'Father' or what?'

Sean smiled. 'I'm not a priest yet. I was made a deacon last year. Hopefully within the next couple of years I'll be made a priest. Call me Sean – now and forever.'

'Okay – Sean. What's going on?'

Sean took another sip of tea and, wiping his lips, continued, 'You remember the earthquake in Haiti back in 2010?'

Vinnie had to look up at the ceiling to remember it and clear his head of other distracting thoughts. 'Of course. It was a terrible thing. All those poor people.'

Sean nodded. 'Unfortunately, it's still a terrible thing. A friend of mine – a Father Miguel Courtois, who is based in Miami, Florida – has been running a mercy mission to and from a small town in Haiti that was devastated by the earthquake. We met in Nottingham. Father Miguel was one of my lecturers. We've kept in touch over the years. He needs my help. He tells me that the situation there is worse than hopeless even many years after the initial earthquake.' Sean took another sip of tea. He put his cup back down and looked deeply at Vinnie and said, 'My help is you!'

Sean waited for Vinnie to react and didn't have to wait long.

'My help?' said an open-mouthed Vinnie. 'How could I possibly help this priest and the people of Haiti all the way from Ballinasloe in little old Ireland?'

Sean replaced his teacup. Looking into Vinnie's eyes, he said, 'Vinnie, I know you to be a great engineer. I also know that you have a great heart. It doesn't take much to also learn that you are not run off your feet with work presently. I know you to be a good Christian, albeit maybe a temporarily lapsed one. I'd like you to look into your heart and see whether you could offer your services to these poor people who badly need your help and expertise. Is that something you could do for me – for yourself?'

Vinnie let out a gasp of air. He stood up, circled the kitchen floor, and settled his hands on the sink, peering out the window. His thoughts ran from his sickness to his work, then to his mother. There was no doubt that Sean had blown his bubble of self-pity away to kingdom come. What was he saying to him?

'Sean, I couldn't possibly be of any use to these people. I'm not qualified to start rebuilding their lives. Besides, I don't even speak Spanish.'

'It's Creole, actually, not Spanish. That's not a problem because Father Courtois speaks the language fluently. He also knows all of the natives and will guide your every step. He'd do it himself if he had the knowledge that you have. He needs a professional to understand the geography and the engineering requirements. All of these things you have. Father Courtois has all the rest.'

Vinnie dragged his foot along the floor. He looked up, saying, 'Let me think about it, but don't hold your breath.'

'That's all I needed from you, Vinnie. I know you'll do the right thing.' Sean stood up and, smiling at Vinnie, said, 'You know, we haven't seen enough of each other since our school days. We should rectify that situation. How about you and I go out for dinner some night and maybe having a drink or two?'

'That'd be great. Anytime,' said Vinnie, slightly perplexed.

Sean smiled broadly. 'I must be off. How about Thursday night? We could meet around seven for a pint and then have something to eat, just the two of us.'

'Okay, great,' said Vinnie as Sean bid his goodbyes by shouting to Mrs. Baker up the stairs.

As Sean left, Vinnie sat down in the sitting room and contemplated what had just happened, rubbing his left arm as he did so.

Christy took another slurp of his Smithwick's shandy. He still shuddered when he thought how close he had come to being implicated in old man Cronin's murder. Thank God he had used a throwaway phone to make contact with Harry, giving him the information he needed about Cronin's movements that fateful night. *Why the hell did they have to kill him?* he thought. He always used a throwaway phone for all of his gambling transactions. An inner voice had guided him to use it in any discussions with Harry Devlin – and boy, was he glad he did.

The police had interviewed Christy a number of times. They suspected that Dino and Fonsie had inside information. How else could they have known that Cronin would have all of that cash on that particular night? It was his new manager, Mick Mullaly, who had destroyed their 'inside man' suspicions when he told them that it was very well known around the town that Mr. Cronin was retiring that day. It wouldn't have taken a thief long to figure out that he might be carrying a lot of money. That more or less convinced the police to leave Christy alone. There was no paper trail linking Christy to him. He never signed any of the documents. He knew that Cronin would have thought he had signed all the chits, but Christy was smart enough to avoid implicating himself.

Now, if he could only rid himself of that scoundrel Devlin once and for all. Unfortunately, his gambling was an addiction. He was into

Harry, and therefore Boxer, for about five grand. That meant he was their slave. He was also terrified knowing that he would be dead if he ever revealed any information to the police. Besides, he had nothing to gain from doing that.

'Hello, Christy.' Christy turned with a start to see Sean behind him. 'How have you been?'

Christy fumbled for words, saying, 'Okay. Can't say I've ever seen you in here before. Do you not support your father's pub?'

'I'm meeting Vinnie Baker. He suggested we try Maud Millar's Pub. What's the beer like?'

'It's beer, same as any other, I suppose.' Christy finished off the rest of his pint. 'I've got to be going. I'm late already. Nice seeing you, Sean.'

Christy made his way quickly to the door, just running into Vinnie, who was making his way inside.

'Hey what's the big rush there, Christy?' With that, Christy was gone. 'He was in a bit of a hurry,' suggested Vinnie as he made his way towards the bar counter.

'Yes, I haven't run into him in a long while. I hope he's doing okay,' said Sean.

Vinnie got the barman's attention and ordered a pint. He said, 'Christy will always be running, I'm afraid. I heard he's a bit addicted to gambling. Not a good gambler by all accounts.'

Sean ordered a pint of Guinness too, and both men made their way to a vacant table by the window.

'So tell me, have you reached any decision about what we discussed the other day?' asked Sean.

Vinnie downed a good dollop of stout, and wiping his lips, he said, 'Sean, I need more time to think about it. That's a good thing as I'm not discounting it altogether.'

'Of course. Take all the time you need, Vinnie. I'm not going to force you to do anything you don't want to do.'

Vinnie paused in thought. 'I've been studying up on Haiti. I googled it, and to be honest, it looks horrendous. The whole country was destroyed.'

Sean pursed his lips in soulful thought. 'Certainly the better part of it was destroyed. According to Father Miguel, there hadn't been much to destroy at best because the country had already been in a perilous state before the earthquake. I feel it is my duty as a priest and a citizen that we should always try to help those who are worse off than we are, especially as tragedy always seems to befall those who least deserve it.'

Vinnie took another slurp of his drink. 'That begs a question, Sean. Why does God allow these things to always happen to the poorest in our society? Why does he inflict sickness and hardship on those who haven't done anything wrong? When you consider the badness of some people, and yet they always seem to escape any punishment.'

Sean smiled and, leaning forward in his chair, said, 'You know, Vinnie, it's an honest question, and many people always ask it, especially when a tragedy strikes. But it's not an act of God. People construe that someone should always be responsible for wrongdoing, and when that person is unidentifiable, they blame God. God made us. He put us here, but he doesn't interfere with us. He gave us everything we need to lead a good life. He also created this amazing world we live in and made us kings over it to do with it what we please. He also gave us rules to follow. Unfortunately, mankind has always deemed it to be his world, not God's. Man has a happy knack of forgetting about God when things are going well and castigating Him when things turn against us. We should learn to live our lives as God intended us to live them – to love Him and to love our neighbor. They are the two most important commandments, as reiterated by Jesus himself. That's all God asks us to do – pretty simple, really, when you think about it. That's why I'm asking you to do the trip to help these people in Haiti, to love your neighbor as you would yourself.'

Vinnie smiled and said, 'Did you ever consider becoming a politician, Sean? Because you'd be damned good at it.'

'I think that religion and politics should always be in opposite corners, Vinnie,' added Sean, smiling and drinking his Guinness.

Vinnie looked out the window and finished the last dregs of his Guinness. He announced, 'I'll do it. To hell with it. I've not got much going on at the moment anyway. How long do you think this Father Miguel will need me for?'

Sean spluttered his drink and, laying it down on the table, said, 'Vinnie, that's wonderful news. Father Miguel told me that if you could just spend a few weeks apprising yourself of the problems, then that would be enough to steer you in the right direction. Obviously they can't afford to hire an engineering firm because they simply have no money.' Sean looked hopefully at Vinnie and continued, 'They wouldn't be able to pay you any money. They will give you free board and lodgings, though. You won't need any money because the natives are very friendly.'

Vinnie waved away Sean's concerns with 'I don't need the money. Besides, if it's only for a few weeks, maybe . . .' His thoughts were about to disclose his sickness, so he cut himself short from saying anything further other than, 'Well, you'd better be buying me a lot of pints seeing you cajoled me into leaving my native land.'

They both laughed as Sean willingly ordered another couple of pints.

Over the following three weeks, Sean and Vinnie became very close. They contacted each other daily while Vinnie served his notice with his firm. The firm told him that they were proud of his mission to Haiti and that his job was secure and would be waiting for him on his return.

Sean took the opportunity to further Vinnie's understanding of the gospel. Vinnie at first rejected any thoughts of revising his lapsed Christianity but relented knowing that Sean was doing it for his own good, not anybody else's. They discussed the Bible and especially Jesus's time on earth. When Sean explained in concise terms how Jesus definitely existed, Vinnie became more relaxed. He understood things a lot more clearly, just as the disciples probably did when Jesus was around.

The three weeks flew by, and Sean drove Vinnie to Dublin Airport, where he was to catch the connecting flight from London to Miami and then to Port-au-Prince. As he drove up to the departures drop-off, Vinnie grabbed his bag.

'I hope I'm able to do some good while I'm over there.'

'I know you will, Vinnie. I can't thank you enough for this.'

'It was my decision, Sean, but I thank you for your friendship. I didn't tell you, but I've been going through a pretty rough patch these past couple of months.'

Sean put his fingers to his lips in a blessing motion and said, 'Vinnie, I know about your troubles. Be good, my friend, and we will stay in touch by phone. When you return, your sickness will be gone.'

Sean turned and got into his car. He sped off, leaving Vinnie staring in his wake.

'How did . . .?' His words were lost in the noise.

The Healing.

Bridie studied Dr. Oluha's face as he labored through the day's patients and also the long-term ones.

'We have a problem with beds, Matron. We cannot sustain the standard of care unless we utilize all available beds for those who need them the most. For example, there's a . . .' He trawled through his notes, finding the one he needed. 'Here it is. A certain Mr. Baggie – something or other. He doesn't appear to have a first or second name. Anyway, he's been here for a long time. He's dying, Matron. There's no point in having him here clogging up our system. We should move him to a hospice. Do I have your permission to do so?'

Bridie looked at her doctor. She thought how amazingly odd it was that even though they took a vocational oath, they always seemed to forget about it when it really mattered. Doctors had an uncanny, in-built coldness towards their fellow man.

'I know old Baggie. He's been here longer than I have. In fact, he was here during my mother's time. I cannot throw him out onto the street. If he's dying, then so be it, but he is deserving of our fullest care and attention – regardless,' she said, beginning to get angry.

Dr. Oluha looked at Bridie with a couldn't-care-less attitude. 'So be it. But I want it noted that he leaves my ward. I don't want his type eating away at my budget.'

Bridie tried to maintain her composure. Instead, she was matter-of-fact when she said, 'Leave it to me, doctor. I will make sure he doesn't eat into your budget. Is there anything else?' she asked disdainfully.

'No, that about covers it.' With that, the doctor took his leave.

Bridie sighed as she pondered poor old Baggie's life. God knows he never had anything going for him, only the odd comfort of spending his nights curled up in a warm hospital pretending that nobody knew he was there when all and sundry turned a blind eye to his existence. She didn't know what he did on a daily basis. She was always too busy to think about him. Now he was leaving this world. She wondered about him. She was about to cry when Rosie knocked on her door.

'Bridie, I'll be taking the night shift. Is that okay?'

Bridie shook her head to bring herself back to reality. 'Yes, yes, of course, Rosie. Are you sure you'll be okay on your own?'

'I'll be fine, Bridie. Don't you worry about a thing.' Rosie closed the door and went on her way.

Bridie gathered her papers together, yawned, and thought to herself that she should be heading home. It was late, and she wanted to cook Dan his favorite dinner. Besides, for the first time in a long time, they had two full days off together.

Rosie checked her logs. Everything seemed to be in place. She looked at her watch; it read 11:47. It was time to do her rounds.

Checking in at the nurse's station on the first floor, Rosie noted that everything was in place. She double-checked the nurse's roster. There were no problems that couldn't be handled. Moving up to the second floor, she went from room to room. Apart from the usual coughing and occasional snoring, she was happy to move along, having checked everybody's charts.

While she was in room four, Rosie thought she heard an unusual sound. Moving along the corridor in the direction of the sound, she was now sure that the sound was someone talking. She came upon the resting room, as they referred to it, where they had lodged poor old Baggie. *God help him all the same,* thought Rosie. *The poor divil was going nowhere*; *now he's talking to himself in his sleep.* She hoped he ended up in heaven, as God knows he had no life here on earth.

She approached the door to his room. She noticed that it was ajar. She tried to look inside the room, but it was pitch black. She heard voices. As she squinted her eyes, she could see Baggie talking to someone. *God,* she thought, *maybe Baggie had family after all?* Rosie couldn't make out who or what he was talking to. He was deep in conversation. It was the only time in the past few weeks she had seen or heard Baggie in any coherent way. He had always appeared to be comatose. Deciding not to interfere, she backed away, making herself disappear. After what seemed like an age, the door to Baggie's room opened fully, and she missed seeing who came out. She darted back into Baggie's room.

Baggie was smiling to himself. 'Baggie, Baggie, are you all right?' asked Rosie, but Baggie lay there, all the time smiling, seemingly at perfect peace. Rosie made her way over to the window, which overlooked the car park. She looked down and saw a figure sneaking towards a car. She continued to stare downwards. It was only when the dark figure clicked the lights on his car that she got a good look at the driver. It was Sean! *What was Sean doing talking to Baggie?* she wondered.

Sean looked up in her direction. She could have sworn he smiled at her. She partially waved at him, but he ignored her and got into his car. He turned the engine and drove away calmly.

Rosie looked back towards Baggie. He was asleep.

Bridie woke up clinging to Dan. She loved his big, brawny chest and his muscular, hairy arms. She couldn't have been happier if she had tried. Smiling to herself, she was happy with her life. Dan seemed happier too. They needed to talk, and this coming two days was the perfect time for them to share their troubles and their woes.

She crept from the bed and made her way downstairs. She put on the kettle, followed by the grill. She was going to start their weekend together the best way she knew – with Irish sausages and the best of bacon and eggs, followed by Ma Baker's soda bread and a big dollop of butter, washed down with mugs of Irish tea. That would make her man more than happy. God, she thought to herself, how lucky she was to have a wonderful man who loved her so much, two sons, and a daughter who thought the world of her and a job that suited her very being.

Bridie heard Dan moving upstairs. She decided to get a move on. Within minutes, Dan appeared.

'What's that you have going on, girl?' he asked, knowing full well it was the Irish breakfast that triggered every part of his anatomy.

'Sit yourself down there, boyo, and you'll see why you married this sexy little kitten.'

Dan laughed aloud. He picked up yesterday's paper and threw it aside when he saw that nothing in it interested him. 'You know, Bridie, I was thinking.'

Bridie turned around in his direction, saying, 'You know that can be fatal, Dan Robinson?'

Dan looked up at her. 'If you were one of my customers, I'd throw you out on the street for a remark like that.'

'Go on,' said Bridie, laughing.

Dan threw back a mouthful of tea. 'I was thinking that maybe I should go to mass.'

'Mother of divine sorrows, Dan Robinson. Are you gone out of your mind or what?'

Dan looked at her, saying 'No, listen. It's just that things have been going well for us – reasonably well, that is – what with all the financial problems we've been having. I thought that maybe we should go to Sean's church. I believe they have an eleven o'clock mass or service or whatever they call it. It would be nice to support him and all like. What d'you think?'

Bridie smiled her usual smile that said, *I adore you, Dan Robinson*. Not wanting to let him off that easily, she continued, 'And what exactly brought this conversion on?'

Dan twisted in his chair. 'Nothing, really. You know that I sold my interest in the property and that I put the proceeds against the loan.' Dan thought for a second and corrected himself. 'That is, the bank took the proceeds and put it against the loan. Anyways, it managed to reduce the loan by about a third. I feel that maybe I owe God something in return. If it wasn't for him [*and the flick of a coin*, he thought to himself], maybe . . . who knows?' He paused, letting the conversation end peacefully.

Bridie raised her eyebrows, thinking that now was as good a time as any, seeing he was in the mood. Placing a full plate of the finest Irish breakfast in front of her husband, she added, 'Dan, if you don't mind me asking, how much in debt are we?'

Dan cut some rasher, and, adding it to a slice of sausage and some egg, he finished the mouthful before saying, 'Girl, you don't have to be knowing all about that sordid stuff.'

'Dan Robinson, I'm your wife, and a problem shared is a problem halved. For God's sake, man, tell me how much we are up to our necks in it. I've a right to know.'

Dan took a swig of tea and placed the mug down on the table. Looking up at his wife, he said, 'Bridie, I'm sorry for being a mad eejit. I got us into this mess, and by God, I'll get us out of it.' He looked out the window and, finding the right words, said 'about two-hundred fifty thousand euros, give or take, including interest.'

Bridie tried not to gasp too much. She gathered herself and asked, 'Is that after paying off the money you received from the sale of the land?'

'I'm afraid so, girl.'

Bridie shuffled her way towards the sink. 'It doesn't leave us with very much, does it?'

Dan furrowed his brow. 'I'm afraid not. In fact, it leaves us with nothing, girl. I don't know when the bastards will be looking for a full repayment. They'll probably take the business away from me, and that's a fact.' Dan looked out the window again, pushing his unfinished plate away from him.

Bridie made her way towards him. Putting her arms around him, she said, 'I'm sorry for ruining your breakfast. I'm sorry for ruining our weekend together asking you all of these questions. It's just that it's been playing on my mind all the time. I know you're just trying to protect me from all of it, but I have to know. I love you, Dan Robinson. Always have, always will. I don't give a tinker's curse if we do go down the Swannie without a paddle. You can use me as a paddle anytime, anywhere.'

Dan pulled her towards him, saying, 'Bridie Robinson, I've always loved you and I always will, for the very words you've just spoken to me. I can't believe I could ever do anything wrong as long as I have you by my side.'

Both of them embraced as if they were about to leave this world forever.

Tuesday morning arrived without a fuss. Bridie decided to leave Dan peacefully asleep while she made her way to the hospital.

It had been a pleasant two days away from everything. She and Dan had cleared the air somewhat. Obviously the loan wouldn't go away, but at least they both knew the circumstances. There was nothing worse than being left in the dark, regardless of the good intentions.

As Bridie arrived at the car park, she could have sworn she saw Baggie walking out of the hospital. She thought to herself that she needed a strong cup of tea, or maybe coffee for that matter, as her eyes were obviously playing tricks with her.

Bidding her good-mornings to everybody she met, she made her way to her office to be met by Rosie, who seemed more than a little agitated.

'What's up, girl?' asked Bridie, thinking that she didn't need any drama for her first day back at work.

'You're not going to believe this, Bridie. Baggie has gone!'

'I'm sorry to hear that, Rosie. You know we were expecting it to happen. Was it peaceful in the end?'

'No, Bridie, not that gone. He's discharged himself. He's alive and kicking. In fact, he left here whistling!'

'Rosie, Baggie had only days to live! Get yourself together, girl. Sit down and tell me what the hell is going on.'

Rosie grabbed a chair and sidled up to Bridie's desk. 'Bridie, none of us can believe it. Dr. Oluha and Dr. O'Reilly are flabbergasted. They've been upstairs all morning. Baggie was, as you say, meant to be dead. I'm telling you, Bridie, that he walked out of here without a care in the world. He even shaved!'

Bridie leant back in her chair. *It was Baggie I saw as I drove in! How is that possible?* she thought. *I'd better go and see the doctors right away.* 'I'm going upstairs,' she barked at Rosie, practically running up the corridor. Rosie decided against saying anything about seeing Sean the previous Saturday night.

As Bridie arrived at St. Margareth's ward, she saw the two doctors in deep conversation.

'It's just not possible, doctor,' said Dr. Oluha as Dr. O'Reilly pored through the charts and printouts, trying to decipher how a clinically dead person suddenly arose from his sickbed, shaved himself, and walked out of the hospital – unaided!

'I need answers, doctors,' said Bridie as she confronted the two men.

Both of them looked at her askew, not wanting to be the first to be embarrassed. Dr. Oluha looked towards the patients in the ward. Dr. O'Reilly, looking fed up, shouldered the responsibility by saying, 'Bridie, I don't know what to say to you. This man had practically no liver, three of his arteries were closed, and he had a collapsed lung. There is no medical reason for him to have a complete recovery like this.'

'That's not good enough, doctors, because I just saw your patient walking out of here whistling "Yankee Doodle Dandy." Now, get me some answers!' Bridie said furiously as she turned on her heels and headed back down the corridor, leaving two befuddled doctors in her wake.

The dead arose.

Bishop Benny stood in the vestry with his hands leaning on the small altar. Breathing a large sigh, he turned to Peter and Sean. 'Men, can you split the work between you today for Sunday mass? Peter, you do the gospel and split the readings between yourself and Sean. Sean, you do the announcements.'

'Yes, Your Grace,' they said in unison.

Peter looked over at Sean and asked of the bishop, 'Your Grace, is everything okay with you?'

Bishop Benny looked into Peter's eyes. 'I'm afraid my Martha had a bad night last night. She's actually had a bad week. It's very much hit and miss, I'm afraid. My heart cries out for her every time I see how much pain she is in. I just wish I could share her pain.' He looked at the crucifix, turned back, and said, 'We'd better say mass.'

When Peter opened the vestry door, he noticed that there were considerably more people present in church than was normal. The eleven o'clock mass was always the highlight of the week, as the congregation knew it was the bishop's mass. That always guaranteed the largest attendance. But today there appeared to be a lot more attending.

Sean took his seat near the podium and looked down into the pews. He smiled as he saw Linda smiling back at him. He had a pleasant surprise when he also saw his mother and father sitting beside her. He raised his eyebrows at Linda, who smiled back with hunched shoulders.

Bridie had a good look around to see if she knew anybody and looked shocked to see her Rosie a few rows back. She had no idea that Rosie even attended mass, let alone the Anglican one. She stared at Rosie, trying to get her attention. It was then she noticed the rather striking old man sitting next to her. He was well dressed, and she wondered if that was Rosie's stepdad.

The bishop began. 'Almighty God, unto whom all hearts are open, all desires known, and from whom no secrets are hid; cleanse the thoughts of our hearts by the inspiration of thy Holy Spirit, that we may perfectly love thee, and worthily magnify thy Holy Name; through Christ, our Lord. Amen.'

When the time came to read the announcements, Sean looked at the audience and said, 'I want to ask for your special prayers today for Martha, the bishop's wife, who is very ill. Many of you know her well, and she has gone through much pain these past months. Also pray for our bishop, who appreciates your prayers on his wife's behalf.'

Benny looked down at Sean, and tears welled in his eyes. Sean continued with the normal announcements.

During the Communion, Bridie managed to get a good look at the old man walking from the altar behind Rosie. Where had she seen that face? She definitely knew him! It was when he was just a few feet away from her and just before he made his way back to his seat that it hit her. 'My God, it's Baggie!' she whispered audibly. How could it be? Dan touched her arm, letting her know that she could be heard. Bridie blinked a couple of times. It was then that Rosie spotted her and smiled back at her.

Sean turned to the congregation at the end of the mass and said, 'The mass is ended; go in peace,' to which they all replied, 'Thanks be to God.'

As the congregation marched out of the church in single file, they were met and greeted by the bishop and Sean. When most of them had moved along, Sean took his mum and dad, together with Linda, aside.

'It was great seeing you all in church. To what do I owe this pleasure?'

Dan smiled, saying, 'If the parents can't go and see their own son say mass, then there's something wrong with them.'

Bridie jumped in. 'I was surprised too, Sean. It was your father's idea, and I'm delighted. Your mass is identical to the Catholic one.'

'We are all Catholic, Mum. No matter. I'm delighted you came. You're going to have to do the same again next week as the bishop has asked me to give my first sermon.'

'That's great, Sean,' added Linda, hugging him.

'It's only the 7:30 mass, the early one, but it's a start and a great honor.'

'We wouldn't miss it for the world,' added Bridie, at the same time looking around for Rosie. 'Did you happen to see Rosie by any chance? She was with some gentleman I think I know.'

'I did see her earlier, but she's gone now,' said Sean. 'I want to take us all to lunch – my treat.'

'Great stuff, son. Let's go,' enthused Dan.

Martha coughed heavily and erratically. Benny wiped her brow, whispering to her that she was going to be just fine. He encouraged her to cough up any bile that she needed to; he told her not to be embarrassed, that he was always there for her. Benny knew how Martha reviled bad manners or having to do something in public that should remain private. Her will couldn't obey what her body was forcing her to do.

These past few weeks had been the worst for her. Benny had seen her through rough patches, but this seemed interminable. He had called the doctor about a half hour ago. He was more than worried. Martha looked deathly, and Benny was frightened.

He heard the doorbell, and telling Martha to be strong, that the doctor had arrived, he left her to answer the door. As he opened the door, the doctor could see by his face that things were not good. He asked Benny to wait outside while he examined her. He was accompanied by his nurse. It was obviously bad because Benny had never known the doctor to bring his nurse with him.

'Can I do anything, doctor?' asked Benny in hope more than in asking.

'It's best that I see her alone for now, Your Grace. I'll call you as soon as I have finished my examination.'

The nurse offered to make Benny a cup of tea, which he declined. There was nothing he could do but wait.

Peter carried the candles from the vestry towards the altar. He always loved the way that Mrs. Harte, the housekeeper, dressed the altar with beautiful flowers. He had no idea where she obtained them from; all he knew was that they were always fresh. He adjusted the candlesticks and marked the pages for tomorrow's readings. It was then he thought he heard voices from the back of the church.

Turning around, he saw three figures down by the baptismal font. He slowly edged his way down the center aisle, trying to make out who the people were. He stopped in his tracks when he recognized Sean with two other men. Climbing into the nearest pew, he decided it was best to not interfere. Instead, he tried to listen to their conversation.

It wasn't long before he realized that Sean was performing a baptism. One of the men he recognized as the new member of the congregation, someone whom Sean apparently knew quite well, as he seemed to be hanging around the church quite a lot. The other man was a stranger to him. After about ten minutes or so, Sean shook their hands and blessed them, bidding them goodbye.

When Sean had locked the main front door, Peter called out softly, 'I didn't realize you were doing any baptisms tonight, Sean.'

Sean looked at Peter and smiled. 'Our work is never ending. That was a new member of our congregation I just baptized.'

Peter nodded, asking, 'Who was the elderly gentleman? I seem to recognize him.'

'That would be poor old Baggie. He is from my hometown. He brought the new disciple to me. He's a good and loyal servant, our Baggie. You can trust him. . ... How is the bishop?' added Sean.

'Not good. I believe the doctor has been called. They're all over at the main house as we speak.'

'I should maybe drop over and see if there's anything I can do,' added Sean.

'I'd love to help out myself, but I arranged to meet up with Shirley,' said Peter. 'I promised her that we'd both go out for dinner. Did I tell you that we have set a date for our wedding?'

'No, you never mentioned it. When is the happy day?'

'September twenty-fifth. I was hoping you would marry us,' Peter said, smiling.

'Alas, as I haven't yet been ordained, that's a matter I'll have to leave to somebody else. I know the bishop would not be averse to performing the ceremony, but I suppose under happier circumstances.'

'Yes, I don't think he has any thoughts for anything else right now other than for his Martha.'

The doctor closed the bedroom door and looked at the bishop. He indicated for them to be seated.

'I'm afraid it's not good, Your Grace. Martha's dying. She won't last the night.'

Benny broke down completely. The tears rolled down his face, more in exhaustion and acceptance of the fate he knew was coming to his beautiful wife. The doctor and the nurse tried their best to console him. The doctor offered him some sleeping tablets, but Benny refused saying, 'I'll stay awake with my Martha until the end. I will pray for her and with her. We will spend these last few hours together, doctor. I thank you all the same. Can I go and see her now, please?'

'Of course, Your Grace. Would you like the nurse to stay with you?'

'That won't be necessary. I would prefer to be alone with her.'

'We'll let ourselves out, Your Grace. I'm terribly sorry for your troubles.'

'Thank you, doctor. I'll go to her now.'

The doctor indicated to the nurse that they should take their leave.

Within minutes, the house was silent. Benny made his way to Martha's bedside. Taking her right hand in his, he started to pray.

Martha remained unconscious. While he prayed, the tears rolled down his face. 'What am I going to do without you, my love? What's the point of trying to live a life by myself when all I ever wanted was you?'

As he spoke and prayed, he felt someone was in the room with him. At that moment, a hand touched his shoulder. He didn't jump with fright; it was as if he expected it. He looked up and saw Sean reaching down and taking Martha's left hand in his. He looked up to the ceiling and prayed silently, earnestly. Benny stopped crying. He felt that he was being transported to some heavenly place. He felt the surge of power enter his body and transfer to Martha. After what seemed like an eternity, he saw Sean open his eyes and say, 'Martha, you will be well.'

Benny looked at his wife and up at Sean. 'What's happening, Sean?'

Sean bent down and whispered in Benny's ear, 'She was merely sleeping. She will be well again. You must not tell anyone of this.'

Benny stared deeply into Sean's eyes and saw something calming in them. Their blueness looked straight through him. It was as if he was in total control of the situation. Benny felt himself become exhausted, and with that he fell fast asleep.

When he awoke the next morning, Benny heard the birds chirping. The rays of sunlight were peeping through the slit in the curtains. He shook his head and felt that he had been in a dream, somehow drugged. He thought back to the night before and wondered whether the doctor had indeed given him the pills that made him sleep. Then he thought he remembered Sean in the room.

He looked at Martha. She was gone. He bowed his head, leaning it on the mattress, and started to cry. It was then that he felt a hand rub the back of his head. A voice said, 'What is my bishop crying about?'

Benny looked up, startled. He saw Martha looking at him, eyes wide open. 'Martha, what's happening?'

'I don't know, love. Perhaps you could tell me. I can tell you this – I am starving and dying of the thirst. Is there any chance of a cup of tea?'

Benny smiled, jumped up on the bed, and caressed and kissed Martha with joyful abandonment. 'Oh Martha, Martha, I thought I'd lost you.'

They stayed in that pose for a long time.

Sean fastened his Roman collar, tidied his hair, picked up his Bible, and made to leave his bedroom. As he opened the door, he saw Bishop Benny sitting on a chair outside his room.

'Your Grace, is everything okay?'

Benny looked up at Sean, too exhausted and exhilarated to stand up. 'Things couldn't be any better, Sean. I've just put Martha back to sleep. I can't thank you enough for what you did for her. Sean . . .' Benny stalled his words, trying to ask what he needed to ask but at the same time not wanting to embarrass his deacon.

Sean helped out by saying, 'What's God's will can never be undone. All I did was pray, and God, our heavenly Father, answered my prayers. It was not her time to leave this world or to leave you. Come, you must be exhausted. You should eat and then get yourself to bed.'

Sean helped Benny to his feet and led him down to the kitchen.

The following Sunday, Bishop Benny prepared to say mass. He was in exuberant form. He hadn't looked or felt that way in a long time.

Peter entered the vestry and was happy to see his bishop smiling again. 'I couldn't be happier with your great news, Your Grace. How is Martha this morning?'

'It's a miracle, I tell you, Peter. She is healthier now than she ever has been. It's beyond words.'

With that, Sean entered, and Benny stopped talking and immediately shook his hands.

'I'm delighted to hear your great news, Your Grace. There's no need to shake my hands, I assure you,' said Sean, embarrassed.

Benny immediately corrected himself, saying 'I'm sorry, Sean. It's just that I'm over the moon with all that's been happening. I feel I have been to hell and back.' He smiled glowingly. 'Tell me, how did your first sermon go last week?'

'It was actually two weeks ago, but yes, I was reasonably happy with it.'

'Happy?' exclaimed Peter. 'I can tell you, Bishop, that I've heard nothing but compliments from practically every member of our congregation about Sean's sermon. They told me that they were all uplifted by his words.'

'Indeed. I can't say I'm surprised. Who's doing today's sermon?' asked Benny.

'That'll be me, Your Grace,' said Peter. 'I hope to give Sean a decent run for his money.' They all laughed.

'I want to see you men after mass in my office,' said the bishop. 'I have some news for the both of you.'

Peter looked quizzically at Sean, who returned the look.

The church was three-quarters full with people. Baggie was in the front row as usual, accompanied by the ever-present Rosie. They seemed to get along so well together. Then there were the new recruits whom Sean had recently baptized, together with stranger faces that were more than welcome. Linda and Sean's parents were, as usual, in the front row as well.

After the mass, both Peter and Sean made their way to the bishop's office, both wondering what the bishop needed to speak to them about. Finally, Benny made his entrance, beaming from ear to ear.

'I have such great news for the both of you that I'm bursting to tell you.' Peter and Sean leaned forward excitedly in their chairs. Benny sat down and clasped his hands together and said, 'I've been speaking with the archbishop all week. After many conversations, he has given me the go-ahead to sanction both of your ordinations as soon as possible.'

Peter let out an excited gasp while Sean smiled broadly. 'What does this mean, Your Grace?' asked Peter.

Benny beamed. 'We decided not to wait any longer. The parishes need you, and the church needs your services sooner rather than later.' Looking at Peter, he continued, 'Peter, I know that you've been here as a deacon a lot longer than Sean. I am also aware of your impending marriage to the lovely Shirley. For those reasons, I will be appointing you as my parish priest for the town of Tuam immediately following your ordination.'

Peter gasped, saying, 'Parish priest, Your Grace!'

'Indeed. You deserve it, Peter. My man there, Father John Sullivan, is way beyond retiring age and has been asking me – correction, hounding me – for ages, to have a replacement sent to him.'

Turning to Sean, the bishop continued. 'Sean, I want you to remain here with me as my parish priest for St. Nicholas's. Will you do that for me?'

Sean looked at Peter, then back at the bishop. 'It would be more than an honor, Your Grace.' Sean turned to Peter and shook his hand, saying, 'Congratulations, Peter. You deserve it, and I know you'll make a wonderful parish priest.'

Peter beamed. 'And to you too, Sean. What wonderful news. I cannot wait to tell Shirley.'

'On that subject, perhaps you might get your wish and have Father Robinson perform your wedding ceremony?' added Benny.

Peter rose from his seat. 'I can't believe this is all happening. Sean, will you perform the ceremony for me?'

'Delighted to do so, Peter.' Sean looked to the bishop 'When do you propose we will be ordained?'

'As soon as possible. I have tentatively marked in the fourth of August. You have a lot of organizing to do before that, so I'm entrusting all of it over to the two of you.'

'Leave it all to us, Your Grace,' enthused Peter.

'Go now, young men. Go in Christ.'

With that, the two men knelt down, and the bishop said a small prayer before blessing the both of them.

A good thing or a bad thing.

Miami was bigger than big, thought Vinnie as his plane flew over the city approaching the runway. He was in awe at the many weaving highways that seemed to spaghetti their way to every corner of Miami. He smiled as he pictured himself looking through the airport for his ride. He must have passed the little man, now his driver, a number of times before he realized that the sign he was holding saying, 'Senor Vknee Backer,' referred to 'Mr. Vinnie Baker.'

His driver weaved his way at nerve-racking speeds along the highways and through the adjoining streets. Vinnie gave up trying to speak with him since he had no English. He was there to take him to Father Miguel, who was parish priest in one of the suburbs.

Vinnie looked down at his shaking arm. He had noticed that it had tightened on the journey over. He had put it down to the cabin pressure, not having flown since he'd received the bad news about Parkinson's. He held his arm with his other hand to stop its shaking. He wondered again, as he had many times on the trip over, what Sean had meant when he said that his sickness would be gone on his return. How did he know about it? He hadn't told anybody! How would he get better?

Vinnie's mind was refocused when the driver nearly didn't make the next corner, screeching around like a madman. 'Easy on, there, "Man-Well," or whatever your name is. We have loads of time,' said Vinnie, but the driver ignored him, hanging onto the steering wheel.

As soon as he arrived at the church, Vinnie immediately recognized Father Miguel from the e-mailed photograph that Sean had sent to him. He was a diminutive figure of a man, dressed in black with a huge smile. Father Miguel was opening his car door before Vinnie had time to gather his wheelie case from the seat.

'It is so good to see you, Senor Vinnie. I have heard so many great things about you from Sean. We are blessed to have you help us out in our time of need.'

186

Vinnie managed to get both feet on the ground at the same time as Father Miguel pumped his hand as if he wanted to take it away with him. 'Not at all, Father Miguel. It's an honor to be able to help out any way I can.'

'Please, call me Miguel. Forget the formalities.'

'This is a fine church you have here,' continued Vinnie in his tangy Irish accent, obviously impressed with what he saw.

'It's the church of St. Canice. It was built over two hundred years ago, and I am blessed to have been assigned here. Come, let me show you around. You must be hungry and exhausted after your long journey.'

'I'm not too hungry, Miguel, but I could do with an early night.'

'Let's get you some food and put you to bed. We have an early start in the morning. Our flight leaves for Port-au-Prince at eight a.m.'

When Vinnie had washed himself, he settled down at the table and devoured the soup that was given to him along with some fresh oven bread. 'Mmmm, this is very good, Miguel. Just what I wanted. Tell me, what's the plan for the days ahead?'

'We have so much to do. I was there two weeks ago. Things are very bad, bordering on hopeless. My job is to try and prevent disease . . .' He paused and looked at Vinnie. 'I hope you have all of the necessary shots like hepatitis A, typhoid, Tdap, cholera, and rabies?'

'Yes, I got the full house of shots weeks ago, as soon as I told Sean I would come.'

'That's fantastic. You can never be too careful. As I was saying, our job is to try and prevent sicknesses, such as the ones I just mentioned, to try and give the people some hope.' Miguel paused, contemplating the predicament. Putting his hands to his face and wiping his eyes, he said, 'Before the earthquake happened in 2010, things were bad enough. The government was corrupt. There was and still is a criminal culture that pervades. The capital was destroyed as well as most of the surrounding areas. The country was always poor; now it is even poorer, if that is possible!

'The town I am responsible for is a small fishing community of about five thousand families. They are mostly Christian, mixed with the usual tribal beliefs. The town is called Vil Bondye a, or "God's town" in English. Most natives refer to it simply as Bondye. It's about a three-hour drive from Port-au-Prince along the coast. Its nearest town is Anse-a-Veau, a town that has swollen to around fifty thousand as people left the city. I was originally stationed there, but a number of Christian churches are looking after the needs of the people as best they can. I then moved further west, along the coast, to help these people. You will see how things are when we get there tomorrow. The flight is short enough. I'm hoping that my driver will be there to greet us and take us to Bondye. I can see that you are tired. Come, you must get your sleep or you will be no good to anyone tomorrow.'

Vinnie nodded in agreement as tiredness began to overtake him. He bid his good night and said he would be fine in the morning.

It was on one of these 'normal' days when the guard appeared at Fonsie's cell and announced that he had a visitor. Fonsie was more than a little surprised since he had no kin. Nobody ever looked for one Alphonsus Murphy, just as one Alphonsus Murphy never looked for anybody else – unless there was a financial benefit.

He shuffled his way along the corridors led by the guard and was shown into the room reserved for inmates of a different caliber. He was surprised to see a good-looking man waiting for him. He made his way to the chair, directed by the officer. He stared down at his guest, not knowing what he had done to welcome such a moment.

Sean looked at Fonsie with compassion and said, 'You probably don't know me. My father served you drinks in his pub – Dan's – down in Ballinasloe.'

Fonsie looked towards the ceiling, smiling. 'Jasus, Dan's – now, that brings back memories. Your father, you say. You must be the adopted one.' Fonsie looked over Sean's head, taking in his surroundings.

'Yes, I'm the adopted one.'

'So what are you doing here with me?' asked Fonsie, not unreasonably.

'I'm a deacon in the Anglican church in Galway. It is my . . .' – Sean hesitated for a second, then continued – 'desire to see that any locals from my community get to see their priest or simply to have a chat with people they might know.'

'Have a chat, you say? It's been a long time since anybody bothered having a chat with me.' Fonsie appeared agitated as he looked around him. He saw the screw sitting in the corner listening to their every word. 'Do you have any smokes, Father?'

'No, I don't smoke, but I'll make sure to remember to bring some the next time I'm here.'

'What makes you think there will be a next time, Faddah?' Fonsie exaggerated the word 'Father,' making it appear as if he were mocking Sean.

'Tell me, Fonsie, I understand that you were never incarcerated before now. How are you coping?'

'I'm doing okay. It's not the Shangri-La Hotel and that's for sure, but I suppose it's probably better than being dead.'

'If you like, I can bring you some reading material. I'm allowed to do that, am I not?' asked Sean of the officer at the back of the room, to which he nodded his affirmation.

'What sort of reading materials?' asked Fonsie. 'Are we talking some porn here, Faddah?'

Sean smiled his nonchalant smile, trying to put Fonsie at ease. 'I was thinking more like inspirational material, something that will stimulate your mind in a different direction. You cannot give up hope, Fonsie, that maybe someday you will get released from this prison.'

Fonsie looked distrustfully in Sean's direction, saying, 'This hellhole will take me to my grave and probably hell at that.' He still felt very uncomfortable in Sean's presence, particularly knowing that the screw was listening to his every word. 'You can bring me the book *Oliver Twist*. I always liked the thievery aspect of that particular book. You could say it was right up my street,' he said, laughing at his own humor.

'I'll certainly bring that for you, and I'll pick some other books I deem appropriate.'

'Two minutes,' said the officer, indicating that the meeting should wrap itself up.

'Do you mind if I say a prayer for you, Fonsie?'

'Nah, I don't like prayers or praying. Never have, never will. You keep that one for yourself, Faddah. This one's on me.'

Fonsie stood up and continued to laugh as the officer led him back to his cell. Sean looked down at the floor and said the prayer he was going to say anyway.

As he made his way outside the prison and walked towards his car, Sean noticed a familiar figure making his way into the prison. The person in question noticed Sean straightaway and continued to gaze at him as the two men passed each other, carefully examining each other without saying anything. Harry Devlin smiled slyly in Sean's direction as he made his way through the entrance gate.

Peter and Shirley laughed aloud as they made their way across Eyre Square, both feeling elated having finalized the negotiations for their wedding reception.

'Oh, Peter, I simply can't wait for everything to happen. First your ordination, then our marriage, and also your transfer to Tuam as parish priest no less. It's all too much.'

Peter checked the traffic both ways before saying, 'I know. I couldn't have asked for things to work out as brilliantly as they have done. Our marriage is the most exciting part for me, although I have to admit that knowing I'll finally become a priest after what seems like an eternity is somewhat more than consoling.'

'Have we time for a drink?' asked Shirley in all of the excitement.

'I haven't time, love. The ordination is only two weeks away, and I have to prepare myself. There are a million things to be done. I have to say that the bishop is a new man now that Martha is back on her feet again.'

'Whatever happened to her to bring on such a rapid recovery?' enquired Shirley.

'I guess you have to put your faith in God to answer that question, my lovely, because the doctors are totally flummoxed. Anyway, I'll leave you and love you.'

They kissed, and both went their separate ways.

Peter arrived back to his lodgings, and as he entered through the kitchen, he was taken aback to find Mrs. Harte crying at the kitchen table. Not wanting to interfere, he made to go back out again when he heard her say, 'I'm sorry, Father. I didn't hear you come in. Can I make you a cup of tea?'

Peter closed the door and decided to see if he could help. 'Are you upset about something, Mrs. Harte? I couldn't help but notice that you were crying when I first came in.'

The housekeeper wandered over to the sink, and taking a glass of water, she turned to Peter and said, 'I'm sorry, Father. I know you have a lot on your plate, what with your ordination and the wedding and all . . .'

She suddenly went quiet before Peter said, 'Mrs. Harte, we've known each other a number of years; you can trust me to be discreet.' He sat down, waiting for his words to melt through.

'I know, Father,' Mrs. Harte said as she made her way to sit down at the table. 'It's my niece, you see. She's had polio all of her life. She's such a gorgeous wee thing,' she said, holding a photograph of her niece. 'Here's her picture.'

Peter took the photo and thought how strikingly beautiful the little girl was. She couldn't have been more than twelve or thirteen. She had long black hair and a radiant smile. 'She's a gorgeous wee girl, no doubt, Mrs. Harte,' he said, handing back the photograph.

'I'd do anything for her . . . but my sister and I have received very bad news. You've met my sister, Father?'

'Yes, I've met her a few times, whenever she's come to visit you. I think I met your little niece once too.'

'Apparently she's dying. She got an infection – from where we don't know. We expect it was the school, but you never know. They can't cure her.' With that, Mrs. Harte broke down completely.

Peter grabbed the glass of water and handed it to her and encouraged her to take a sip. 'Is there anything the doctors can do?' he asked.

'Nothing, nothing at all.' Mrs. Harte suddenly stopped crying. Grabbing Peter's hand, she pleaded with him, 'But maybe you could have a word with Father Robinson. He did great things for the bishop, and I heard he's done wonderful things for other people too. Please, Father, can you do that for me?'

Peter was taken aback. He studied Mrs. Harte's face and saw that she was indeed serious. He said, 'But Father Sean is not a doctor. He doesn't have miraculous powers that I know about. What makes you think that he has?'

'I've heard it from some locals, Father. I have a nurse friend at Galway Regional Hospital who told me that Sean goes down there every week and that some people have walked out of that hospital with not a thing wrong with them. I know for a fact that the doctor who was looking after the bishop's wife is totally flabbergasted at her amazing recovery. I don't care what people say; I just want my niece to be well again. Can you at least ask him for me?'

'Well, why don't you just ask him yourself?'

Mrs. Harte shuffled her feet and said in a shy way, 'Because I know he doesn't like me. Every time he sits down to one of my dinners, he goes all quiet on me. I don't like the way he looks at me. To be honest, I'm a bit afraid of him. There, I've said it!'

Peter laughed aloud, much to Mrs. Harte's shock and annoyance. 'Why are you laughing?' she erupted.

'Mrs. Harte, Mrs. Harte,' he said, smiling and nodding his head from side to side. 'I suppose it's probably time for a few home truths. There's no easy way of telling you this, so I'll tell it to you straight. Sean, like most Irishmen, loves his grub. You put a big plate of flowery spuds and a big dollop of Irish butter in front of him, accompanied by a large filet of steak, and you are guaranteed his cooperation like a lapdog.' Peter took Mrs. Harte's hands in his and lovingly told her, 'Mrs. Harte, you can't cook to save your life.' He let the words sink in before he continued, 'You see, Sean was warned by yours truly the

192

day he arrived here that he'd better make alternative arrangements if he wanted to gain any weight or not lose too much. I had warned him that, despite the fact that you are a wonderful housekeeper, your cooking abilities leave an awful lot to be desired.'

Mrs. Harte sat open-mouthed. She was totally dumbstruck and aghast. 'Well, I never,' she managed to spurt out. 'Do all of you feel the same way?'

'I'm afraid so.'

'Even the bishop?' she asked.

'Especially the bishop,' acknowledged Peter. She dried her eyes with her tissues and blew her nose. Peter continued, 'So you see, Mrs. Harte, it's not that Sean dislikes you; it's that he's always afraid what dish-delish you might confront him with. I have seen him slip off to McDonald's the odd night for a Big Mac and fry.' Peter smiled and then said, 'But I promise you that I will mention your niece to him. I don't know what good it will do.'

Mrs. Harte came out of her shock at his words and smiled broadly. 'Oh, thank you, Father. Well, I just don't know what to say. I think I'm going to say good night now, Father, and I might just make history tonight by ending my life of abstinence.'

Peter smiled as Mrs. Harte made her exit. His smile dissipated when he thought further about what she had had to say about Sean. Sure, he had suspected as much that maybe, just maybe, Sean's prayers were heard by the Almighty, but for people to be talking that way about him – well, he didn't know if it was a good thing or a bad thing.

The problem.

Miguel had not been exaggerating when he said that Haiti was in a bad state. Vinnie looked out from inside the car at what could only be described as a war zone. Even the cars had bullet holes riddled through their metal. The roads could only be described as giant potholes. The people looked like zombies, aimlessly wandering around with no perceived plan. The shops could only be barely distinguished from the other buildings by the display of a beer or soda sign saying, 'Buy Coke here.'

Vinnie appeared to be the only Caucasian in sight when they arrived at the airport. There was a sea of tiny brown faces looking at him as if he were the angel who would take them away from this awful place. He waded through their bodies alongside Miguel, who seemed to know where he was going.

Miguel soon selected his driver, a chap by the funny-sounding name of 'Misery,' which was very apt, considering their circumstances. Miguel could see by Vinnie's reaction that he was in shock. 'Don't worry, my friend; you'll get used to it. It gets even worse as we leave the city.'

'How could it be any worse than this?' asked Vinnie incredulously.

Miguel explained, 'In the nights following the earthquake, many people in Haiti slept in the streets, on pavements, in their cars, or in makeshift shanty towns, either because their houses had been destroyed or they feared standing structures would not withstand aftershocks. Construction standards are low in Haiti, as you can no doubt observe.'

Vinnie nodded his agreement as he continued to gaze open-mouthed at the passing buildings.

Miguel continued, 'The country has no **building codes**. Engineers have stated that it is unlikely many buildings would have stood through any kind of disaster. Structures are often raised wherever they can fit. Some buildings were built on slopes with insufficient foundations or steel supports. It has been estimated that about two million Haitians lived as **squatters** on land they did not own. The country also suffered from shortages of fuel and potable water even before the disaster.

'Port-au-Prince's **morgue** facilities were overwhelmed. Two days after the earthquake struck, a thousand bodies were placed on the streets and pavements. Government crews manned trucks to collect thousands more, burying them in mass graves. In the heat and humidity, corpses buried in rubble began to decompose and smell. Some described the situation as a scene from hell. Everywhere, the acrid smell of bodies hung in the air. It's just like the stories we are told of the Holocaust – thousands of bodies everywhere. You have to understand that the situation was true madness, and more and more bodies were found in numbers that cannot be grasped. It was beyond comprehension. The government buried many in mass graves, some above-ground tombs were forced open so bodies could be stacked inside, and others were burned. Mass graves were dug in a large field outside the settlement of Titanyen, north of the capital. Tens of thousands of bodies were reported as having been brought to the site by **dump truck** and buried in trenches dug by **earth movers**.'

They rode in silence. Miguel finally shut his eyes and grabbed himself some sleep. Vinnie found it impossible to close his eyes, even when they had left the city and were travelling along the coast. He took in the contrasting beauty of the ocean as it crawled up the beaches. He saw many makeshift tents along the way housing, or trying to house, the wretched bodies inside. Every now and then, they had to stop the car and try to untangle themselves from a jam of traffic and people and animals as they blocked the roadway. *Roadway* was a misnomer because most could barely be given the title of road – more like battered holes.

Vinnie thought about how people back home in Ireland complained about the recession and how 'hard' things were for them. *Holy Jesus,* he thought. *This is recession and more. This is indeed hell on earth!*

After three hours, they passed the town of Anse-a-Veau. Miguel was speaking to the driver. They appeared agitated.

'Is everything okay, Miguel?'

'Yes, Vinnie. My driver is concerned that we may not have enough fuel to reach Bondye. It's about another hour away. I feel we'll just about make it. I have done this journey many times.'

'That's reassuring, Miguel,' said Vinnie, crouching down in his seat and hoping that Miguel had his numbers correct.

Another hour passed, and they spluttered, literally, into the town known as Bondye. The villagers were amassed on the main street as they slowly crawled up the hill. Then the car stopped, and Miguel said, 'Okay, we made it – just. We have a little walk. Follow me, Vinnie.'

Vinnie clambered out from his seat and gazed at the locals, who gazed back at him in wonderment. It was obvious that his pale skin made him a celebrity. He followed Miguel, who led him up the hill, passing ramshackle houses with no roofs until they finally reached the top.

'Welcome to the town of Vil Bondye a, my friend,' said Miguel as he spread his arms wide, like Michelangelo displaying his masterpiece.

Vinnie took one more step to view the painting. What he saw couldn't have shocked him any more than he had been shocked already. There was nothing but faces looking up at them. Down one side of the street were tented houses – if you could call them that. The other side had nothing remotely resembling a dwelling, just empty spaces filled with barely breathing bodies. Some of the faces smiled at Miguel, and some children ran up to him to greet him. Behind this charade of attempted joy stood a beauty like none Vinnie had seen in the past two days. The ocean in the background was stunning as it washed the shoreline. He could see three boats in the distance. They appeared to be fishing vessels. Apart from that, there was little activity.

Miguel could see the reaction on Vinnie's face. 'Come with me, my friend. It's not as bad as it looks. It's much worse!' He smiled as if his black humor was acceptable, as if he were used to saying and thinking that way.

At that precise moment, Vinnie wanted to turn and run back to Ireland – to anywhere other than this madhouse.

Vinnie awoke the next morning not having a clue where he was. His watch read 12:30. Was that a.m. or p.m.? What day was it?

He climbed out of his bed – if it could be called a bed. He had climbed into it in such a daze, having been presented with some fish or other alongside something they said was a local vegetable. He didn't remember much after that other than complete panic setting in and wondering what his best escape route should be. He thought about telling Miguel that he had just received word that his mother had died. He had read that in some book where some guy always used that excuse if he was in dire circumstances. These were dire circumstances, let there be no doubt.

Vinnie looked around his hovel and saw that he was alone. *What time is it?* he kept asking himself. It was funny how westernized people always needed to know what time it was to be reassured, when in actual fact, in a place like this, time didn't matter one cahoots.

Vinnie dragged his way to the opening that doubled for a door. Peering outside, he saw that people were actively going hither and thither, to what or to where he had no clue. He wondered where the bathroom was. Standing outside, he tried to get someone's attention, anyone's attention, to no avail. What was he supposed to do? He wandered up the hill, then back down again as if he were in some dream world. Hopefully someone would drag him away, slap his cheeks, and give him a good dollop of Irish whiskey, followed by the word 'Surprise!' and everything would be all right again.

'Senor Vinnie, good morning,' said a voice – from where, he didn't know.

'Good morning,' he shouted back to no one in particular.

'Over here,' said the voice. Vinnie turned to his right to see Miguel being followed by about a dozen women carrying various bowls and boxes.

'Could I speak with you a moment, Miguel? I have some bad news that needs your attention.'

'There is never time for bad news, Senor Vinnie; that is something we have lots of. Come, let me introduce you to my girls.'

The girls all giggled. How could they giggle in this environment? What could possess them to find anything humorous in this hellhole? Vinnie thought.

'This is Bona, this is Maya, then Susa, and so on and on. All you have to remember is that they all have an *a* at the end of their names.' The girls all laughed again.

Vinnie followed Miguel. His 'bad news' could wait a moment longer. Maybe Miguel had some rich vein of gold to show him that needed his expertise to unearth.

'Over here, Vinnie.' The girls laid their pots and boxes on the gravel. Miguel put them all in a single line. 'These,' he beamed, 'are my professional staff. They are more qualified than the best of nurses – even doctors. They can perform any operation without proper anesthetics or proper medication. They can cure people better than the Christ child Himself. Now, is that saying something, or is that saying something, as you English comedians might say?'

Vinnie swallowed hard. What could he say? He looked at these girls and had nothing of note to say to them other than to smile, which was hard. He smiled harder, and then somewhere from within, he said, 'I am delighted to meet you all.'

They all shouted, 'Hooray!' which he understood, and his smile became normal.

Vinnie wandered aimlessly through the next couple of hours, not knowing what he should be doing. Eventually Miguel introduced him to Brownie. 'Brownie will be your manservant. He has good English and excellent Creole. He is also our greatest thief, so beware, Senor Vinnie.'

Brownie smiled a great big smile and said, 'Great thief,' and both he and Miguel laughed.

Miguel pushed himself down on a rock beside Vinnie. 'Vinnie, I know how hard this is for you. Trust me when I say that. I arrived here under orders from my church. I thought they had sent me to hell. In actual fact, they had. I thought of every reason and excuse to get out of here, but nothing worked. I know what's going through your mind. Believe me, Vinnie, when I say this – God has plans for each and every one of us. I am a man of the cloth; you are not. Regardless of attire, His plans remain.' Miguel got up and said, 'Come with me. I need to show you something – the something as to why you are here.'

It took them over an hour to climb the hill, which was about a mile from the village. It was a hill of shale, which made it difficult to get their footing. Miguel stopped along the way, pointing out various features of the topography. They had a great view of the village set against the sea in the background.

'I must teach you some Creole, Vinnie, as we climb. Not much further to go. Repeat after me. The word *alo* is guess what?'

'That's pretty easy,' smiled Vinnie.

'It's not so bad. Creole is based on the French language, as you know. For example, to say *goodbye* is very similar to the French *au revoir*, so you can say the French word and they'll understand it. Finally, always say thank you, which is *mesi*. Think of the great Argentinian footballer. Easy, no?'

'I think I'll get the hang of it.'

They continued their climb, finally reaching the apex. Miguel looked down the other side and, pointing far away, said, 'There is our river.' Vinnie looked off in the distance and could make out the water winding its way down to the ocean. Miguel looked at Vinnie and said, 'You see, Vinnie, that river used to flow over there.' He pointed back towards the village. 'Some one and a half miles that way.'

'Holy crap,' exclaimed Vinnie. 'You mean to tell me that the earthquake shifted the entire riverbed?'

'Yes. Not only that, the river now flows through impossible terrain that's useless for habitation. We thought that we could move the village towards the river itself, but there's absolutely nothing there for us. Where the river enters the sea makes it too dangerous to moor our remaining fishing vessels. You can see how strong the current is even from here. Then there's the land. Whatever meagre soil we have down at the village, it's enough to grow our local potatoes, but there's nothing on this side to grow anything.'

Vinnie took in a 360-degree view. To a tourist, it was picturesque; to someone trying to live there, it was purgatory. 'Is there any point in moving the villagers to the nearest town – what's it called?' asked Vinnie

Miguel said, 'Anse-a-Veau. No. That town has already been flooded with more refugees from Port-au-Prince than it can handle. Besides, one has to be careful because all of the towns and villages have their own way of operating. There is no police force. All of the towns are ruled by bandits of one type or another. You don't have to know the horrible things that have been happening all over Haiti. There's been corruption on a wide scale, even within the aid agencies. There's widespread raping and pillaging. It's the law of the bandits, my friend. I can assure you that Bondye is different. The women and children are safe here, primarily because our overlord is very strict about that. He's somebody you do not want to cross. But I suppose he's the best of a bad lot. His name is Gouvene Perseguidor. Everybody calls him Sayil. He's a big brute of a man, a fisherman who saw the opportunity and became the self-appointed leader of Bondye. No doubt you'll come across him. He will be fully aware of your presence.'

Vinnie looked back to the village, saying, 'You say there are about ten thousand people in the town, correct?'

'Yes, that is about right. Probably around five thousand men; the rest are their wives, children, and extended families. I call it a village, but it is populated enough to be classified as a town.'

'How do they live? What are the food and water supplies like?' asked Vinnie.

Miguel sighed. 'The problems are many, I'm afraid. They exist primarily on what the fishermen manage to catch. Unfortunately, due to the problems obtaining diesel for the boats, they have to go fishing whenever the weather is best suited. They cannot go out every day, which they would need to be doing in order to feed such a number. We get a certain amount of supplies from the agencies – primarily medical supplies and bottled water. But we get only what's left after they have supplied the main towns such as Anse-a-Veau.

'We have been lucky to a large extent in that we have been able to control any outbreak of cholera. Other towns have not been so lucky. It's believed that the cholera stemmed from the United Nations peacekeepers who came here immediately following the earthquake from Nepal, where there had been a serious outbreak. Many thousands have died as a result. My staff and I concentrate on ensuring that everybody bathes in the sea every day. The only clean water is what's available to drink from the supplies. We have nothing to wash our hands other than to bathe in the ocean.'

'Have you tried bucketing the water from the diverted river?' asked Vinnie, obviously becoming very concerned for the townspeople.

'It's too far away. The people would be exhausted walking this terrain and would spill most of it.'

Vinnie contemplated the information Miguel had given him. He shook his head in despair. 'I'm going to need a few days to examine the topography in greater detail. I need to do measurements, check the soil, foundations – everything. I'll also need help. Can you get me a list of able-bodied men and their levels of expertise? For example, I'll need carpenters, bricklayers, plumbers, electricians, anybody who has any qualifications in whatever fields they work in.'

'I can arrange this for you.' Miguel breathed out a long breath. 'Vinnie, you have no idea what your presence does for me and for these people. Just to have someone else from the outside who cares is enough to lift everybody's spirits – mine particularly. Come, we have lots to do.'

Take up thy bed.

Sean and Peter read the final part of the ordination ceremony. Bishop Benny said, 'That's great men. There should be no problems when we do the real thing tomorrow. Are you all excited?'

Peter was about to answer when he saw Mrs. Harte bringing fresh flowers for the altar.

'Absolutely, Your Grace,' said Sean, looking at Peter.

'Yes, of course, Your Grace,' agreed Peter.

'Okay, then, I'm expecting a full turnout of parishioners, having announced it from the pulpit these past two weeks so everybody's excited. It's been a long time since we had an ordination, let alone a double ordination.'

As the bishop made his exit into the vestry, Peter turned to Sean. 'I completely forgot to mention to you that Mrs. Harte had asked me to ask you to look in on her niece.'

Sean waved his hand, saying, 'Don't worry; I already spoke to her, and I've seen her niece. By the way, have you noticed how the food has improved these past weeks? I had a filet mignon the other night that was as good as anything you'd get in any of the top restaurants. I also find myself running down for breakfast ever since she started making black and white pudding as good as my mum's.'

Peter laughed. 'I think Mrs. Harte finally got the message somehow. I believe she's actually taking cooking lessons.' They both smiled gaily. Then Peter looked at Sean and asked, 'By the way, how is her niece?'

Before Sean had time to answer, the door to the vestry opened, and both of them were surprised to see Martha gingerly walking towards them. Benny was in the background, smiling, as she approached Sean.

'I'm sorry to interrupt your rehearsals, gentlemen.'

'Not at all, Mrs. O'Dwyer. It's great to see you up and about,' added Peter.

She turned to Sean, and taking his hand, she kissed it, saying, 'Sean, I don't know what I can say to you to thank you for your prayers. I understood from Benny that you were a great help during my hour of need. May God be with you always.' At that, she looked up at Sean into his piercing blue eyes. There was a prolonged silence as they looked at each other.

'I believe your faith alone has saved you, Martha.'

'Thank you,' she whispered. A tear welled in her eye as she turned and made her way back to the vestry. Benny watched her go by and smiled back at Sean.

Peter looked at Sean and was about to ask him what that was all about when Sean said, 'Come with me, Peter. I want you to help me buy you and Shirley your wedding present. I have no idea how to go about doing it. It shouldn't take too long. Will you do that for me? We'll have precious little time between now and the day you get married.'

Peter said, 'Okay, let's go. We can go over to Brown Thomas. I know that Shirley has left something called a wedding list or something at that store. You can pick something out.'

Sean nodded happily and said, 'I must bring the donations with me and deposit them in the night safe. I forgot to do it last week.' He grabbed the leather folding wallet.

They left the church grounds and walked down Churchyard Street. As they made their way down Buttermilk Lane, they were confronted by four guys who didn't look too friendly. 'Hey, look what we have here – a couple of priests, and my guess is that they have a present for us.'

The biggest of the four held out his hand. 'Hand it over and you won't get hurt. Do anything else and you won't be saying any mass for a long time.'

Peter was very nervous. He looked towards Sean, who appeared calm and unperturbed. 'There's no need to do anything like that. Go in peace,' said Sean.

The four of them laughed out loud and reached out to grab the leather wallet. Sean tried to resist, but they wrenched it from him by pushing him backwards against the wall. Almost immediately one of the four gang members was pushed forward to the ground while another was thrown against the wall, landing with such force that he fell down unconscious. The other two had barely any time to look around before they too were punched senseless. Peter grabbed onto Sean, totally terrified. A large figure of a man confronted them.

Sean said, 'Relax, Peter. I know this man.' As they viewed the carnage that was before them, Sean looked up and said, 'Gabby, it's so good to see you. You couldn't have come at a better time.'

Gabby smiled and said, 'I'm only glad I was in the neighborhood to help out. These thugs won't be bothering anybody for a long while.'

Peter stood terrified and confused, half hidden behind Sean.

'Peter, allow me to introduce my great friend, Gabby Doyle, from my hometown of Ballinasloe. We have been friends since I was a child. As you can see, they don't come any bigger than Gabby – or smarter, for that matter.'

Sean led Peter out from behind him. Peter offered his hand, which Gabby made disappear as he enveloped it in his own massive hand. 'It's wonderful to meet you, Mr. . . . . eh, Gabby. Any friend of Sean's is a lifelong friend of mine,' said Peter, obviously shaking with fright. 'If you don't mind, I think I need to sit down somewhere, preferably in a pub. I believe I'm out of breath and not used to seeing such . . . excitement.'

Gabby smiled, saying, 'It's a pleasure to meet you, Peter. It just so happens that I'm in Galway with my wife, Angela. We are staying at the Skeff Hotel on Eyre Square. It's a sort of a treat for her since we've been working extra hard this past year.'

'Perhaps we should be moving away from here,' said Sean, looking down at the bodies strewn around.

'Good idea. Let's go across the square to the nearest pub,' begged Peter.

'First, let me deposit this money at the bank,' insisted Sean.

'I'll do that for you, Sean,' said Gabby. 'Go across to Garvey's Pub, and I'll meet up with you there. Mine's a Smithwick's.' Gabby took the wallet while Peter led Sean to Garvey's.

'I'm not the better of that altercation at all, at all,' muttered Peter as he downed a mouthful of Irish whiskey, then coughed and spluttered. 'Holy God, if any of our parishioners see us in here drinking the night before we are due to be ordained, I don't know what the bishop would say.'

'Don't worry about a thing. We'll be fine,' Sean assured Peter as Gabby made his entrance.

A number of people looked around, wondering why the bar had gone darker than normal. They turned around in their stools when they saw the size of Gabby.

'Ah, a Smithwick's,' smiled Gabby as he gulped down half of it in one swig. 'You know, the main reason we're here is that we wouldn't miss your ordination ceremony for anything. Are you both excited?'

'It's wonderful, Gabby, and I'm delighted that you both came. I am blessed to have such a friend as you.'

'And a big friend, I might add,' said Peter as he finished his whiskey, finally relaxing. 'Who were those people, and should we call the police?'

'I don't think it'll be necessary to call them,' said Gabby. 'I don't believe they'll be bothering anybody for a while.' Gabby turned to Sean. 'I did see our friend Harry Devlin around the corner. It wouldn't surprise me if he had something to do with it.'

Sean nodded, saying, 'No matter. All's well that ends well. I really should be going. Peter, I want to get your wedding present.'

'Okay, Sean. I'm good to go, as the Americans say.'

'Once again, thank you Gabby for your help,' said Sean. 'We'll see you at church tomorrow?'

'Wouldn't miss it,' said Gabby as he raised his glass in a toasting gesture.

Peter followed Sean, having once again thanked Gabby profusely, as Gabby smiled in return.

Bridie shouted up the stairs, 'Come on, Dan! We don't want to be late!'

'I'm coming, I'm coming. Hold your horses, girl,' said Dan as he made his way downstairs, trying to fix his tie. 'I haven't had to wear one of these things in years. I think it's gotten smaller for some reason!'

'Methinks your neck might have got a little bigger, me big man,' Bridie said, smiling as she helped him out.

"Tis a great day for the Robinson family, Bridie. I couldn't be happier.'

'I know, Dan. I can't believe where all of the years have gone. It seems like only yesterday that I was picking him up from outside the hospital main doors.'

'God! Do you think there'll be many there?' asked Dan as he shoveled a thick slice of bread into his mouth.

'Not for the want of trying. Molly and Kevin said they'd meet us at the church. I've been on the phone all week ringing everybody we know. They've all said they wouldn't miss it for the world. Sure I don't think any of them have ever been to an ordination in their lives.'

'I heard Gabby and his wife will be there. There's also the other man's family, so that should make a decent-sized crowd,' enthused Dan.

'Peter's a lovely man,' said Bridie. 'His wife's name is Shirley, so don't be forgetting, now.'

'I won't, girl. Come on. We'd better be going.'

Rosie parked her car at the front of her house. She beeped the horn and looked towards the front door. A minute later, Baggie appeared and looked more than handsome in his new suit. He climbed into the passenger seat as Rosie pulled out onto the main street.

'We'd better get a move on, Baggie. We don't want to be late.'

'Thank you for buying me this new suit, Rosie. I don't deserve it.'

Rosie looked over at Baggie. She still couldn't believe that this was the same man she had cleaned up after on so many occasions. She had scolded him and at times run him from the hospital. Then there were times when she felt utter compassion for him. Most of the time, pity had replaced her anger. Now he was more than a man of mystery. She had taken him in when Sean asked her not to say anything about his visit that night and requested her to look after him until he was fit again. How could she have refused? She was in the midst of something miraculous, of that there was no doubt. She had seen a man walk from his deathbed!

Rosie shook her head as she had done a million times since that fateful night. She still didn't have the words to work out what she should do. She decided instead to do what Sean had asked of her. She genuinely believed that if he had asked her to walk on water, she would do it for him.

She looked over at Baggie. Rosie had since learned that Baggie was now Sean's number-one go-to person, and it appeared he was more than capable. Of course he was; hadn't she found out bits and pieces from him as she tried to cajole him with alcohol – which he refused, with food – which he ate, and with charm – which he smiled at?

Then one night he told her everything. He had been a teacher in one of the secondary schools up in Dublin all of his life. He didn't know he was an alcoholic until one day he was fired having been allegedly missing for over a week, a week he remembers nothing about. He started to drift around the country. He lost his wife in a divorce. He thankfully – as he said himself – had no children. Finally, he had made his way to Ballinasloe, and there he had rested for the past thirty-five years or more, as far as he could remember. He had thought he was due to die that night until he opened his eyes and saw Father Sean praying over him. They spoke, and he found his body transforming beneath him as Sean prayed even more. All he remembered after that was Sean telling him to sleep, that tomorrow he would be well again and that God needed his services.

Rosie had sat in silence as he recounted his story. She had a thousand questions, but Baggie had no answers. She did know that he would do anything for Sean, so much so that he had dedicated his life to Sean – literally.

Peter was nervously waiting for the bishop to appear. Sean smiled at him, saying, 'It's a wonderful day for the both of us, Peter. I am so happy for you. Being nervous is a good thing. It means that you are focused.'

'I don't see you being the slightest bit nervous, Sean, and I'm delighted for you too. I just wish we could get started.'

'We still have a bit of time. Don't be worrying.'

Then the back door to the vestry opened, and Bishop Benny appeared dressed in his full refinery.

'Your Grace, you look incredible,' spluttered Peter.

'You sound like my wife, Peter,' the bishop laughed. 'Don't worry, men; we will get the proceedings under way shortly. It's a joyous day for the entire Anglican Church and an even more joyous one for me. My lovely Martha is not only well, as you all know,' he said, turning towards Sean and smiling, 'but she has also volunteered – or should I say demanded – to play the organ for today's hymns and marches. How about that, as they say?'

'Wonderful news,' added Sean.

They then heard the reeds burst into tune outside the door. Bishop Benny smiled. 'That's my favorite march she's playing.'

Dan turned his car for the second time, looking for a parking space. 'Jesus, why aren't there some spaces available? Has the world gone mad or what?' he said, getting annoyed.

'Stop taking the Lord's name in vain, Dan Robinson. Have some patience. We'll find somewhere. There must be a funeral going on or something. That would explain the large crowds.'

'But why would they have a funeral today of all days?' asked Dan, which Bridie couldn't answer. Finally, he found a space and managed to cram his car into it. 'How's about that for parking?' he said proudly.

Bridie ignored his boasting and said, 'Come on, let's be getting over there. Oh, there's Molly and Kevin. Thank God they're not late. Oh, there's Linda.'

Everybody was dressed in their best clothes. Most of the ladies wore special hats and carried rarely used handbags. The men were all suited and tied.

'You look fabulous, Linda. Is that a new dress?' asked Bridie.

'Absolutely. This is a special day for me too. I can't wait to see Sean. I know he and Peter have been rehearsing it for weeks.'

Linda, Bridie, and Dan greeted people they knew and smiled at others they didn't know, gradually making their way into the church, which was ribboned and dressed in flowers and bouquets of various sizes and colors. They were ushered down the aisle to the front row and sat themselves down beside Rosie and Baggie. Kevin and Molly followed, which filled up the front row on their side. Peter's family was on the other side, and the two families saluted and smiled at each other. Gabby and Angela made their way into the row behind them, and Bridie was delighted when they were joined by Judge Conran and Frank O'Connor, both of them acknowledging their arrival.

After about five minutes, the organ blared open, announcing that the ceremony was about to begin. Everybody turned around to await the procession, which was arranging itself at the front entrance. Bridie gasped when she saw that the church was full to the rafters and people were actually standing at the back and around the sides. Then an altar girl carrying a beautiful golden cross led the procession up the main aisle. She was followed by a dozen men and women singing from songbooks, all in perfect falsetto and baritone harmonies. Then a woman priest, dressed in priestly clothes, carried the Bible aloft, and people blessed themselves as she passed.

Then Bridie's heart beat harder and her eyes welled up as she saw her Sean and his friend, Peter, step in unison up the aisle, their hands folded together in prayer like two little boys who had become real men. They smiled and stayed focused as they neared the altar, never looking away from the main crucifix over the altar. The whole procession was capped off with the entrance of Bishop Benny, decked out in the finest splendor of blue and golden vestments. All of the congregation joined in the singing as if it were the last day on earth for everybody.

Bridie looked at Dan as the tears streamed down her face. Dan wrapped his arm around her and let his voice join in harmony with everybody else as the first hymn drew to a close.

The ceremony was magnificent. Sean and Peter did everything to perfection. Had they made a mistake, nobody would have noticed because all and sundry were captivated by the proceedings as the bishop led them in prayer and song. Nobody could deny that the whole ceremony had the perfect balance for such an occasion. Bridie thought that it was even more powerful than a civil marriage. She could feel a heavenly bond between her son and God, if that were possible, as she looked at how fervent he looked. He was saying the prayers alongside Peter and the bishop as if he were alone with God Himself.

Bridie turned around a couple of times to see how people were reacting. There wasn't a dry eye in the house as far as most of the women were concerned. Even some of the men were trying not to display the emotions they obviously felt. She didn't know most of these people. She felt that most people were staring at her Sean. She looked back up at the altar. Peter was on one side while Sean was on the other. She looked back again at the congregation and was sure that most people's heads were turned towards Sean. Everybody applauded loudly and enthusiastically when the bishop announced that his diocese was the proud possessor of two new priests. It was then that Sean and Peter visibly relaxed and smiled broadly, taking in the acclamation they so richly deserved.

Then the mass began, and both men took up their new positions at the altar. Bishop Benny gave a warm sermon concentrating solely on his two new priests, their families, and the congregation as a whole. The time came for Communion, and Bishop Benny announced that all of the children wishing to receive the sacrament should come up first to the altar with their parents or guardians. There were shuffles as the ushers got people organized.

Both Dan and Bridie thought they heard audible gasps from behind. Turning around, they couldn't see any fuss until people started staring at the center aisle as a young girl, accompanied by two old ladies, led the rest of the children. Some people put their hands to their mouths in shock as others enquired of the people around them as to who they were or what was happening. Peter sorted the chalices on the altar. He turned around with the chalice containing the wine and nearly dropped it as he gaped at Mrs. Harte accompanying her sister and the young girl. 'This is Mrs. Harte's niece,' thought Peter aloud. The housekeeper had shown him her picture that night a few weeks back. But this was a girl who had been in a wheelchair all of her life. This was the girl with polio!

There was a hushed silence as the trio knelt down at the altar in front of Sean. Everybody stopped as Sean walked towards her, laid his hand on her head, and smiled. 'The body of Christ,' he said, continuing, 'The body of our Lord Jesus Christ, which was given for thee, preserve thy body and soul unto everlasting life. Take and eat this in remembrance that Christ died for thee, and feed on Him in thy heart by faith, with thanksgiving.'

'Amen,' said the little girl as she waited for the wine chalice. When she had received it, she stood up and walked with her hands clasped in prayer to the tears of joy of all those who knew her.

The rest of the children followed. Sean distributed the hosts of Communion and stopped in his tracks when he saw the next communicant lift his head and open his mouth to receive. It was Father Rice. He gazed softly at Sean, who smiled back at him and gave him the host. Dan and Bridie followed and couldn't have wished for anything better in their lives at that moment than to receive Communion from their son. Judge Conran and Frank O'Connor had discussed whether their Catholic church allowed them to receive Communion from an Anglican priest, and the judge assured Frank that all was in order.

Shortly thereafter, the mass was ended, and everybody marshalled slowly out into the clear blue sky to be met and greeted by each other. The Wilson family introduced themselves to the Robinson clan, and they all got on terrifically. Sean and Peter greeted and thanked everybody for coming. The bishop wouldn't take his arm away from Martha, who had to field so many questions from well-wishers enquiring about her health. She assured them that she couldn't have been better, all the time looking over in Sean's direction.

Bridie couldn't help but notice how many people were encamped around Sean. She barely knew any of them. When she managed to grab hold of Rosie and enquired of her who all the people were crowding around her Sean, Rosie smiled and said he was very popular. 'Sure why wouldn't he be, having a gorgeous mother like you?' she ended, making her escape rather than try to explain the unexplainable.

Bridie blushed and smiled. Before she could hold on to Rosie, Dan touched her shoulder and said, 'Molly and Kevin have been asking me what we're going to do for lunch.'

'Good God, Dan Robinson, can you not just stop thinking about your stomach for once in your life?' she exclaimed, annoyed.

Sean approached his mum and dad. 'I'm sorry for not coming over earlier. I have been ambushed by good wishes. It's been a surreal experience. I can't thank both of you enough for everything you've done for me.'

'Sean, who was that little girl they were all fussing over when she went up for Communion?' asked Bridie, but before he could answer, he was tapped on the shoulder by Father Rice.

'Father Rice, it's wonderful to see you again,' said Sean. 'How good of you to come. Have you met my parents?'

Father Rice smiled broadly. 'I couldn't have missed your special day, Sean. I know of your parents. I met Bridie when you were a little boy. Do you remember me, Mrs. Robinson?'

Bridie opened her mouth and then said, 'Yes, yes, I do remember you that day . . .' She broke off, not wanting to make an issue in front of Dan. 'How have you been, Father?'

'Couldn't be better.' Turning to Sean, he said, 'Sean, my heartfelt congratulations. The church has gained two great disciples today. Godspeed go with you, my son.'

'Thank you, Father Rice. Will you not stay for something to eat?'

212

'No, I must be off, but thank you all the same.'

Sean took Linda by the hand and said, 'Do you think everything went well? I'm sorry for ignoring you. It wasn't intentional. From now on, I will have eyes and ears only for you.'

Linda leaned her head against his chest. 'Sean, it was the most beautiful day of my life. Don't worry about me; I'm fine. To see you up on the altar and to know that you are now a fully fledged priest lifts my heart. I am always here for you.'

'I am always here for you too, Linda. Remember that forever.'

Anna.

Vinnie looked down at his drawings and examined his calculations for the umpteenth time. 'This is hopeless,' he said to himself. He stood up and scratched his head.

He wondered if the package he had sent to himself would arrive, and if so, when? He needed his tools. He needed his theodolite, cross staff, levelling staff, and optical squares. All he had been able to bring with him were his compasses, steel tape, and tracer. He reckoned he could equip himself with his own designed plane table and drawing board from materials around the town. How he was to make land-measuring chains was anybody's guess. From his initial calculations, drawn from his observations and estimates, this was an impossible job. There was no heavy equipment, not even a tractor for pulling away any rubble or loose soil, let alone moving any boulders. How was he expected to do this?

As Vinnie paced the floor, Miguel popped his head through the curtain that acted as a door. 'Vinnie, I have someone here whom I'd like you to meet.' He drew back the curtain to reveal a beautiful woman with sparkling brown eyes and long dark hair. 'This is my chief nurse and . . . how do you say it in Ireland? Ah yes – chief bottle-washer, Anna.'

Anna smiled and curtsied. Vinnie was taken aback at her beauty, the first nice thing he'd seen since he had arrived at this horrible place. 'I'm very pleased to meet you, Anna,' he said more than enthusiastically. 'Do you speak English?'

'Yes, I have good English, but you need to speak slowly for me to understand you.'

Vinnie smiled again when Miguel said, 'I would be lost without my Anna. I leave everything to her when I'm back in Miami. She runs the hospital for me and has saved many lives. Come, let us show you around our town.'

Vinnie decided to say nothing to Miguel just yet about his despair. Instead, he followed Miguel and Anna as they introduced him to some of the locals. Everybody smiled at him with toothless and semi toothless grins. The older ones had drawn and haggard skin while the children and younger folk had beautiful skin. The children played merrily like every other child around the world. Vinnie shook his head in amazement that, despite the hardship and poverty around these people, they still found time to smile amongst their troubles. He saw women boiling pots of sweet-smelling brews. Miguel had him sample some.

'It's so good. What is it?' Vinnie asked.

'The people are renowned for cooking with spices they grow themselves. Most of it is just broth made mainly from vegetables or fish bones. If the catch is big, then they will add full pieces of fish to the pots, and their bellies will be full for another while. Anna and her staff have instructed all of the women to keep their houses and bodies clean. The last thing we want is an outbreak of cholera. The women are great at that; the men not so.'

As they walked through the streets, Vinnie was surprised and impressed at some of the things he was seeing, such as how some of the walls of the buildings had been freshly painted and that one or two houses had motorbikes. Most of the men stood around in groups and remained aloof from him.

'Don't worry too much about the lack of sociability of the men, Vinnie. They'll come around in time.'

'Or when Sayil lets them,' added Anna.

'Yes, unfortunately, everything we do has to get approval from Sayil. No doubt you'll be meeting him soon,' added Miguel.'

As they walked, little Brownie came running up the street excitedly. 'Senor Veenie, your box eez here!' he shouted.

Miguel spoke to him in Creole and told Vinnie, 'He's saying that a big box has arrived addressed to you.'

'That'll be my tools from Ireland. Great. Now I can get to do some accurate work. Miguel, I'm going to need some men to help me plant stakes in the paths I mark. Can that be arranged?'

'Yes, I'll get you all the help you need.'

Vinnie was happy for the first time since he had gotten there. He walked quickly back to his house and found that Brownie had already emptied the box and placed all of his tools on the table. He checked, and everything seemed to be there. He decided to get to work right away.

Within the hour, he could be seen heading for the hills accompanied by Brownie, five men, and a donkey laden with sticks and tools.

It took a number of days for Vinnie to do his calculations. At least now he had the correct tools to give him accurate information. Having reached the main river, he understood the impossibility of trying to divert it back towards the town. However, he came across one feeder tributary that would have enough momentum to force its own route – if it could be dammed.

Having run some tests, he noted that the quality of the water was good. He was also assured of this when he found fish living under pebbles and rocks. His calculations told him that he would have enough of a flow to take the tributary down the first mountainside and along half of the flat land at its base. His major problem, then, would be to try to find a way to pump the river along a bedrock, just enough to push it over the remaining hill and down the other side. From there, he didn't see a major problem in getting it sourced back through the town and into the sea. Fresh water was crucial for the town's survival and possibly the only way it could support itself. It was also the basis for avoiding disease. If that could be provided, then Vinnie would have achieved what Sean would have expected of him.

That was the positive side or ideal dream, but the practicalities of achieving it were enormous. First, there was no heavy equipment. How were they to shift the million tons of rocks and shale? Everything was so badly eroded that he couldn't find any forest to give him the necessary wood to construct frames for leverage. The main river was so badly silted that it left him with no other option than to try to divert the tributary. He would have to sit down with Miguel and point out the problems and the unbelievable obstacles that were in their way.

Vinnie said, 'Orevwa,' to the men as he and Brownie arrived at his house. He was dead tired. As he pulled the curtain, he was surprised and delighted to be greeted by Anna. A fire was lit, and the smell of food wafted throughout.

'Welcome, Mr. Vinnie. I hope you are hungry,' said a smiling Anna.

'What a nice surprise. Is this all for me?' asked Vinnie as he looked into the boiling pots.

'And me,' blurted Brownie, already pushing himself into position at the table.

'Sit down, the two of you. I will serve you your dinner. You have both worked hard today.'

Vinnie sat down and stared shyly at Anna as she ladled a soup of potatoes, vegetables, and some food that Vinnie couldn't recognize. Brownie pushed his spoon into his bowl and slurped the soup until it was half-eaten in a matter of minutes.

'Take your time, Brownie,' Anna said and repeated it in Creole. 'So tell me, Senor Vinnie, how was your day?'

Vinnie relished the taste of the food and couldn't take his eyes away from Anna at the same time. 'Insurmountable is one word that could be used.' Anna creased her forehead. 'Sorry, I meant that the problems are huge,' added Vinnie. 'And please call me Vinnie. There's no need for Senor.'

'Okay . . . Vinnie,' she said, emphasizing the word playfully, 'What sort of problems do you have? Maybe my listening will help?'

Vinnie smiled. 'Before I tell you, can you tell me what's in this dish, because the taste is magic?'

She laughed. 'Maybe when I tell you, you might not think it's so magical.' He looked afeared in an exaggerated way that made Brownie giggle. 'It's a dish of potatoes, local vegetables, and seasoning. I also added some mango for sweetness, salt, and some meat.'

Brownie butted in. 'Meat! Yum-yum.'

'I would have thought meat was hard to come by around here,' said Vinnie.

'Not for special guests such as you, Vinnie. Some of the women I know offered it to me, and I accepted it on your behalf. The locals are a very proud people, and it would be insulting to them to refuse their generosity.'

'Well, it's delicious, and if I may, I'd like some more if there's any available.'

'Ah, like Oliver Twist, no?'

'Yes, just like Oliver.' As Anna filled his bowl, Vinnie continued, 'Without any heavy drilling or moving equipment, I fail to see how we can do anything other than move the smaller stones and shale. We would also need pumping equipment to push the water up around five hundred feet to get it down the other side. They're just a couple of the major obstacles.'

Anna said, 'Have you spoken to Father Miguel about this?'

'No, haven't had the chance yet. I expect I'll speak with him tomorrow.'

'Have you met Sayil yet?' asked Anna.

'No, can't say I've had that dubious pleasure.'

'Then after your dinner, I will take you to him. You have to meet with him, or you will get nothing and nobody to help you around here.'

Vinnie looked over his spoon and suddenly lost his appetite. 'Gee, do we have to do it tonight? I'm fairly knackered.'

'No time like the present, as you people say, right?'

Vinnie sighed. 'You're right. I'm not on vacation here. There's work to be done. What am I going to say to him? I don't speak Creole.'

'You just stand there and smile and look important. I will do all of the talking.'

Ten minutes later, Anna led Vinnie down the road about a half mile until they came to a stop outside a tavern. Two men approached them. The men asked Anna something, and she responded. Vinnie stood there, not knowing what to do. Anna nodded for him to follow her.

As they entered the bar, they were confronted by about six rough-looking men. Vinnie was taller than all of them, but he didn't fancy getting into a fight. From the back of the bar came a big muscular guy, about the same height as Vinnie. He was obviously the man of the hour – Sayil – and he didn't look happy. Anna launched into a litany of words, to which Sayil responded angrily every now and again. Vinnie stood there as Anna pointed to him. After about fifteen minutes and following some harsh words interspersed with the occasional laugh – or it could have been a smirk – Anna indicated to Vinnie to shake Sayil's hand. Vinnie obeyed, and with that, the two of them turned and walked out.

They were about halfway down the street, and Vinnie could remain quiet no longer. 'So what happened in there?'

Anna looked back to make sure nobody was around. 'We got what we came for.'

'What did we come for?' asked Vinnie.

'You'll see tomorrow morning. You get your sleep. Tomorrow is a busy day for everybody, and I have a lot of things to organize.'

Vinnie watched in awe and wonderment as Anna left him in her wake. She walked hurriedly down the road and out of sight. Vinnie couldn't help but notice that she had a terrific figure.

Engaged

Shirley studied herself in the full-length mirror. 'Do I look fat in this, Linda?'

'Not a bit of it, Shirley. You have a wonderful figure.'

'Oh, Linda, I'm so excited and happy. Imagine, I'm getting married on Saturday.'

Linda smiled. 'I'm delighted you chose me as your bridesmaid.'

'And why wouldn't I? We've become the best of friends since we got to know each other, haven't we?'

'Yes, we have. I know Peter is Sean's best friend too. They get on so well together.'

'I know. Peter is always going on about how "Sean did this" and "Sean did that." You'd swear they were brothers.'

'I suppose they are brothers in a way. Tell me, where have you decided on the honeymoon?'

'Well, we can't go abroad because Peter starts as the new rector in Tuam in about two weeks, so we're travelling around Ireland, staying at bed and breakfasts and the odd hotel. We'll be grand. We can always do something later in the year or maybe next year. God, it's hard to believe that another year is gone.'

'I know, Shirley. I don't know where the time goes. What's your new house like in Tuam?'

'It's fine. Nothing modern about it, but you could say it's quaint.'

'That's like saying that an ugly person has a great personality,' said Linda as the two of them laughed loudly.

'It'll do us for what we want. Besides, Tuam is only a stone's throw away. It's not like we're going to the moon.' Shirley changed her expression as she gingerly enquired, 'What about you and Sean? Is there any sign of you two tying the knot anytime soon?'

Linda shrugged. 'I don't know. I'm always half-expecting Sean to propose to me, and just when I feel he's about to say the words, something happens, like a phone call or some emergency or other. I know we love each other. It's just that it will happen when it happens, I suppose.'

Linda looked a little down, so Shirley said, 'Come on. Let me get out of these clothes, and we'll whip ourselves over to the Shangri-La and have some champagne and a bite to eat.'

Linda smiled brightly and nodded her head in obvious agreement.

Sean thought Fonsie looked a lot more relaxed compared to the previous times he had visited. Fonsie flipped through the pages of the magazines Sean had brought with him. 'So, how are you feeling today?' asked Sean as he handed him two packets of cigarettes.

'Why are you being good to me? I don't know you. Are you hoping that you'll convert me?'

'It's not like that, Fonsie. I care for you just as much as I care for all of my parishioners. Would you like me to hear your confession?'

Fonsie looked up from the table. 'Are you working with the cops now, Faddah?'

Sean smiled. 'If you feel you are up to it, perhaps we could examine your conscience. This is solely between God and you, not the police.'

Fonsie fiddled with the cigarette box. 'Naw, Faddah, I don't think I'm ready for that just yet. Besides, I couldn't remember half the sins I've committed.' He grinned a semi toothless grin showing tobacco stains.

'Well, whenever you feel up to it, all you have to do is call me. I'll be back again next month.'

'Listen, Faddah, I do appreciate what you're doing for me. I suppose your God knows that I haven't been the best of candidates for forgiveness, but maybe one day, if I'm spared, I'll maybe come around to His way of thinking.'

Bishop Benny and his wife, Martha, together with all of the Wilson family, were in attendance as Peter stood at the foot of the altar awaiting the arrival of his beautiful bride. Sean was dressed in white vestments for the occasion, his first wedding as a priest. The organ announced the arrival of the bride in the usual manner, and Linda looked radiant in pink as she preceded Shirley, accompanied by her father. A good crowd of onlookers were there to gawk as they always do, especially the women. Peter looked splendid in his Scottish kilt, a last-minute decision in honor of his family's Scottish tradition. Everything went without a hitch as Sean performed the ceremony to perfection. The bride and groom kissed, bringing the wedding to its conclusion.

Later, Sean and Linda dined with the Wilson family and Bishop Benny and Martha. The wine flowed and the stories were many as they regaled each other of their lives in England and Scotland before they had immigrated to Ireland. One of the Wilson clan had a magnificent baritone voice, and he led the ensemble in renditions of 'Danny Boy,' 'The Streets of Athenry,' and many more, which lifted each person's spirits to new levels.

As they drove back to Ballinasloe, Sean and Linda remembered back through the day and discussed how everything had gone so well. Sean stopped outside Linda's house and said, 'Linda, I probably haven't been the best of company as far as being your boyfriend is concerned over these past months and years.' He looked her in the eyes and held her chin gently in his fingers. 'But I want you to know I love you deeply, more than anything in the world.'

They kissed longingly, and Linda said, 'Oh, Sean, I love you so much. You make me more than happy. You don't have to apologize for anything.'

Sean opened the glove compartment and handed her a small box. He said, 'That's why I don't want to wait any longer. Will you marry me, Linda?'

Linda looked at the box and opened it. She couldn't help but choke up as she took the ring and put it on her finger. Looking back at Sean, she threw her arms around him. 'Of course, my darling. I thought this day would never come.'

The next day, Linda couldn't wait to tell her family and texted everybody she knew while at the same time filling up her timeline in Facebook. As a result, she was kept busy the entire day answering phone calls and texts from all of her friends. They all asked the same thing – when was the big day?

Meanwhile, Sean kept it low-key, telling only Bridie on the phone, who screamed with delight at hearing the news. She also asked when the big day was, and Sean kicked for touch, like all men. 'I don't know, Mother. For the moment, we are officially engaged. Would that not suffice?'

'Well, maybe for now. Sean, I couldn't be happier.'

'Happy about what?' asked Dan, overhearing part of the conversation.

'Sean and Linda are engaged,' she said holding her hand to her mouthpiece. 'Okay, Sean, run along, and I'll talk to you later,' insisted Bridie, knowing Sean was in a hurry. She hung up.

'That's great news altogether,' said Dan as Bridie sat down at the table.

Bridie crisscrossed her hands and said, 'I can't believe he's finally proposed. I know Linda has been waiting a long time for this moment to arrive. I must call her. I'm sure she's over the moon.'

Sean knocked on Bishop Benny's door. 'Come in,' said Benny. Sean apologized for interrupting. 'Not at all. Sure I was only saying a few prayers. What can I do for you, Sean?'

'I'd like to start a new campaign to help the down and outs. What I have in mind is having what I call a "Day of Hope" when we gather all the destitute children in the town and surrounding areas and help them prepare for school. I was thinking of organizing it for around August next year, just in time before the new school year starts.'

Benny scratched his chin. 'A Day of Hope, you say. It sounds intriguing and obviously for a very good cause. Where did you dream this up?'

'I'd heard of it from some of our American churches where it works very successfully. It means that every child will get a free haircut, medical checkup, and dental and eye examinations, as well as a good breakfast and/or dinner, and they'll be sent home with free schoolbooks, writing materials, and all the things they'll need for the school year. Once we get it established the first year, then the second and subsequent years should be a lot easier. I'd have to find qualified medical people, stylists, and the like who will offer their time free of charge for the day. It's a new concept for our parish and probably the country, for that matter, but I believe it will be well worth it. I also believe that it's the right thing to do. As our Lord said, we need to be able to teach when their bellies are full and when they are happy, not when they're sad.'

Benny smiled and said, 'Of course, Sean. I have absolutely no objection. Are you sure you'll have enough time, together with all of your other duties, to organize this as well?'

'Oh, I'll have lots of help.' Sean rose, kissed Benny's ring, and made his exit.

Saul, Saul...

Vinnie opened his eyes. He could have sworn he had heard a lot of mumbling going on somewhere. He shook his head and listened intently. There was definitely something going on outside. He jumped out of bed and brushed his teeth. He put on a tee-shirt and a pair of shorts.

Pulling back the curtain, he was greeted with a sea of smiling and quizzical brown faces. He looked further. The faces went down the street and around the corner. 'What's happening?' he said to nobody in particular, thinking that there must be some sort of emergency.

'They are your volunteer force, Vinnie,' said Anna as she approached from the side of the building with little Brownie beside her.

'What do you mean, Anna?'

Anna smiled radiantly and said, 'You told me last night that you didn't have any heavy equipment to do the bulldozing and the lifting. Well, here's your heavy equipment.'

Vinnie looked down the line again. There must have been over a hundred faces looking back at him. 'But what am I to do with them? How can they help me?'

'Vinnie, think. These people will work night and day for you. They will not moan or grumble. They believe you can get them their river back.'

Vinnie stood open-mouthed, looking into Anna's eyes. 'Why would they believe that?'

She smiled back at him. 'Because I told them!'

Vinnie looked incredulously at Anna, who smiled her magnetic smile back at him and said, 'Are you going to do this or not?'

A silence occurred as the people seemed to sense that something was wrong from the way Anna spoke. Vinnie looked at the poor wretches again. He looked back at Anna and then at Brownie.

'Okay, God damn it, why not? All we can do is make a balls of it, I suppose.'

Brownie looked at Anna and said, 'What is "balls of it"?'

Anna smiled. 'It means he is confident and very happy that he can do it.'

Brownie smiled again, and speaking in his native tongue, he told everybody that the white man was a god who was going to fix the river. The crowd all mumbled agreeably, some smiling as if they had won the lottery. Vinnie wondered why they were all so happy because he certainly wasn't.

After organizing the men into able-bodied and not-so-able-bodied lines, Vinnie told Brownie to lead his line one way up the hill while he went the other way. He was to stop when he saw Vinnie stopping. The easiest thing to do was to try the simple things first. That way, everybody would be able to see that they had some affect, and hopefully that would encourage them.

Had Vinnie been working with professionals, it wouldn't have mattered. He remembered he was constructing a bridge once in Connemara, and he had to use labor supplied by the unemployment exchange. They became disheartened after a few days when they saw that their work amounted to very little. They hadn't realized that they were doing the most important part by creating a solid foundation. Instead, Vinnie made them build four pillars, two on either end of the bridge. It meant nothing to the construction and was valuable only from an optical viewpoint, but it had a tremendous effect on their demeanor. They then worked even harder and with purpose in completing the bridge. Vinnie was also happy with their work, despite the fact that they had no qualifications. This experience crossed his mind as he made his way up the hill. Perhaps there was a chance that they could achieve something even if none of them spoke any English or had any experience. What else had he? He had no other alternative.

About a half mile up the hill, Vinnie stopped the two lines. They were about twenty yards apart. The day before, he had made the carpenters plant the marking stakes at strategic points along the way. The stakes went all the way to the river, about another mile away. He asked Brownie to get everybody's attention so he could explain what he wanted them to do. Brownie was to make sure that he translated Vinnie's words correctly. Vinnie waited anxiously for Brownie to issue his instructions in Creole. Then suddenly, and much to Vinnie's shock, the men lined up as he had planned and started to shift through the shale, leaving the heavier rocks and stones, and throwing the loose, smaller stones and shale to one side. This was to be the bedrock needed to guide the river through the town and down into the sea. This was the relatively easier part but was labor intensive all the same.

Vinnie was amazed at their productivity. They bent down and acted like a cold-planer machine used to lift asphalt from a roadway. They didn't stop until Vinnie got worried that maybe they needed a break. He called time, and Brownie told the workers to sit and drink. They did as they were told but continued to stare at Vinnie. Vinnie asked Brownie why they were staring at him.

'They are wondering why you wanted them to stop working.'

Vinnie chuckled to himself, thinking that he'd have the unions on his back if this happened back in Ireland. 'Fine. Let's get back to work, then.'

Brownie started the gangs again, and they continued with their work for another two and a half hours. Vinnie sat drinking water, totally amazed at their tenacity and dedication. Perhaps this wasn't the craziest scheme after all!

Around midday, Vinnie turned around to see what all the noise and excitement was about. He put his hands to his head in wonderment when he saw a line of over a dozen women coming up the hill carrying baskets of food and drink for the workers. In the distance, he could see another lot of women starting the same journey. He also recognized Anna directing them from afar. She caught his eye and waved. He smiled and returned her wave with a mock gesture of thanks. These people were something else, Vinnie thought.

Every day for the next two weeks, Vinnie was greeted by the same hundred faces encamped outside his house each morning waiting for him. It wasn't long before those two weeks became a month. Vinnie finally completed the final stretch of riverbed, the one that approached the town and the sea. It looked good, and he was pleased with the results.

The part he wasn't looking forward to had arrived. He and the townspeople looked out towards the valley that offered them a challenge equivalent to parting the Red Sea. Vinnie felt deflated as he led his men down the degraded hillsides, slipping down the slopes. When they reached the part that levelled out, they looked back up the hillside, knowing that they had to run a river back along the way they came. Silently, everybody realized what a daunting task lay ahead of them. They looked to Vinnie. He felt their anguish was even greater than his. He turned away, more to hide his own fear and lack of confidence. He thought how generals who led their men into battles against overwhelming odds must have felt. Yet sometimes even the outnumbered forces won. He thought how the townspeople were depending on him. He thought how Anna and Miguel had put their trust in him.

Vinnie took a deep breath, turned around, and saw how his men were sullen and awaiting their instructions. He pumped his arms into the air and bellowed out a huge 'hooray!' over and over. The men looked at each other in amazement and confusion until Brownie also started shouting, 'Hooray! Hooray!' without knowing why he was doing it. Then all men started doing the same until soon there was a crescendo of voices all shouting, 'Hooray!' in unison. They all danced in circles like crazy people, finally sitting down with exhaustion and exhilaration. They all laughed together as Vinnie looked at them wondering where he could start.

Brownie stood up and pointed backwards. 'Senor Veenie, it's Father Miguel.'

Vinnie was glad to see Miguel. He needed to talk to somebody – anybody!

Miguel smiled at his townsfolk and sat down beside Vinnie. 'Great progress, my friend. I see my people look very happy.'

Vinnie tried his best to look confident, but it didn't last. 'Miguel, I'm sorry, but this part is impossible without heavy equipment. You see that ridge up there?' He pointed upwards, and Miguel confirmed by nodding. 'As soon as we try to move any of those big boulders, the whole thing will probably come crashing down. I need that ridge because it's the only way to have the elevation we need to run the river. If we have to come down to the valley, we wouldn't have any pumping mechanism to pump it back up. I need that gradient.'

Miguel could see how earnest Vinnie was. His despair upon arrival and over his first few days in Bondye had been replaced with a new enthusiasm. It was the enthusiasm of a committed person, not one of hopelessness. He could see that Vinnie needed a shoulder to cry on, as everybody does from time to time.

'Come, you have done great work thus far. You all need a good meal and some gaiety. Let's go. I have something organized for all of you.' Miguel told his men to make their way back and get ready for a fiesta *Tan li yo selebre*, which translated meant 'it's time to celebrate.'

He walked with Vinnie back along the trail. 'Vinnie, when I have troubles, I always speak with God. He never lets me down. It doesn't happen immediately, but he always answers. You should try it.'

Vinnie smiled back at Miguel. 'I think we'll need a lot more than prayer to fix this problem, Miguel. More like a miracle is needed at this stage.'

They walked back slowly, and Miguel changed the mood by explaining how the fiesta worked. 'Villagers love to celebrate, and they do it with great enthusiasm. I have always got a little supply of beer put aside for such an occasion. Tonight we will use up our supply and pray that it will be replenished soon. Anna and the womenfolk have been working all day, cooking and baking. They have surpassed themselves in your honor.' They parted and agreed to meet up as soon as they had washed and changed their clothes.

Vinnie lay down on his bunk bed and gazed at the ceiling. 'To hell with it. Let's get drunk!' he said aloud to himself. He washed as best he could, longing for a nice hot shower, which had been missing from his life ever since he'd arrived there. Come to think of it, a lot of niceties had been missing from his life. He looked down at his left arm. *Funny, I had forgotten about that. It hasn't shaken at all these past weeks, and I haven't experienced any pain either!*

An hour or so later, Vinnie made his way in the direction of the noise. The night sky was clear and full of stars. People came up to him, laughing and patting him on his back and shoulders, saying, 'Mesi, mesi V-Nee.' He laughed and smiled back at them as someone pushed a bottle of beer into his hand, which he gushed down quickly, wishing it was a Guinness. There were hundreds of people everywhere and musicians played wildly on their instruments as fires blazed in grates along the streets, sending out wafts of great aromas indicating that food was being served.

Amidst all of this surreal gaiety, Vinnie's eyes were drawn instantly to the most beautiful sight he had ever seen in his life. Anna's smile was electric, breathtaking. Her white teeth contrasted against the hue of the flames that lit her complexion. She looked at Vinnie playfully, waving at him to come over. She offered him some food; then, before he had time to eat it, she took his arm and dragged him reluctantly into the middle of the other dancers. She danced for him while he moved from side to side. Everybody clapped and sang like there was no tomorrow. For the first time in a long time, Vinnie was totally relaxed, charmed and mesmerized by Anna.

Miguel looked on with joy seeing Vinnie and Anna together. His idea that they might hit it off was paying off. *Never underestimate the wiles and charms of a woman in times of difficulty,* he thought. He also noticed Sayil in the background with his small army of cronies. He wasn't happy, that was obvious. As long as he kept out of their way, then Miguel didn't care.

With sweat dripping down his face and chest, Vinnie begged Anna to stop. She laughed. 'You are not fit, Vinnie. You need to exercise more.'

Vinnie grabbed a chair and was handed another beer, which he relished. Anna took a plate, and they tucked into their food with delight.

'You know, it's times like these that make it all worthwhile,' Vinnie said, all the time totally at ease in Anna's company. He noticed she stared at him a lot, a stare he enjoyed.

As the people disappeared slowly during the evening, the festivities were coming to an end. Anna brought out a small cup. 'Taste this.'

'What is it?'

'It's our local liquor. Go on; you will enjoy it.'

Vinnie tasted it and licked his lips. The sweet flavor was powerful.

'That's your dessert,' she said, laughing.

'I had other things in mind for dessert,' said Vinnie coyly.

'Aha, you are not as shy as I thought,' Anna responded, playfully digging at his ribs.

Vinnie gently woke up to the morning sun. He had just had the best sleep in a long time. He smiled to himself as he remembered the night before. He thought about Anna, naturally. He turned in the bed and drifted his finger down her naked back. She was simply gorgeous. She was sleeping comfortably.

After a few moments, Vinnie looked at his phone, which told him he was late. He'd better get ready as his tribe of workmen would be waiting for him outside. He kissed Anna on the neck, and she made a purring sound. He dressed himself quickly and opened the curtain. To his shock, there was nobody around. Was it because he was with Anna? he wondered.

Vinnie stepped outside and looked around, but there wasn't a soul in sight. He walked down the lane but could see only children playing in the distance. He went back inside and shook Anna awake. 'Anna, Anna, there's something wrong. Nobody has arrived for work.'

'What?' she said, rubbing her eyes and pulling the sheet up to cover herself when she realized she was naked. 'That's impossible. Today is only Friday. They know they have to work today.'

She climbed into her clothes and walked quickly outside, followed by Vinnie. They spent the next ten minutes looking around as Anna inquired of some of the local women about the men.

'Come on,' she said. 'We'd better find Miguel.'

They made their way to the makeshift church that acted as Miguel's headquarters. Sure enough, he was working at the altar. He turned around.

'I know what you're thinking. I have some bad news. It seems the men have been instructed by Sayil's men to down tools and stop working for us. I don't know why. I saw him last night at the fiesta, and he didn't appear happy. I was just on my way to see him now. You might as well join me and give me some support.'

All three of them walked quickly towards the tavern that acted as Sayil's office. As they approached, some of his men tried to stop them, but Miguel was having none of it. He pushed them aside and made his way through the door. Vinnie thought they seemed afraid of Miguel – maybe it was because of his priest's attire?

Sayil was sitting down, drinking something from a bowl. He had a large glass of beer beside him. Vinnie thought he didn't look well, certainly not as well as he had the first time he saw him.

Miguel conversed with him in Creole. They had a raging argument. Anna tried to interfere, but Sayil insisted she shut up by having his men take her and Vinnie out of the tavern. They waited outside for almost a half hour before Miguel reappeared. He looked sullen and was shaking his head.

Miguel said, 'It's not good. I don't know what's wrong with him. He's always in bad form, but today he's angry for some reason. He told his men to stop working for us.' They made their way down the street, and Miguel continued, 'I think it's something tribal. These animals don't like to see their people enjoying themselves, so probably having the fiesta was a bad idea.'

'I think there's more to it than that, Father,' added Anna. 'Some of the women told me that he's not happy because his fishing boats have not had any luck this past week. If he doesn't have a good catch, he doesn't have any bartering power. He's able to get good money for his catch, which he can trade for anything he needs in the bigger towns.'

Miguel considered her words. 'That would make more sense, Anna. It also creates further problems for our river project. It means our people will go hungry again.'

They walked the rest of the way to the church in silence. Vinnie didn't know anything about Sayil other than that he was a tough guy and somewhat immovable. 'Did you think he didn't look well, Anna?' asked Vinnie.

'I can't say I did. I was so concerned about not losing my temper with him.'

'That didn't work, then,' added Vinnie, smiling at her.

'There's nothing we can do until he changes his mind,' said Miguel, obviously disappointed. 'What will you do, Vinnie?' asked Miguel, looking hopefully at him.

Vinnie raised his eyebrows and looked at Miguel, then Anna. He smiled. 'I can't very well abandon ship at this stage. I have a lot more surveying to do. That'll keep me busy for a number of days. Besides, I have someone nearby whom I've taken a real fancy to,' he said, smiling.

Anna blushed as Miguel said, 'Aha, I see you two have formed a little partnership.'

Anna blushed again. 'Father, it's not so.' She dug at Vinnie's ribs.

Miguel changed the mood. 'Okay, let's give it a few days, and hopefully our friend Sayil will come around.'

Have faith.

'Faddah, I think I'd like you to hear me confession,' said Fonsie.

Sean looked at him, surprised. He thought Fonsie looked different today for some reason. 'I saw Harry Devlin on my way in. He seemed to have just visited somebody. Have you any idea who?'

Fonsie shifted in his seat. 'I expect he was in with Dino. He sees Dino a lot.'

Sean took out his stole, and, placing it around his neck, he closed his eyes and asked Fonsie to confess. Reading from a pamphlet Sean handed him, the inmate said, 'Bless me, Father, for I have sinned. It's been . . .' He stalled and said, 'I don't know how long it's been, Faddah.'

'It doesn't matter, Fonsie. Did you examine your conscience?'

Fonsie looked at Sean. 'Yes, I think I did.'

'Then tell me your sins.'

'I stole a lot, Faddah. Many times. I don't know what I stole, but I stole a lot.'

'Are you truly sorry for what you did?'

'I am, Faddah, in a lot of cases. There were times I was glad I stole from some people 'cos they deserved it, really. I mean, they had loads of money anyway; they wouldn't have missed what I took.'

Sean smiled. 'It doesn't matter whether you think they deserved it or not. What matters is that you are sorry for having committed a sin. What really matters are that you're not going to sin again.'

Fonsie looked up at the ceiling. 'I don't know whether I can say that I'm not going to steal again, but if I ever get outta here, I'd say I'm going to change me ways.'

Sean nodded. 'What about anything else? Have you committed any other sin?'

'There's loads, Faddah. I don't think I ever hurt anybody – physically like – always in their pockets, you know, like?' Fonsie looked again at the officer sitting behind him, then back at Sean again.

He looked troubled. Sean said nothing, letting him come to his own conclusions. Finally, he stuttered, 'I never killed anybody, Faddah.' Fonsie looked at Sean for assurances. 'I mean, I was there and all . . . the time of the killing.' He looked around at the officer to make sure he wasn't listening. 'It was Dino, Faddah. He did the killin', not me.' Sean looked on silently. 'I don't know why he did it. There was no need. We just wanted the money like. I had to say nothin'; otherwise, Dino or Harry or Boxer would kill me.'

'That's enough. It's time,' said the prison officer loudly.

Fonsie looked scared. Sean looked at Fonsie. 'For these and for all of your sins, I grant you absolution. In the name of the Father, the Son, and the Holy Spirit, amen.'

Fonsie looked at Sean. 'Am I free to go now, Faddah?'

'Not free in that you can leave this prison, but yes, you are free in your soul. You have to continue to repent, Fonsie. You must go from here and never sin again.'

'I'll try, Faddah. I will try.'

The officer led Fonsie back to his cell as Sean looked on.

Molly and Bridie spoke feverishly in the kitchen. Dan interrupted them by saying, 'What's the big noise going on around here?'

Bridie smiled at Molly. Turning to Dan, she said, 'Molly just told me that she and Andrew are engaged and going to get married in April. Isn't that great news?'

Dan looked in amazement, then smiled and stepped forward to hold Molly in his arms. 'I couldn't be happier. My only little girl is finally getting married. Andrew is a fine young man. He'll take great care of my little girl.'

'Daddy, I'm not your little girl anymore. I'm in my thirties, and it's about time I was getting married.'

'You'll always be my little girl, make no mistake about it.'

Molly looked at Bridie and back at Dan. 'Daddy, I want to get married at the Shangri-La Hotel. Is that okay?'

Dan looked wide-eyed, then at Bridie, who opened her eyes to tell Dan to say yes. 'The Shangri-La it is. If that's what my girl wants, then that's what she gets. How many are you thinking of inviting?'

'Well, Andrew's family is huge. There must be at least a hundred and fifty of them. So that, together with our family and all of my friends, I'd say around two to three hundred.'

Dan sat down. 'Holy God, that's a fierce number of people there, Molly. Are you sure we need to have such a big wedding?'

Bridie could see how anxious Dan had become and said, 'Not at all. We'll invite whoever you want to invite, Molly.'

'Thank you, Mum,' said Molly, hugging Bridie as Dan scratched his head, wondering how the hell he was going to be able to afford it. 'I have to go and tell Andrew that it's all set. Oh, did I mention that I'm going to ask Sean to do the ceremony?' With that, she skipped from the kitchen with obvious excitement.

Bridie looked at Dan. 'Don't worry, big fella. I'm sure you'll find a way to get us through this,' she said hopefully.

'Yeah, it'll be grand,' replied Dan without any enthusiasm.

The three days flew by, and Anna and Vinnie became even more attracted to each other. They saw each other for lunch and dinner and at night they slept together.

They were having breakfast when their solitude was torn by the sound of Father Miguel in obvious distress. He burst through the curtain. 'Anna, Vinnie, I have terrible news.'

Father Miguel drank from a glass of water sitting on the table. Vinnie and Anna watched as he tried to sit down, but each time he tried, he jumped up again and paced around the floor.

'Sit down, Miguel. You're making us both nervous,' said Vinnie, wondering what could have possibly happened.

'It's Sayil. He's dying. Worse, he has cholera! Oh, my sweet Lord, what are we going to do?'

'Cholera!' shrieked Anna. 'When did this happen? How did this happen?'

Miguel finally sat down and tried to calm himself. 'You know he goes up to Port-au-Prince every weekend?' Anna nodded. 'You also know that they have a huge cholera problem there? I don't know why he goes or what he does up there, but it's obviously something illegal. Some of the men just told me that they've cordoned off Tavern Street. His men won't let anybody in or out. He won't let any medical staff in to treat him.' Miguel finished the water and continued. 'Besides, we have nothing to treat him with. We don't have any medicines. This is unbearable. It won't be long before it spreads, and we'll have an epidemic on our hands.'

Vinnie looked towards Anna, who had begun to perspire. She sat herself down and put her head in her hands. 'That bastard deserves to die.' Realizing what she had just said, she added, 'Forgive me, Father. It's what I feel. I know it's wrong, but it's the way everybody feels about him.'

'Don't worry about it, my child. At the moment, I am in your camp, God forgive me.'

'Should we be getting everybody out of the town?' asked Vinnie.

Miguel looked at Anna. 'I don't know what the best thing to do is. We could make sure that the area is closed off, but there's no way we can prevent it from spreading if one of his men contracts the disease, and that's a real possibility. Somebody had to carry him into his bed; someone has to feed him. It's a horrendous disease capable of wiping out a whole town of this size in weeks. The people are very scared. I've no doubt everybody knows about it by now. It won't be long before there will be a mass exodus. We will not be able to prevent anybody carrying the disease from leaving the town if they decide to run.'

They sat in silence. At that moment, Vinnie's phone rang. It showed a Skype call from Sean. 'It's Sean. Excuse me, everybody; I need to take this outside.'

'Tell Sean I was asking for him,' said Miguel. Vinnie nodded.

Outside, Vinnie could already see that there were more lights than usual on in the town. He could also see the first signs of people moving their belongings on donkeys and carts. It had started already.

'Sean, thank God you rang.'

'What's wrong, Vinnie?'

'Sean, this is a nightmare. There's a guy here who runs the town by the name of Sayil. He's just contracted cholera. The whole place is in a frenzy. Not only does this guy run the whole town, but he was the one who stopped his people from working for us in reclaiming the river just as we were making some progress. But we also need heavy equipment. Sean, I'm sorry for crying on your shoulder, but we are totally lost here.' Vinnie looked at Sean as he considered what he had told him.

'Do you know a woman called Anna?' asked Sean.

Vinnie knocked his head backwards slightly. 'Yes, I know a woman named Anna. Why?'

'You must get Anna to visit this man Sayil, and tell her to place her hand on his forehead while at the same time saying the Our Father. Do you understand?'

Vinnie looked again at his phone, thinking this was crazy. 'Get her to put her hand on him! Sean, the man has the pox. He has cholera, for God's sake. Anna will get it too if she goes near him!'

'Vinnie, do you trust me?'

Vinnie had his mouth open, and his forehead was creased in wonder. 'Trust you?' He looked at his hand. He had answered the phone with his left hand. He hadn't been able to do that for months. He also noticed that he had forgotten all about his own disease because it seemed to have disappeared. He turned his face towards Sean. 'Yes, yes, of course I trust you, Sean.'

'Then do as I say. When she has done this, tell Miguel to say a mass by the man's bed until he sleeps. Then wait three more days and ring me. I will tell you what you need to do.'

The phone went dead. 'Sean, Sean, can you hear me?' But the communication was gone.

Vinnie stood outside, thinking, *I must be going mad. Holy crap, how am I supposed to get Anna to do this? How did Sean know about Anna?*

He walked back into the kitchen. Anna and Miguel were sipping hot coffee. 'Could I have one of those? If you have any whiskey, I'd appreciate it too,' said Vinnie without smiling.

'What's happening, Vinnie? What did Sean say?' inquired Miguel.

Vinnie caressed the coffee to warm his hands, then took a deep mouthful and swallowed, letting the heat hurt his throat. Then he took a big breath and put his hand on Anna's. 'Anna, do you trust me?'

Anna looked at him quizzically. 'Why, Vinnie, do you ask me that?'

'Because I'm going to ask you to do something I don't think I could do myself.'

'What do you mean?'

Vinnie looked at Miguel. 'This concerns you too, Miguel.' Miguel looked pensive. 'I've been speaking with Sean. He asked me to ask Anna to go into Sayil's house and lay her hands on his forehead and say an Our Father.'

Anna opened her eyes in shock. 'No, no, I will not do this. This is crazy.' She jumped up, but Miguel stood up too and held her by her arms.

'Listen to him, Anna. I know this Sean. He is a wonderful man. He is a priest. He has special gifts.' Vinnie looked up at Miguel. Anna said, 'What do you mean, he has special gifts?'

Miguel said, 'When I lectured in Nottingham University, Sean, as you know, was one of my students. He was capable of keeping the students and the lecturers spellbound by his discourse. The man is a genius. But he also cured people. We were sworn to secrecy.' Miguel looked up to the ceiling. 'Forgive me, Father. If Sean instructs us to do something, then we must do it. We must have faith.'

'But Father Miguel, I have no immunization for cholera. I will get this disease too if I go near him.' Anna started to cry.

'My child, I assure you, if Father Sean told you to go, then you will be safe.'

Vinnie coughed for attention, saying, 'He also wants you to go, Miguel.'

Miguel looked at Vinnie. 'What?'

'I'm afraid so. He wants you to say mass by his bedside until he falls asleep. Then we are to wait three more days, and I'm to ring Sean for further instructions.'

Miguel pondered Vinnie's words. 'Then so be it. I will be with you at every moment, Anna. Does that convince you?'

Anna looked at Miguel, wiping her eyes, then down at Vinnie, who was sitting down looking back at her. He said, 'I will be beside you too, Anna. I'm not going to let the woman I love do this on her own.'

Anna threw herself into Vinnie's arms. 'Oh, Vinnie, I love you too. Promise me you will stay with me at all times.' She kissed his face and head.

'I promise you; I promise you.'

They kissed, forgetting about Father Miguel, who interrupted them to say, 'We should do this right away before we lose our courage. Come.'

Vinnie took Anna by the hand, and they followed Miguel down to Tavern Road.

The five thousand.

Bishop Benny couldn't have been happier if he'd tried. He whistled as he organized his desk. *So much correspondence used to cross my desk; now everything is done by e-mail,* he thought to himself, *and I still haven't a clue how to work it! I must make a note to go and do a computer course before I retire.* God knows, even older parishioners were sending him e-mail, and he didn't know if he was replying to the right people. He chuckled. *What matter? Now my Martha is fit and well. I am a happy man.*

There was a knock on his door. 'Come in,' he responded.

Sean opened the door a little. 'May I interrupt you, Bishop?'

'Anytime, Sean. For you, anytime.'

Sean closed the door. 'You know I'm organizing my Day of Hope for the disadvantaged in our community?'

'Yes, of course. How is it going?'

'It's going very well. I have only one problem. I was wondering – if I could be so bold – if I could hand the reins over to you. I've so many things to do, I hadn't realized it was going to take up so much of my time.'

Benny looked at him, not knowing what to say. 'Can I get you some help from outside?'

'No, it's not that. I have all the help I need on the ground, so to speak. My able-bodied friend Baggie is more than capable of doing all the footwork for me, and he has lots of help as well. I need someone in authority to be the overseer, that's all. I would like this project to become the norm across the whole country in the future, and maybe it'll spread across the world.'

'You sound as if you won't be around, Father Sean. Is everything okay?'

'Everything is fine. I would greatly appreciate it if you could do this for me.'

Sean looked his appealing best as Benny looked into his blue eyes. 'Of course I'll do it for you, Sean. You know that. Will someone show me the ropes?'

'I'll arrange that. Thank you so much, Your Grace. It means a lot to me.'

Sean closed the door behind him. Benny sat down and pondered what had just happened. It was a little over two weeks to the Easter festivities. Maybe the burden of too much work was getting to him, he thought. Then why did it sound as if he wasn't going to be around? Benny decided to ring the archbishop.

'I hope Sean won't be late. I'm getting nervous,' said Molly to Andrew.

'He'll be here,' assured Andrew.

Then the chapel doors opened, and Sean made his way up the aisle. 'I'm sorry I'm late. I had so many things to do.' Sean looked at Molly. 'I know you're nervous, but don't be. This will go like clockwork. Is Dad coming?'

'He said he'd be here with Mum.'

Then the door opened again, and in rushed Bridie and Dan. 'I'm sorry we're late. It was your father, as usual,' Bridie said with disgust and looking back at Dan, who shrugged his shoulders, deciding to say nothing.

'It doesn't matter. I was late myself,' said Sean. 'Okay, let's go through the readings and our rehearsal.'

Sean guided them to where they would be sitting, then asked Andrew and Molly to show him the readings they wanted. He agreed with their choices. After about a half hour or so, they were finished, and Molly breathed easier. 'Thank God that's over. Will you all come for a wee drink?'

'I'm afraid I have too much on my plate. It's a week on Saturday at eleven, right?' confirmed Sean.

'That's correct, Sean,' said Andrew.

'You'll be giving the bride away, Dad?'

'Aye, I will, and you'd better look after her.' He mimicked throwing a fist at Andrew.

'I will, Mr. Robinson. She'll be all mine,' he said as he kissed Molly.

They made their way down the aisle towards the exit. Sean tapped Dan's shoulder. 'Are you okay, Dad? You look worried.'

'I'm fine, son. I'm a little sad at losing Molly, but sure it had to happen sometime, what?'

'Yes, it did.'

Dan turned on his feet and walked towards the door again when Sean said aloud, 'Don't worry, Dad. Everything will turn out right for you; you'll see.'

'What's that, Sean? Sure everything is fine, I tell you,' Dan said as he continued on his way with Sean smiling at him from behind.

They came to a barrier on Tavern Road, about two hundred yards from the tavern itself. Three men with sticks stopped them. Miguel was having none of it. He produced a large crucifix and said something in Creole that made them stand back. Vinnie and Anna climbed over some of the boxes making up the makeshift barricade and followed Miguel as he strode with purpose to the bar. The men were afraid to come any closer.

Miguel gingerly opened the door and asked if anybody was in there. When there was no reply, he walked in. Vinnie took Anna's hand and encouraged her to follow him, all the time reassuring her with a smile.

They could see something at the end of the room. The smell in the room was odious. Anna went over and opened the two small windows to let in some air. Vinnie put his shirt to his mouth, unable to breathe the stench. Miguel brought a lit candle closer to the form lying on the bed. It was Sayil.

He looked desperate. He was sweating profusely, and his face was covered in sores. His breathing was labored; then he broke into a cough, and phlegm and bile came running from his lips. Miguel grabbed a cloth and wiped his mouth. He tried to speak, and Miguel told him to be quiet, that they were here to help him. His eyes were closed and appeared to have scabs on them. Sayil was trying hard to

243

speak, so Miguel bent his ear closer to him. There were some muttered words, and Miguel lifted his face, saying, 'He says he's blind. He hasn't long to live.' Both Miguel and Vinnie looked at Anna. 'Anna, you have done the hard bit; you are here. Let's do what Father Sean said, and then you can go,' said Miguel, pleading with her.

Anna took baby steps towards the bed. Vinnie thought she was going to run. Then she lifted her arm and stretched it out, laying her hand on Sayil's forehead. She started to say the Our Father, and a calm came over her. It was palpable as Vinnie stared at her. She finished the prayer and fell back into Vinnie's arms, exhausted.

'Take her outside for some air, Vinnie,' said Miguel as he set up a crucifix and some holy water and lit two candles. He then started the mass in Creole.

Vinnie used a piece of wood to fan Anna, who sat down with her head bowed. 'Are you okay, my love?' asked Vinnie, concerned.

Anna tried to look up, saying, 'I need to keep my head down for a moment or two. I feel dizzy.'

'You did great in there, Anna. I am so proud of you.'

Anna glanced up at him. 'I hope our faith will make sure we remain well, Vinnie. I have to tell you that I don't remember doing anything. Did I say the prayer?'

'Yes, you did everything perfectly. You put your hand on his forehead, and you recited the Our Father.'

'I don't remember doing it.'

Vinnie encouraged Anna to walk slowly back with him to the house. She needed to lie down and get some rest.

Miguel appeared two hours later. 'How is Anna?'

'She's sleeping. I think we should let her sleep. She's been through a lot. How are you, Miguel?'

Miguel put his stole on the table and undid his cassock. 'My friend, I am, as you Irish say, knackered.' Vinnie smiled. Miguel looked at Anna and said, 'Come, let's leave Anna asleep and talk outside. I'll bring a couple of beers.'

'That would be great.'

They sat outside. There was a chill in the air, but neither men cared. They slugged their beers; then Miguel wiped his lips.

'You know, when you told me what Sean had asked of you, I was skeptical,' said Miguel. 'My faith is obviously not that strong.' He looked up to the skies. 'But while I was saying mass, a feeling came over me that I've never felt before. It made me feel warm inside, sort of serene or trancelike. It was a strange feeling, but I felt protected in some way.'

'I couldn't believe what Sean said, either. Tell me, have you been speaking to him since I arrived here?'

'No, I haven't. Why?'

'He knew about Anna. He related to our problems here like he already knew what they were.'

Miguel thought some more. 'When I said earlier that I'd seen Sean cure people, I wasn't lying. All of us at the seminary witnessed him curing a fellow student who became ill very suddenly. After Sean blessed him and touched him, the student recovered immediately.'

'Are you saying it was a miracle?'

Miguel squished his face. 'I don't know, Vinnie. I'm not a great believer in miracles. I do believe in Jesus's miracles. They have been proven beyond any doubt. You were saying that we have to wait three days and then contact Sean again; is that right?'

'That's what the man told me. How is Sayil?'

'He fell asleep. I think he'll probably sleep for three days. I'll stay up there with him. He needs somebody to look after him. You get your sleep. I'll see you tomorrow. Good night, my friend.' Miguel finished his beer and strolled down the street.

Vinnie sat there for another ten minutes. Then he moved back inside to look after his lovely Anna. As she slept, he watched her. They had said they loved each other. He had never loved before. He had feelings like he never had before. *God, she is gorgeous*, he said to himself. He lay down beside her, and a few minutes later, they were asleep – together.

The next day, Miguel reported that there was no change in their patient. By the middle of the second day, he said that Sayil seemed to be breathing more easily and that the saliva had also stopped running from his mouth. That night, Anna and Vinnie looked in on Miguel. They were no longer afraid. They were shocked to see Sayil sitting up in his bed drinking soup. He was still blind, but he was talking a little. On the third morning, he stood up for the first time, and Miguel stood back aghast when Sayil opened his eyes and announced that he could see. He started to cry and went down on his knees. Miguel said that Sayil was attempting to pray, something he had never done before. Miguel helped him back into his bed and comforted him by praying.

Anna did her nursing duties and changed his bed linen for fresh ones. She also cooked him proper food. By the end of the third day, Sayil was sitting at his table, a very humbled man. He remained quiet as he listened to Miguel praying. Vinnie told Miguel and Anna that it was time to ring Sean. He stood up and went outside.

He Skyped Sean and was answered immediately. 'How is our patient, Vinnie?'

'I think you probably already know that your plan worked. I don't know how it worked, but it worked. He's alive, and the cholera seems to have disappeared.'

'Can he see again?'

'Yes, he can see. What do you want me to do now, Sean?'

Back inside the tavern, Sayil was asking lots of questions. He wanted to know if the gringo was the one responsible for making him better. Miguel said that Vinnie was partially responsible, but that it was Anna who had been the significant one. Sayil went to his knees and started to kiss Anna's hand, telling her that he was sorry. Anna recoiled at first but then took pity on him. He was no longer the demon he once was.

Vinnie reappeared with a worried look. 'What's wrong, my friend?' asked Miguel.

'Is everything okay, Vinnie?' inquired Anna.

Vinnie sat down at the table and looked at all three of them. 'I've been speaking to Sean.' He looked at Miguel. 'You'd better do the translation. He told me to tell Sayil that he is to launch his fishing vessels immediately. He will capture a lot of fish. How, I don't know. Why, I don't know. That's what he said.'

Miguel looked puzzled. 'Did he say tonight?'

'Yes, right away.'

'But Sayil is not fit enough to walk, let alone fish in these waters.'

Sayil spoke, getting Miguel's attention. Miguel explained what was being said. Sayil listened intently. When Miguel finished speaking, Sayil stood up and said something. He then left like a man who had just eaten a good steak.

Vinnie asked, 'Where's he going?'

Miguel stared at the door. 'He's gone fishing!'

Vinnie and Anna made their way back to the house. Anna washed some dishes while Vinnie looked on. 'Anna, there's something I have to do back home in Ireland.'

Anna turned and looked at Vinnie, worried. 'Why do you have to go back? Are you married?'

Vinnie laughed. 'No, nothing like that. I have eyes and body only for you. Sean, my priest friend, told me my mother is sick. She's all alone, and I want to make sure she's cared for. I've spent a lot longer here than I ever thought I would, especially not having accomplished anything. But I promise you I'll be back as soon as I can. Do you trust me?'

Anna smiled. 'After you told me to touch a diseased person and now you ask me if I trust you?'

He smiled. 'I shouldn't be any longer than two, maybe three weeks. Will you be okay?'

'Of course I'll be okay, knowing you are coming back to me.'

They kissed longingly, made love, and fell fast asleep.

Vinnie and Anna were awakened the next morning by shouts and screams coming through their window and curtains. Both of them jumped up in the bed. 'What the hell's all the racket?' said Vinnie.

He jumped out of bed and pulled up his shorts. Anna did the same, and they both looked out to see people running wildly towards the small harbor. Vinnie and Anna looked at each other. 'We'd better see what's up,' said Vinnie as they both walked to a trot, then started to skip, joining the rest of the people.

Miguel spotted them and came running back to meet them. 'Oh, Vinnie, oh, Anna, it's a miracle, a miracle I tell you,' he said, hugging them and crying.

'What happened, Miguel?' asked Vinnie.

'Come, see for yourselves.' Miguel pushed his way through the now-frantic crowds. Reaching the top of the line of people, he pointed to the fish spread out in a row stretching along the sea-front.

'Holy crap, what are they?' asked Vinnie, staring at the biggest fish he had ever seen in his life.

'Tuna, my friend – great big yellow fin tuna.'

'How many of them are there?'

'I believe there are 153,' added Miguel. Then he took Vinnie aside. 'Vinnie, do you know what this means? It means salvation for the whole town. Some of the fishermen have told me that they weigh on average about two-hundred-fifty to three-hundred pounds. That's worth about a million dollars. Do you hear me? A million dollars!'

Vinnie gasped, then shook his head. 'But has this ever happened before?'

'No, Vinnie, never before.'

At that moment, Sayil came forward, took Vinnie's hand, and started to speak uncontrollably and unintelligibly. Miguel put his arms around him, trying to calm him down. They talked intently as Sayil said one thing after another, animated with his arms held wide and looking out to sea. Anna started to cry and went to talk to some of the women, who were all crying. A number of men came and touched Vinnie, rubbing their hands on his tee-shirt. He looked to Miguel to help him.

Miguel shushed Sayil and said, "Vinnie, he has an incredible story. He said that they went out as you asked them. The sea was becalmed. He thought it would be hopeless to try to fish under those conditions. Then a storm brewed, and one of the boats got into difficulties. Then . . .' Miguel broke off.

'What?' asked Vinnie, dying to know.

'He said he saw someone walking on the water, Vinnie. Then a great load of fish appeared from nowhere. They practically threw themselves into their boats. Their nets were cast and were full in minutes. He had never seen anything like it in his life. He and all the fishermen are very afraid. They believe they saw God.'

Vinnie sat down. This was too much to take. 'That can't be. He's obviously hallucinating after his sickness.'

'Then how do you explain the catch of fish and the fact that these tuna are very rare for these waters? They are usually found in the northern Gulf, not here!'

Vinnie looked at the tuna and had to admit he was spooked. 'I don't know.' His phone rang. It was Sean. They did FaceTime this time.

Sean looked happy as he smiled on Vinnie's phone. 'Did everything happen the way I said it would?'

Vinnie looked exasperated but happy. 'Yes, Sean, just as you said. Father Miguel is here; he wants to talk to you.'

Vinnie handed his phone to Miguel, who had been waving frantically to talk to Sean. 'Sean, thank you so much from the bottom of my heart. You did not abandon us. You said you would be there for us, and you were.'

Suddenly a scream went out that scared everybody. It was Sayil. He stared at the phone, pointing and saying the same words over and over. Then he fell to his knees and started crying. Others around him started doing the same thing.

Miguel looked open-mouthed at them, then back at Sean. 'You hear what they are saying?' asked Miguel.

Sean smiled. 'Have faith. Peace be with you always.' Then the phone went dead.

Vinnie looked in astonishment. 'What's happening, Miguel?'

Miguel smiled a great big smile, and with tears in his eyes, he said, 'They say that the man who walked on water – was Sean.'

Dial M.

'Well, speak of the divil himself! If it isn't the great Father Sean Robinson in the flesh, as we live and breathe,' goaded Harry as Sean walked towards the gathering.

'How are you, Sean?' asked Vinnie. 'That was a great service you put on for Molly.'

'Thank you, Vinnie. I'm so glad you could make it. More to the point, how is your health?'

'I'm completely cured, Sean. Of course, you knew that.'

Sean looked at Vinnie, immediately acknowledging with a nod and saying, 'Your Haiti trip was successful?'

'You could say it was more interesting than successful. Thank you for keeping me informed about my mother.'

'How is she?'

'She'll be okay. Her sister, my aunt, is going to move in with her until she's able to look after herself.'

'And how is Anna?' Sean asked, smiling.

'She's a beautiful woman. I'm going back to Haiti on Wednesday. I'm determined to finish that project now that we have the finances to do it. Miguel was able to get a couple of iceboats from Jamaica and had the fish for sale in Miami and Japan by the end of last week. It was incredible.'

Sean turned to Christy and Harry. 'You're all looking well. What have I been missing?' he said as he accepted a glass of wine from Vinnie.

'Vinnie was telling me how you cured his mind and probably his body at the same time. Is that true?' enquired Christy.

Sean smiled. 'Curing the body is probably easier than curing the mind. Let's say we enlightened each other with a happy outcome. Will you be coming to mass tomorrow, Christy?'

'I don't think so, Sean. I haven't been to church in a long time.'

'I'll certainly be there. What time is it at, Sean?' inquired Vinnie.

'Eleven o'clock is the main mass. I think you'll find it enlightening.'

Their attention was shifted to a slight commotion over at one of the tables. Kevin was engaged in a heated conversation with somebody. Sean made his way over. 'What's the problem, Kevin?'

'This eejit here of a manager, a Mr. . . . . What did you say your name was?'

The other man looked hassled and replied, 'Mr. Halpin, owner of this establishment.'

'Mr. Halpin here screwed up. He says that we don't have any wine for the wedding. That the wine I arranged, 'said Kevin, slurring his words and obviously the worse for wear after consuming one too many, 'was ordered weeks ago by my father.'

Sean tapped Kevin on the shoulder 'Let me handle this, Kevin. I'm sorry, Mr. Halpin. Let me introduce myself. I am one of Dan Robinson's sons. My name is Sean.'

'I'm pleased to meet you . . . Sean. Please, call me Matt.'

'Nice to meet you too, Matt. Kevin is correct; our dad did order the wine.' Sean looked over Halpin's shoulder. 'I think if you look in that room over there, you'll find it.'

Halpin turned in the direction that Sean indicated. 'That's the cleaning room. We would never put it in that room. Besides, if what you say is true, you are talking about a lot of wine, probably two dozen cases!'

'I'm aware of that. Would you please check?'

Matt Halpin shook his head, certain that he was correct. He took out a bunch of keys and opened the door. To his amazement, the room was half full with boxes of wine, all marked *Beaujolais 2014*. He counted the boxes. 'One, two, three . . . fifteen . . . twenty . . . twenty-four.'

He turned to find Kevin smirking. 'See? I told you we Robinsons are not stupid,' said Kevin as he hiccupped.

'Don't let it worry you, Matt,' said Sean. 'Perhaps you could make sure that everybody is served.'

Matt Halpin scratched his head. 'Yes, yes, I certainly will. This is . . . not right. I'll have to see my managers. That wine should never have been stored in there.' Matt went out, tut-tutting to himself.

Kevin turned to Sean. 'How did you know that the wine was in that room, Sean?'

'No matter. Let's get back to the celebration,' he said as he led Kevin back to the bar, reminding him to be careful with his drinking. 'This is my older brother, Kevin, everybody,' said Sean as he introduced him to Vinnie and Christy, noting that Harry had already positioned himself with two girls at a nearby table.

Peter reread his sermon for tomorrow's mass. He wasn't entirely happy with it. He still hadn't settled with his new congregation in Tuam. The locals had been used to the former 'old man's' pitch. The congregation were going to have to be slowly converted to the new 'young man's' way of thinking. It was so different from the congregation in Galway city, especially since Sean had arrived on the scene. The Galway church was always full to the rim every Sunday, and even the early 7:30 mass was nearly always half full. *No matter,* he thought. *Give it time, Peter; just give it time.*

'There's somebody at the door, Peter. Will you answer it? I'm making the dinner,' shouted Shirley from the kitchen.

Peter came out of his deep thoughts. 'Okay, no worries. I'll get it.'

He opened the door to reveal Sean standing there. 'Sean, what a pleasure. Come in, come in.'

Sean stepped forward. 'I was passing by. I know it's been remiss of me not to have shown my face before now.'

'Not at all. You know you are welcome anytime. And besides, you have been a lot busier than I. Tell me, how was Molly's wedding?'

'Fabulous. Everything went like clockwork. In fact, it's still going on at the Shangri-La. I had to make my exit because I've yet to prepare my sermon for tomorrow.' Sean looked down at the table. 'I see you are doing the same.'

'Yes, nearing an end to it. My congregation is a very old one, I'm afraid, not like yours.'

'Give it time, Peter. You'll see.'

'Can I get you something – a coffee, something stronger, perhaps?'

'Nothing for me. I just called over to see you and Shirley.' Sean turned towards the sideboard. Picking up a phone and cradle, he said, 'What's this?'

Peter smiled. 'That, my friend, is one of those old-style phones, the sort that was used before everything went digital and, God save us from all harm, the mobile generation. My mother – Lord, rest her – used to be the artistic director at a theatre in Leeds when we lived there before we came to Ireland. I remember her telling me about a production called . . .' Peter put his fingers to his lips, thinking. 'Yes, that's it, *Dial M for Murder*. It was a successful movie at that time by Alfred Hitchcock. The play ran for nearly a year. She kept that phone as a memento and gave it to me before she died, telling me to always think of her.' Peter lowered his head. 'I know she's in heaven now.'

Sean smiled, saying, 'I know she is.'

'Sean, what are you doing here?' asked Shirley, coming in from the kitchen. 'Peter, you never said Sean had arrived.'

They chatted some more, and Sean bid his goodbyes and best wishes to Shirley. On his way out, he turned to Peter. 'I don't know when I'll get the chance to see you again, but whenever you are up in Galway, will you look in on Benny, make sure he's okay? I asked him to do something for me, and I just want to be sure that he finishes it.'

Peter looked at Sean, confused, and said, 'Absolutely. You know that I would. I'd do anything for you, Sean – you know that.'

Sean smiled and bid his farewell. Peter watched as Sean drove off, all the time wondering why he felt that Sean was saying goodbye for the last time.

Easter Week.

The people filed into the pews. Father Rice climbed into the back row and slid behind a rather tall man in the hope that he would not be seen. The archbishop had told him of his concerns, having received a phone call from Bishop Benny. He didn't know what to make of the bishop's concerns other than to suggest that he attend today's mass and listen to what Sean had to say.

There was certainly a huge crowd, more than at the Catholic church, by his reckoning. Father Rice could see Bridie and her husband in the front row alongside Linda, Sean's fiancée. It was good that Sean was getting married and settling down. The organ played the entrance hymn. Everybody stood as the procession was led by the little altar girl carrying the crucifix, and everybody blessed themselves as she passed them.

Sean brought up the rear of the small procession. He reached the top of the altar, bowed, and turned to the congregation, and said, 'Blessed be God – Father, Son, and Holy Spirit.'

The people responded, 'And blessed be his kingdom, now and forever. Amen.'

The lessons and the psalm were read, and then Sean walked to the pulpit to read the Gospel. It was from St. John's account of the Last Supper. Father Rice thought that it was odd because that would normally be kept for Good Friday, which was only days away. Everybody sat waiting for the sermon. Sean adjusted his papers and looked out at his audience. He appeared to look at everyone individually. Father Rice felt it too.

This could be my last sermon! This could be your last day on earth! Imagine if God appeared before you all now and told you that this was to be your last day in this life. Would you be afraid? Would you be excited? The Gospel tells us that on the last day, there will be a huge torment in the skies as the heavens are opened to reveal the Son of man in all of his glory. Jesus has told us to stand erect and look up to the heavens and not be afraid. Which one would you be? Would you be the one who stands erect or the one who cowers? This is the true test of faith.

But we should not be awaiting the last day with fear. Instead, we should be awaiting it with joy. That's a hard thing to do. I don't deny that. But if your faith is truly strong, then you will have no fear. You must ask yourselves if you are living the commandments that God gave to you. Do you love God with your whole heart, with your whole soul, and with all of your mind? As importantly, do you love your neighbor as yourself? Leaving the first commandment as a given, let's examine the second one. It's not always easy to love your neighbor when that person holds a weapon to you. The weapon could be a sword, or it could be a word. What do we do? The answer is in the Gospel.

Show me where Jesus used force against his neighbors or his enemies. He had many enemies. The Pharisees and the Romans attempted to kill him on many occasions, yet they were afraid because the people loved him, and they were afraid of the people. When they did get close to capturing him, he simply slipped away. Throughout the Gospel, you will find that whenever Jesus was faced with adversity or anger, he slipped away; he made off in a boat or went into the desert. Jesus never involved himself in any violence, even though he stirred up so much resentment amongst the authorities.

We should learn to do the same in the face of adversity. We can show our love by walking away. Remember this: your faith has saved you and given you credence; your spirituality has guided you. At the Last Supper, Jesus said to his disciples that they should eat his flesh and drink his blood in remembrance of him. When Jesus was taken away from them and crucified, all of his disciples abandoned him and disavowed all knowledge of him, as they were afraid.

I am wondering if that were the case today, if Jesus were to walk amongst you, would you also abandon your faith because of some outside fear? Would your faith be strong enough to withstand ridicule and condemnation from other sources? Does your belief extend to defending and promoting your steadfastness? We are all tested at some stage in our lives. We never know when or where that test will take place. But we should always be prepared for that eventuality, for as the Lord has told us, 'You never know the moment nor the hour.'

Sean looked down at the audience, and he saw that they had listened well.

'I have some announcements. As some of you may know, we have been working hard to arrange our Day of Hope this coming July. On that day, we will be helping the poorest in our community to get their children enrolled in our schools. I have some great helpers . . .' — Sean looked down at Baggie and his friends in the third row, who smiled back at him — 'who have been working tirelessly to enlist the help of doctors, nurses, opticians, and hair stylists with great success. Now we need many volunteers to help us on that great day to cater for their breakfasts and dinners and to lead them around the buildings. We estimate that we will have over three hundred children on that day. Any of your services would be greatly appreciated. Finally, next Wednesday is the last day for our children's Bible study class before the summer break. All children are asked to attend at five p.m. for one hour. Please stand for the Nicene Creed.'

As mass ended, Sean greeted his congregation as usual outside the front doors. Linda, Bridie, and Dan stood to one side awaiting the final people to leave after shaking Sean's hand. Father Rice came up last and shook Sean's hand. 'A fine sermon, Sean. It reminded me of the sermon you gave when you were twelve.' They both smiled.

'We have come a long way since then,' said Sean.

'I hope to see you on Easter Sunday. I can be here to help you out if you'd like,' said Father Rice.

'That would be kind of you. I never refuse help.'

They confirmed their phone numbers and said that they'd see each other later in the week. Father Rice left, not feeling secure in the knowledge that that would be the case.

Sean turned to Bridie. 'How are Molly and Andrew? Did everything finish off okay last night?'

'Oh, Sean, it was wonderful. You were wonderful too. They've gone off to Tenerife on their honeymoon, happy as little piggy's,' said Bridie, smiling.

Dan looked uninterested and distant. 'Are you okay, Dad?' inquired Sean.

'Sure, son, I'm grand. Do you fancy a pint?'

Sean took Linda's hand. 'If you don't mind, I'd like to take Linda away for a few hours since there's not much time to be alone these days, especially with the week I have ahead.'

'No problem, son. I'll take your mother off to the Skeff for their buffet lunch. It's always good.'

They bid their goodbyes, and Sean told Linda to get the car while he locked up the church.

As they drove, Linda remarked, 'That was a heavy sermon today, Sean. What did you mean by it being your last one?'

Sean kept his eyes on the road, looking straight ahead. 'I didn't mean that it would be. I said it might be – that everybody should be prepared.'

Linda hummed, 'Well, I want to hear many more of my future husband's sermons, and that's an order,' she said, smiling.

Sean contemplated saying something else but decided the time wasn't right.

The good wine.

Dan sat at the table in the kitchen, looking through the bills. *God, was it only four days ago they had the wedding, and already the bills are in front of me?* he thought to himself as he downed some tea. He had lost all of his appetite of late, even refusing dessert the previous Sunday, much to Bridie's surprise. He thumbed through the invoices for the wedding dress, the suit rentals, the limousine, and of course the biggie of big ones, the Shangri-La! 'Fifty-five grand. Oh, sweet Jesus, how am I going to pay that?' he said aloud to no one in particular.

'Is it talking to yourself you are, now? That's always a bad sign,' said Matt Halpin, standing in the doorway.

'What are you doing here? Don't tell me you're wanting to be paid already,' said a startled Dan.

'Not a bit of it, Dan Robinson, and well you know it.'

Dan looked at him. He didn't really know Matt Halpin. Obviously he knew of him. Sure, wasn't he the owner of the Shangri-La, which was known the length and breadth of Ireland? Dan looked warily at him, wondering why he had a big smile across his face. Dan was in no mood for happy faces and said, 'What the divil are you doing around these parts? Ballinasloe is a bit outside your territory.'

Matt sat down and put a bottle of the Beaujolais wine on the table in front of them. He playfully wagged his finger in Dan's direction, saying, 'As if you didn't know, Dan Robinson. Sure aren't you the brains that runs this whole town?'

'I wouldn't say that, but I'm curious, and I'm listening.'

'I don't know what little game you're playing, but I admire your bravado.'

'I have no idea what you're talking about, Mr. Halpin. I really don't.'

'Please, call me Matt. All of my friends do, and it would be my honor to have you as a friend.'

'Matt it is, then. Now, will you play your cards?' Dan asked, getting a bit annoyed but at the same time not wanting to be rude.

Matt shuffled in his chair. Leaning both arms on the table, he said, 'You see, I was flummoxed when your lad, Sean, told me that the wine you had ordered was to be located in the cleaner's room. We'd never put wine into that room. My manager confirmed it for me. Never knew a thing about it, he said. So I poured the wine out as instructed, and pretty soon my waiting staff were coming back to me telling me how everybody was enthralled with the wine. They wanted more and more.'

'Aye, it's a good Beaujolais, to be sure,' interrupted Dan.

'Good Beaujolais! I knew immediately it wasn't anything like a Beaujolais. This wine, my friend . . .' – he pointed to the bottle on the table – 'is none other than a Rothschild. Being a sommelier myself, I take great pride in knowing my wines, which is part of the reason for our success. I couldn't for the life of me figure out what a Rothschild was doing in a Beaujolais bottle. Then on examining the bottle, I found out your little secret.'

Matt looked to see Dan's reaction. Dan looked him back in the eye, not having a bull's notion what the man was going on about. He decided to stay dumb, as they say. 'Go on,' said Dan.

'Ah, a true card player if ever I saw one. Never giving a tell away.' Matt took the bottle in his hand, and looking at Dan at the same time, he flicked the corner of the Beaujolais label. A small bit came unstuck. Then he put his forefinger and thumb to the corner and pulled it off like a magician pulls a rabbit from a hat. 'Ta-da!' he sang.

Dan looked at Matt Halpin, then back at the bottle. He still had no idea what was going on but decided to play a card. 'Well, you got me. I didn't think you'd notice.'

'Notice?! Not notice a Lafite-Rothschild when I see and taste one? My friend, asking a sommelier to distinguish between a Beaujolais and a Lafite-Rothschild is like asking a duck how to swim in water,' he said, emphasizing his knowledge and the name of the wine sitting in front of them.

Dan still hadn't a bog's notion what was going on. He led another card. 'Is there any crime in pretending it's something other than what it is?'

'Not a crime, Dan – no, sir. I admire your little game. You didn't want your daughter or anybody else thinking that you were showing off buying expensive wines, so to hide any embarrassment, you deftly placed Beaujolais labels over the Rothschild ones. How debonair of you, Dan. You have my highest respect.'

Dan took the bottle in his hands and read the label. He'd never heard of it. He looked again at his admiring fan and said, 'How many of these are left, and how much are they selling for nowadays?'

'That's exactly why I'm here today, Dan. You see, a Lafite-Rothschild would normally retail for around fifteen hundred euros a bottle. Now, we still have nineteen cases in storage for you. By the way, I moved them to our temperature-controlled room. I'm still a little puzzled that there was so much remaining, as I'm sure your guests drank a lot more than that. No matter, as I say, we have nineteen cases at twelve bottles per case, which would give us two hundred twenty-eight bottles. That, at fifteen hundred a bottle, would give, by my calculations, a total value of three hundred forty-two thousand euros.' Matt stopped talking to see what Dan had to say.

Dan's poker face had disappeared. He had lost Matt's diatribe as soon as he had told him that each bottle had a face value of €1,500. He had lost contact with civilization after that. 'What . . . what's the number again?' he spluttered out, trying to regain his composure.

'Three hundred forty-two thousand euros,' said Matt, reconfirming the numbers. Dan remained speechless. 'So, Dan, what would you like me to do with them?'

Dan tried to get his thoughts together but couldn't.

'I knew it. I knew it, Dan Robinson, you old scoundrel. Okay, here's what I propose. Are you ready to hear me out?'

'Go on,' said Dan, hoping that somebody somewhere would smack him over the face and bring him back from noddy land!

Matt continued. 'Bearing in mind that your customer base . . .' – he coughed – 'with all due respect, would not appreciate the finer qualities of same said wine, I am suggesting that I take them off your hands at obviously a much-reduced price. Now hear me out, Dan, before you say anything.' Matt held his hand up to Dan's face. Dan continued staring in disbelief, trying desperately not to show his reactions. 'What I'm suggesting is that I take this fabulous wine off your hands for, say, two hundred fifty thousand, being the current retail price less normal markup, costs of spillage, and whatnot. So, rounded up to two hundred fifty thousand is a fair price, bearing in mind that I'll have it in storage for many years.'

Dan was beginning to come around. There was nothing better than a discussion on money to revive Dan Robinson. He stood up and faced the window looking out onto the yard. He breathed in deeply; then he said, 'I'll tell you what I'll do. You can keep the Rothschild as you outlined if you clean the slate on my daughter's wedding invoice.'

There was a silence as Matt considered it for a few seconds. 'No way, Dan. That means I would make nothing on the wine.'

'But you'd have it appreciate over the years, and you know that. If this wine is as good as you say it is then its value will only increase over time,' said Dan, now wanting to complete the deal.

Matt crinkled his forehead. 'True, true enough. But it's still not a good bargain for me.'

Dan figured he had pushed too far. Now he hoped Matt Halpin wasn't going to withdraw his original offer.

'I'll tell you of another suggestion I have,' said Matt.

'Go on,' said Dan tentatively.

'I've always admired you, Dan, for what you've built here in your business. Like me, you are a man of vision. Despite the recession, you have survived, and thrived by all accounts. You have something I don't have – and that's character. You see, I've had a notion for a long while that I'd like a quaint little operation like yours so that I could then send my overflow by coach down to a place like this, and even have spare top-class accommodation available for them, especially for my American guests.'

Dan interrupted, 'Well now, you see, I don't have any accommodation here!'

'I know that, Dan. That's why I have a second proposition for you. What say you and I enter into a partnership? That is, you and I will rip your building apart and create a masterpiece, just like this wine here.' Matt touched the bottle as if it were a newborn child.'

'Go on,' said Dan.

'I would love to get into bed with you, Dan – metaphorically speaking, naturally – and create an enterprise worthy of the Shangri-La name right here in Ballinasloe. I'm suggesting that I make an investment of one million euros and create a new property. In return, I would take a fifty-percent shareholding in the new venture at no cost to yourself.'

Dan nearly hit the ceiling. He remained calm while inside he was fit to explode. He carried the moments carefully. Finally, he said, 'I like your idea, but for this to work, I have an alternative suggestion.'

'Go on,' said Matt, now no longer in the driving seat.

Dan continued, 'This pub has always been in the Robinson name, and I don't want to change that tradition. How about you invest the one million, and we split it sixty percent to forty percent in my favor?'

Dan waited for his words to sink in. Matt carefully doodled with his pen and paper. 'Done!' he said loudly and held out his hand to complete the deal.

Dan was just about to agree when he said, 'And you'll wipe my daughter's slate clean?'

'You old divil. I need you in my corner, make no mistake about that, Dan Robinson. It's a done deal.' With that, the two men shook each other's hands strongly, all the time smiling. 'What say you and I flick the seal on this here bottle to celebrate?'

'Might as well be hung for a sheep as a lamb – flick it,' said Dan.

Sean watched Bridie as she prepared dinner. 'You know, Mum, that I love you?' he said as Bridie turned around, smiling.

'Of course I do, Sean. What brought that on? she said returning to the dishes in the sink.'

'We never seem to say it enough, that's all. It's something we should all say every now and then, don't you think?'

'Absolutely, Sean.' She turned to him as her hands were still in the sink. 'And I'll always love you too.'

The hall door banged loudly, and an exuberant Dan skipped into the kitchen. 'Boy oh boy, have I got news for you. You're not going to believe what I have to tell you,' Dan blurted out. Bridie had to stall him so she could follow what he was saying.

Dan told them all about Matt Halpin, about the wine, and then about his proposal to invest a million euros in the pub. 'What do you think of that? Yee-haw!' he shouted. 'We have to celebrate. Sean, grab some beers, whiskey, champagne, anything. God, I think I'm going to have a heart attack.'

'You will if you don't sit down, Dan Robinson, said Bridie. 'Are you serious, or are you having me on?'

'I couldn't make it up, now, could I? Of course I'm serious. I've never been more serious in my entire life. It's a miracle, I tell you. Now, where's that bottle opener?' Dan went into the living room.

Bridie turned to Sean. 'I've a feeling you had something to do with this. Am I right?'

Sean looked at her, and a small smile creased his lips. 'Don't make me lie, Mother. I've got to go. Congratulations, Dad. I have to go,' he shouted into the living room. He kissed Bridie and made his exit. Bridie looked on in wonderment and started to cry.

Dan came back into the kitchen. 'Aw, don't be crying, girl; it's time for laughter. After all of these years, we're finally back on top, finally out of the quagmire.'

It didn't stop Bridie from crying, but she was more than happy to see her Dan come back into the real world.

The Cock Crows.

There were fifteen children sitting in two rows at the front of the church for Bible class. Sean asked softly, 'Children, what would you say to Holy God if he came into this church right now?'

Little Nora shot up her hand. 'But Holy God is here right now. He's always here.'

Sean smiled. 'You are right, of course, Nora. He is here all the time. But say He appeared standing here like me. What would you say to Him?'

The children looked at one another, not knowing what to say. Mary Baxter shot up her hand. 'Father, I'd be afraid. I'd probably cry.' The other children giggled, and one or two agreed with Mary, saying they would be afraid too.

'It's all right to be afraid, but just for a little while, until you got used to Him. Say He wasn't scary looking and you liked Him immediately. Do you think you'd have anything to say to Him then?'

The children fumbled in their seats. It was nearly six o'clock, and they knew their mums would be there soon to take them all home. Then at the end of the row, little Marcia O'Donnell pushed her arm up and said, 'I'd ask Him to forgive me.'

Sean swallowed deeply. 'Oh, Marcia, that's the perfect answer. That's the most wonderful thing you could say to Holy God.' A tear welled in Sean's eye when he considered their innocence.

Then the mood was broken as the mothers made their way up the aisle. Sean told them all to have a great summer and to be good as he waved them off. Only Mary and Alice Doyle were left. Sean wondered where Mrs. Doyle was. It wasn't like her to be late. 'Hang on there a few minutes, girls, while I lock up the vestry.'

'Okay, Father,' they said in unison, reading their picture books.

Sean strode into the vestry, then heard a knock on the door. He thought that was strange but figured that Mrs. Doyle must have parked her car up the side of the church. He opened the door, and a voice said, 'Hello, Faddah.'

Sean stepped back and said, 'What are you doing here, Fonsie?'

Then another body came into vision from behind Fonsie. 'You'd better step back inside, Father,' said Dino as he waved his gun at Sean's body, pushing Fonsie ahead of him.

Sean was speechless and stepped back slowly into the vestry. 'I don't know what's going on here, but there's no money here.'

'It's not money we're after, Father. It's you,' said Dino. He pointed to a chair and indicated for Sean to sit. 'Go and check that nobody's in the church,' Dino instructed Fonsie.

'Why aren't you two in prison?' asked Sean.

'Because we escaped, that's why. And I'll be having no more questions from you.'

'But I have nothing to do with you.'

'I'm afraid you do, Father. You see, one of the screws told me that you and Fonsie had a great little chat, and big mouth Fonsie told you everything about a certain murder.'

'But a confession is sacred. Anything said during confession cannot be told to anyone.'

'I don't believe that. You're a witness and a damned good one, as far as I'm concerned.'

Fonsie came back holding Mary and Alice by the hands. 'These kids were outside. I locked the door. There's nobody else.'

'Leave the children. Take me. I'm the one you want. They can do you no harm,' said Sean anxiously, making his way over to take their hands from Fonsie.

'I'm afraid they could be very useful to us as hostages in case things go bad for us. Put them in the car, Fonsie. You move too, priest, and no funny stuff or I'll shoot one of the kids before I shoot you.'

Sean started to sweat. He was pushed in the back by Dino and sat between the children in the backseat. Fonsie drove with Dino in the passenger seat, pointing his gun at the children. The children looked terrified as Sean tried to cuddle them and assure them that they were going to be all right.

'Where are you taking us?'

'That's for you to find out. Relax. We'll be driving a good bit.' They sped off northwards.

Mrs. Doyle couldn't understand why the church was locked. She ran around the back and up to the bishop's house. She knocked frantically on the main door. Mrs. Harte opened the door. 'Goodness, whatever's the matter, Mrs. Doyle?'

'My children are missing. They should be at the Bible school. I went there now, and the church is locked,' she said, stepping inside.

Martha came out. 'What's all the commotion, Mrs. Harte? Oh, hello, Mrs. Doyle. Is something wrong?'

As soon as Martha heard what was going on, she rang the Gardaí. Two hours later, a frantic search took place around Eyre Square. Bishop Benny spoke to two guards, who asked him for details about Father Robinson.

'Sean wouldn't do anything untoward against anybody, let alone children,' he said anxiously, looking across at Martha. 'This is awful, but I'm positive there's a perfectly reasonable explanation. I'm sure that any minute now, Father Sean will come through that door and explain everything to everybody's satisfaction.'

They seemed to have been driving for a long time. Finally, Fonsie turned left up a dark, winding lane. Sean looked out the window to his left and saw a lake. He still held the two girls close to his body. The girls were very quiet. He knew they must be nearly terrified and confused.

'There's the cabin. Park around the back of it,' said Dino as Fonsie parked under a tree.

It was dark, coming up to eight o'clock. Dino opened the side door of the cabin and found a torch. He motioned for them to follow him. Soon he had found candles and placed them around the cabin, on the table and a bench. The cabin was small, only one room with a single bunk-type bed and a sink.

'Sit on that bed with those kids,' he said, barking at Sean.

Little Alice started to cry. 'There, there, now,' said Sean, kneeling down in front of her. 'No need to cry. Father Sean is here with you. I'll look after the both of you. Don't be worrying.'

Alice hugged her sister and put her thumb in her mouth. Fonsie moved up close to Dino. 'What are we going to do with these kids? This wasn't part of the plan.'

Dino looked angrily at Fonsie. 'This wouldn't have happened if you had kept your bloody mouth shut, you dickhead.' He looked over at Sean and the children. 'They'll be very useful to us. Think about it. Nobody knows we're here. They'll all know that those kids have been kidnapped, and the only suspect is that priest. Harry will know what to do. I'm going to send him a text as agreed. See what you can cook up while I'm texting him, and keep an eye on this lot.'

Fonsie opened the cupboard and saw a box of cereal and some bread. There was a cooler with milk, a tray of eggs, butter, and some marmalade. On the floor was a Primus stove attached to a small gas bottle. 'It looks like Harry was here earlier,' Fonsie said to Dino, pointing to the contents of the box.

Sean laid the children on the bed and covered them with the two blankets. He whispered to them to try to sleep as he hummed a tune to them. Alice was the first to sleep while Mary stayed motionless with her eyes wide open, staring at Sean. Sean smiled reassuringly at her, all the time holding her hand.

'Good morning, and here is the seven o'clock news from RTE. Reports are reaching us this morning of a child abduction case in Galway city. We now go over to our chief crime correspondent, Brian Jennings, in Galway. Brian?'

'Good morning, Anne. Late yesterday evening, two girls – Alice and Mary Doyle, aged five and seven years respectively – went missing from the local Anglican church here at St. Nicholas's in the heart of Galway city. It's not known who abducted them, but the last person to see them was a Father Sean Robinson, who has also gone missing. Gardaí have released an all-points alert throughout the country to try and locate the missing children. It's not known at this stage if anybody else was involved in this possible abduction. I interviewed the mother of the two children, a Mrs. Nellie Doyle.'

The broadcast cut to tape. 'My children are missing,' said a frantic Mrs. Doyle. 'If anybody knows where they are, please, please tell the Gardaí.' She broke down crying and was aided by her husband, who was holding her by her arms. 'I don't want to lose my little girls. God, please help us.'

At that, she broke away from the microphones as someone in the background shouted, 'Hang the bastard!'

'As you can see,' continued the reporter, 'an obviously distressed Mrs. Doyle, mother of the two little girls. As you could hear, she was surrounded by angry bystanders. Back to you in the studio.'

The announcer continued. 'In other news, five men escaped from Athlone Prison yesterday afternoon, three of whom have since been caught. The two men on the loose are Daniel Dempsey, five feet eleven with blonde hair, aged 32 and wearing prison overalls. He may be armed and dangerous. The second man is Alphonsus Murphy, five feet five inches tall with brown hair and a partial beard. Both men should be approached with extreme caution. In other news . . .'

Frank Brady turned off the television. He'd heard enough. He was senior detective for the Galway province, having been promoted after the Troubles had ceased and all of the IRA had been put behind bars, many of them due to his hard work and diligence. He didn't miss any of it. He liked the quiet rural city life. Nothing too untoward ever happened, and he had grown accustomed to his new way of life. He thought back to the many times he had put his life on the line, and for what? No more, he swore to himself. No more was Frank Brady putting his life on the line for nobody.

So a bit of excitement at last in Galway. No doubt there was a simple solution to all of this; this was no abduction. He'd never heard of a priest abducting anybody; other stuff, yes, but not abduction. It didn't add up.

Frank made his way into the city, and as he arrived at his office, he was met by his boss, Governor Rhode. 'Morning, Gov. What gets you out of bed before midday?'

'Leave it, Frank. There's a whole brouhaha going on over this priest abduction thing. I want you on it. Take all the men you need.'

Frank raised his eyebrows. 'Is Rome complaining?'

'Those donkey's in Dublin love it when something goes on outside their jurisdiction. They like to throw their muscle about. This is not a special branch case, Frank. Do you hear me?'

'I hear you loud and clear, Gov. I'll get on to it.'

Governor Rhode stormed out, obviously hassled, then turned back to Frank, saying, 'You've got only forty-eight hours, Frank. Then the Romans move in.' Frank always smiled at the way all of the rural police stations referred to Dublin as "Rome."

'I hear you. Pluto, get in here!' he shouted to nobody in particular.

Seconds later, Pluto appeared in his doorway. 'You screamed for me, boss?'

'Get everybody down to the planning room. I mean everybody. We have an emergency.'

'Sure thing, boss.'

Ten minutes later, Frank walked into the planning room and saw that Pluto had done his job. 'Okay, people, we have an abduction situation. Anybody ever had one of these before?' He looked around the room. No hands were raised. 'Great, then you'll have to do exactly as I say, seeing I'm the one who has the experience and because I'm your boss.'

Some of the older guys smiled, leaving the raw recruits wondering whether they should smile or not.

'Pluto, you do the computer trawling. Take two men down to this priest's house and take all of his records, drawings, laptops, and every other top or otherwise. You' – he pointed to the only female policewoman present – 'take two people with you and start the interviewing process. I want the bishop re-interviewed, followed by any member of the church – parishioners and the like. Find out what they thought of this Father Robinson, anything at all, anecdotal or otherwise. The rest of you start ringing around the prisons, hospitals, schools. Let's find out where this priest hung out. Go now!' he shouted. 'Get me results today!' he blared as they left the room.

Pluto looked as the room emptied, saying, 'What about this Father Wilson? And there's also a Father Rice known to have frequented the church – not to mention the Archbishop of Armagh.'

Frank looked at Pluto sarcastically. 'Somehow I don't think the Archbishop is involved, do you?'

'No, chief,' said Pluto as he went about his work.

'I'll deal with the Wilson chap and the Robinson family,' Frank shouted to Pluto.

The news coverage was every hour on the hour. It didn't matter whether you turned on the television, the radio, or social media; it was all about the abduction. Social media went mad saying that the church was always harboring these sex criminals. They had their verdict without a trial. The press was more cautious, waiting on the facts to emerge but still keeping their readers interested with suppositions. That's the way the world worked nowadays, thought Peter as he told Shirley he was just going into town to get some groceries and her medicine.

'Are you sure it's okay, Peter, after all the stuff that's going on?'

'I don't see how it affects us. This is all blown out of proportion. We know Sean. He'd never be involved in anything like this.'

'I know, Peter, but it's been more than twenty-four hours now and still not a sign of those poor wee children.'

Peter left Shirley without responding. Instead, he shook his shoulders and made his way down the road in his car. He arrived at the supermarket and saw what he wanted. As he took a tin of peas down from the top shelf, a young girl who was packing the shelves said out loud, 'You're with that pedophile priest.'

Peter turned to her and said, 'I don't know what you're talking about, you silly girl. Get back to your work.'

Instead, she repeated the accusation, this time more loudly so that other people nearby heard her and saw her pointing at Peter. 'He's with that pedophile priest. I saw him.'

Peter hurried himself towards the cashier. He turned and noticed the girl following him, together with one or two other shoppers. He decided to abandon his purchases and leave the store.

He walked quickly across the street, and entering the pharmacy, he noticed how quickly everybody stopped talking as soon as he entered the shop. He made his way to the counter and asked for a prescription for a Mrs. Shirley Wil... He stopped himself and looked around. Everybody was looking at him.

Finally, somebody broke the silence. 'You are that priest, a friend of that bad one, aren't you?'

Peter responded, 'No, you are mistaken. I don't know the chap.'

'Yes, I've seen you before. You said mass with him down at the Anglican church. You are the same person.'

Peter turned on his heels and made his way across the street to his car. He desperately fumbled with his keys and finally got the engine going as the crowds gathered around his car. He shot off as quickly as he could, all the time looking into his rearview mirror. He finally got to the safety of his house. He turned off the engine and took a deep breath.

Peter made his way inside the kitchen through the back door. Shirley looked at him. 'Peter, are you okay? You look flushed.'

'I'm fine. Just a near accident in the car, that's all.'

'There's a detective in the sitting room waiting for you. He's been waiting about a half hour.'

'A detective? What does he want with me?'

'I expect it's to do with Sean.'

Peter opened the door to the sitting room. Frank stood up to greet him, saying, 'Father Wilson. I'm sorry I didn't give you any notice, but, as you can imagine, things are all urgent these days. I'm afraid we don't have any time for protocol.'

'Not at all, detective. Please have a seat,' said Peter as he directed Frank to the table.

'So I believe you and Father Robinson were bosom buddies?'

Peter looked at the detective, and after ten seconds or so, he said, 'No. I didn't really know the chap very well at all. I'm afraid you're mistaken.'

Frank looked at the priest and knew immediately he was lying. His experience told him to let his words settle before continuing. Then the silence was broken by the shrill of a phone ringing on the sideboard. Both men looked over at the old-style phone as it rung once . . . then twice . . . then a third time. Then it stopped.

'Aren't you going to answer that?' asked Frank, looking in the direction of the phone.

Peter stood up, motionless. He gazed intently at the phone. He strode over and picked up the cradle and the receiver. There were no cables, no wires. He placed the phone back in its spot, fell to his knees, buried his face in his hands, and cried profusely.

Frank stood up and helped Peter to his feet. He nudged him towards the table and sat him down. He offered him his glass of water. It took over five minutes before either man spoke.

'Are you all right, Father?' asked Frank, feeling sorry for the priest.

Peter blew his nose in the tissues and wiped his eyes. He stared at the floor, then at the phone and back at the floor. It took another minute before he finally said, 'I do know Father Robinson. I've known him all of my adult life. I know everything about him.'

'Then why did you lie, Father?' asked Frank.

Peter looked up to the ceiling. Finally, he looked Frank in the face. 'Because I've been subjected to harassment ever since this abduction thing was announced. Locals are accusing me of complicity in the abduction. Apart from that, I'm ashamed of myself. Sean is a wonderful man. He wouldn't harm anybody, detective. I'd give my life for him,' he said, trailing off to look once again at the phone.

'I know you might have sympathies for your friend, Father, but my job is based on facts and evidence. Can you tell me when you last saw him?'

'Why, only last Saturday. He called around to see Shirley and me.'

'How did he appear to you?'

'He looked fine. We talked about our sermons for Sunday mass, and . . .' Peter broke off and turned his head towards the phone again.

'What, Father? What else happened?'

Peter returned his gaze to the detective. 'Nothing, really. We just chatted generally.'

Frank could tell that there was something bothering the priest. There was no point in pushing him at this stage. He would wait until another time. He'd wait and see what developed in the case. 'Okay, Father, that about wraps it up. If you think of anything further, you'll let me know?'

'Yes, yes, of course, detective. And please feel free to drop around anytime.'

'Oh, I will.'

With that, Frank made his exit, leaving Peter still gazing at the phone.

Thirty Pieces Of Silver.

'What have you got?' asked Frank of Pluto when he settled himself in his office.

'Quite a bit, chief. It seems this Father Robinson made a number of visits to the prison in Athlone. Met a guy by the name of Alphonsus Murphy, aka Fonsie – a dirty piece of work, known as a pickpocket and general no-gooder in Ballinasloe. He's also on the wanted list as one of the recent escapees.'

Frank raised his right eyebrow. 'Hmmm, that's interesting. A bit coincidental that he was on the visitors list around the same time as the escape and abduction, don't you think?'

'I do, boss. There's more. This guy Fonsie and another reprobate named Dino for short were involved in a murder a few years back – the killing of a Mr. Seamus Cronin, former bank manager of a local bank in the town. They are both on the run.' Frank rubbed his chin. 'There's more,' added Pluto. 'Apparently, our priest said that last Sunday was his last sermon. A number of interviewees mentioned it. They said they thought it was strange at the time, but they only became suspicious following the abductions. The whole town is buzzing with chatter and innuendo, and don't even go down the social media front.'

Frank said, 'Jesus, this has grown hair and two siblings.'

Pluto smiled at the comment. 'What should we do now, boss?'

'Let's see,' thought Frank as he looked out his window. 'How much of a fund do we have for a reward?'

Pluto looked up, thinking, 'I'd say around forty, maybe fifty grand. Why?'

'Put it out that there's a reward for any information that results in the capture and unharmed recovery of the Doyle children. Make it for thirty big ones. Okay?'

'Sure thing, chief. I'll get right on it.'

Pluto left Frank pondering. 'What the hell is happening here?' he thought aloud.

Harry was waiting for the early morning news. He wasn't able to sleep all night. He read the text and smiled to himself. The plan was working out better than he had expected. It had been easy enough to arrange the riot at the prison knowing Boxer's contacts amongst the screws and the prisoners. All Harry had to do was to supply Dino with enough cash to stir things up. The fact that three others escaped with them didn't matter a toss. Convincing Dino to grab the priest was the real winner. Now all he had to do was get rid of the lot of them. That would solve any problems about anyone squealing in the future, leaving Boxer and him to carry on their business as before.

Harry switched channels, tuning into RTE.

'Good morning. Here is the eight o'clock news. Gardaí are combing the Galway County area as they step up efforts to locate the missing Doyle children. Tempers flared in the city last night as people gathered outside the Anglican church, waving banners and shouting obscenities. Gardaí threw a cordon around the church in case of trouble. In breaking news, Gardaí have also issued a thirty-thousand-euro reward for any information leading to the safe capture of the Doyle children and the arrest of Father Sean Robinson, the main suspect in the abduction. As we enter the second day of the reported missing children, Gardaí are hopeful of an early arrest in the case. We now...'

Harry switched off the television. 'Thirty-thousand reward,' he said. 'That's just perfect. Now I can put the next stage of my plan into effect.'

Christy had a wicked sore throat. He was also coughing a lot. He must have had the flu. *Damn it,* he thought, *I was meant to play cards tonight!* He looked through the medicine cabinet for something to ease the pain in his throat. The doorbell rang. *Who the hell is that at this hour of the morning?*

When he opened the door, he saw Harry standing there, smiling. 'The top of the morning to you, Christy. How is the day finding you?'

Christy looked unwelcoming. Harry was the last person he wanted to see at his house. 'What do you want?'

Harry looked around him and saw that there was nobody on the street. 'Let me come in. I have a proposition for you that is to your advantage.'

Christy looked at him. 'Come in so, but you're not staying long. I have the flu, and I need to get back to bed.'

'What I have to offer you will get rid of your flu in an instant.' Harry looked at Christy and thought he was just ripe for the plucking.

'Go on, out with it. What have you got to say?'

Harry grabbed a chair, saying, 'You know all about this abduction thing with those kids, right?'

'Yeah, it's all over the news. What about it?'

'Well, the police have just announced a nice little reward of thirty-thousand euros for any information leading to the safe capture of the priest and those kids.'

'So what has that got to do with me?' said Christy, getting agitated.

'I'll tell you if you just listen to me. I happen to know where they are holding out.' Harry let his words sink in before continuing.

'How the hell do you know that?' asked Christy.

'No matter how I know; just that I do. I have, as they say, friends who have friends. Now, you haven't forgotten that you owe Boxer fifteen grand, have you?'

Christy had to sit down, and he started to cough again. There was little doubt in Harry's mind that Christy was all too aware of his gambling debts.

'You are also aware that tomorrow, Friday, is the last day for repayment of that fifteen grand. So I have a solution to your problems. I can give you the location of the kidnapping priest and therefore those kids. All you have to do is inform the police. You can claim the thirty thousand, pay off Boxer, and have fifteen big ones left over for yourself. How does that sound?'

Christy stopped coughing. He thought about Boxer and Harry's proposal. Then he asked, 'Why are you doing this? What's in it for you?'

'Good question,' said Harry. 'What you don't know – in fact what nobody knows – yet' – he paused for effect – 'is that Dino and Fonsie are also there with the priest and those kids. By getting the cops in on it, Boxer and I will have no further problems trying to keep their mouths shut. I've been going up to that prison every week since they were sentenced trying to placate Dino to keep him onside. If Dino and Fonsie are out of the picture, then it's a load off your back too. They are the reason why Boxer can't sleep at night. If you clear your debt and get rid of Boxer's sleeplessness, then you are a free man. Get it?'

Christy thought long and hard. It made a lot of sense to him. 'But how do you know the police won't recapture Dino and Fonsie, and then they'll squeal anyway?'

'Because I know Dino, and there's no way he won't come out of where he is without shooting. Now, do you want to end your problems or not?' said Harry, getting annoyed and showing his impatience. Christy bit his fingernails. 'Come on, Christy, make up your mind.'

'Okay, okay, I'll do it. What's the address?'

'There's one more thing,' said Harry. 'When you contact the police, you've to get their agreement that they won't ask you where you got your information. They'll be so keen to locate those children that they'll do anything you want. If you implicate me in any of this, then you also implicate Boxer. You get my meaning?' Harry stared straight into Christy's eyes.

'Yeah, I get you. Don't worry, I'll handle it. Didn't I handle the bank manager for you?'

'Yes, you did, Christy. I have every confidence in you.' Harry stood up. 'They are holding out at Skull Lake, about forty miles north of here. The cops will know about it. There are only two fishing cabins on that lake. The one they want is on the north side of the lake. Have you got that?'

'Yes, I've got it.'
Harry smiled and closed the door behind him as he left.

Easter Thursday

Mary had finally fallen asleep around three o'clock. Sean hadn't slept a wink. It was cold, and he shivered. He stood up, trying to get some feeling in his feet.

'Where do you think you're going?' asked Dino, pointing his gun.

'I'm freezing. We need heat in here. The children will be cold.'

'Turn on that stove, Fonsie. He's right. I'm freezing too.'

Fonsie got up and turned on the Primus. He went outside to relieve himself.

Sean looked at Dino. 'How are the children supposed to go to the bathroom? How long are you going to keep them here?'

'Questions, always bloody questions, eh, Father? You should be more worried about yourself and forget about those kids. Now, sit back down and don't get up unless I tell you.'

Dino checked his phone again. Still nothing from Harry. He had said he would let them know what to do soon. Dino was getting nervous. He knew the cops would be stepping up a gear trying to find them. It wouldn't be long before the helicopters were out searching, if they weren't already.

Fonsie came back in, wheeling a portable heater. 'This was outside, and it has a full jar of gas. At least we'll be able to stay warm.'

'Chief, we might just have something on that reward money,' said Pluto excitedly.

'Why? What's happening?' said Frank, taking another slug of coffee.

'I have someone on the line who will only speak with you. He wants assurances about something before he tells us where the kidnappers are.'

'What makes you think he's genuine?'

'It's the way he's talking. He seems very nervous, not the crank-call type.'

'Are you tracing his call?'

'Yes, we have a trace on it, but it's a throwaway phone. We're trying to get a handle on his location and get a car over to it if we can.'

'Okay, put him through.' The phone on his desk buzzed. Frank licked his lips and said, 'Detective Chief Frank Brady here. What do you have for me?'

'Before I tell you anything, I want your assurances that if you find those children, you won't ask me how I got my information.'

Frank opened his eyes wide and needed to think quickly. To give himself a little more time, he asked, 'Have you any other demands?'

'One other thing. If you do find them, then I need that money by tomorrow, Friday. Understand?'

'I see,' said Frank, trying to get a handle on his caller and knowing that the clock was ticking before the Dublin lot would stick their oars into his case. 'I'll tell you what I'll do. If your information leads to the safe – and I emphasize *safe* – rescue of those children, then I won't ask you any questions. But if a hair on either of their heads is harmed, then I'm coming after you, and you will tell me everything. Is that clear?'

'And what about my money?'

'You'll have your money tomorrow; I guarantee it.'

'I want you to know that I've taped this conversation. Is that understood?' added Christy.

Frank was impressed with his caller. It was a smart move on his part. This was no idiot he was dealing with. 'I understand, and I've no problem with it either. Now give me what you've got.'

A few minutes later, Frank finished writing. He turned to Pluto, who was standing in front of him, waiting anxiously to hear the news. 'Find out all you can on a Christy Welch of this address. Have you ever heard of a Skull Lake about forty miles north of here?'

'Yes, it's renowned for its trout fishing. Take the Mayo Road and then veer off about halfway there. They'd be just muddy lanes from there – no proper roads – so it could take nearly two hours in a car. Will I get a few teams together?'

Frank thought some more. 'No. We need to be very careful about this and keep the press out of it. If we send in our lot of plods, they could make a mess of it. We need professionals.'

Frank took up his mobile and searched his contacts. Finding them, he pressed the button. It had only rung once before it was answered. 'Bill, it's Frank Brady. I need you over here – now!'

Mary lay awake, not saying a word. Alice still slept. Sean asked if she was hungry, but she didn't answer him.

'The children are hungry. They need food,' he called out to nobody in particular.

Fonsie looked in the cupboards. 'There's some tins of beans, a couple of tins of peaches, and some instant mashed potatoes. I could cook something up, I suppose.'

'You need to do something, or these children will get sick,' added Sean.

'I'll do the ordering around here, Father, if you don't mind,' said Dino. 'I believe I'm the one with the gun. Put something on for all of us, Fonsie. I'm going outside for a dump.'

'What about them?' Fonsie asked.

'They ain't going nowhere. I'll just be outside,' said Dino as he closed the door.

Sean decided to use this opportunity to appeal to Fonsie. 'Fonsie, I know this is none of your idea. You've got to help us, or at least make sure the children are safe.' Sean stared at Fonsie, appealing to his good nature.

Fonsie stopped what he was doing and looked anxiously towards the door. 'Look, Faddah, you're right. I never wanted any of this to happen, but Dino's in charge, and I'm not able for him. You can see that.'

'I know, but if you get the chance, perhaps we can both attack him. Two of us should be able for him.'

'No, Faddah. I'm in enough trouble as it is. Look, I don't want any harm to come to those children – I really don't.' He looked over at Mary and Alice. 'I'll do what I can.'

Then Dino came back in. 'Is everything okay in here?'

'Shipshape,' said Fonsie nervously. 'Won't be long before we'll have mashed potatoes, beans, and a big mug of tea,' he said, looking at Sean.

Sean sat back and sighed deeply.

Harry sat thinking about his next message. He had told Christy to get some sleep and get rid of his flu. He knew Dino would be getting nervous, but until the cops got their act together, he needed to keep him happy; he needed Dino to stay where he was.

Harry sent the following text: *Everything looking good. Boxer and me are being closely watched by the cops. They should leave us alone by tomorrow. Am bringing a new car and money for your escape. I'll also bring new clothes. Is there anything else you want? Won't be much longer. Sit it out. HD.*

He sat waiting on a response. Ten minutes passed, and his phone buzzed. Dino's message read, *Hurry up. These kids are annoying me. I need smokes and some beers. What time will you be here?*

Harry had anticipated Dino's every thought – not that it was very hard to do. He immediately responded, *I left beer and smokes under the bed. Be there around midday tomorrow. Stay calm.*

That should keep him there, thought Harry.

Dino jumped up and looked under the bed. Finding a case of Heineken and a carton of cigarettes, he immediately changed his mood. He started laughing. 'Good man, Harry. He didn't forget us after all,' he said, holding the carton in the air and smiling at Fonsie, who smiled back, happy that Dino was happy. Sean thought that it was probably a good thing that they had the distraction of beer and cigarettes; it would keep their minds away from the children, at least for a while.

Governor Rhode walked into Frank's office. 'What's happening, Frank? Rome is breathing down my neck.'

Frank looked at him. 'I've asked for a SWAT team from Dublin. It's run by a close friend of mine by the name of Bill McGlynn. We worked together a lot when I was based in Dublin. He should be here in about an hour.'

Rhode looked surprised. 'A SWAT team? Holy Jesus, Frank, I hope you know what you're doing.'

Frank looked at him disdainfully. 'Yes, I do. That's why you promoted me.'

'I don't mean it like that, Frank; you know that. I mean, why a SWAT team??'

'We know where the captives are; at least I'm nearly positive. We got a hot tip. Bill will be bringing his own chopper, and his team are professionals. They are as good as you'll find anywhere in the world. I need to use them to have any chance of getting those children out of there unharmed.'

'Okay, Frank. I do trust you. Keep me posted.'

Rhode walked out. Frank didn't want to show him or anybody else that he himself was very nervous.

Two hours later, they had landed the helicopter about a mile away from Skull Lake. They were met by Frank and his team. He and Bill shook hands and exchanged pleasantries, but being the professionals they were, they wasted no more time in getting down to work.

They made their way to the lake, getting as close as they could without giving away their positions. Bill got everybody's attention.

'Okay, we've studied the map and the surrounding region. I have a map here of the lake, and there's the cabin. It's small, which is good. The cabin is covered by the lake on the east side; the main door is here on the south; there's one back door on the north side and nothing on the west. We will cover all three sides anyway, while your lot will cover the lake side, Frank, in case they try to run for it that way.'

Frank nodded, saying nothing, leaving Bill to do all of the talking. This was his game. Frank left him to it.

'The major problem I see is that there's only one tiny window there, and it's curtained. That means we'll have only one opportunity to take them down. We are going to take them down, Frank, correct?'

Frank looked Bill in the eyes. 'If we have to, then we have to. My only concern is the children.'

Bill continued. 'We'll have the thermal imaging cameras set up shortly; then we'll be able to scope the bodies. We'll get an idea of where the bodies are, but we won't know who's who. I want three of you on either side of the cabin. Check your radios and go silent,' he said, organizing his teams. 'Frank, I want you to make sure that nobody – and I mean nobody – screws this up from your side. That means total silence – no lights, no coughing, no sneezing, nothing. Is that clear?'

'Clear, Bill. Don't worry about us.'

Bill went off about his work. Frank turned to Pluto. 'You heard the man. Do exactly what he says. Remember, there are two small children's lives at stake here.'

Pluto and his men nodded their understanding. Frank lay down behind a felled tree. It was going to be a very long night, he thought.

Bridie hadn't slept since this whole thing started. Dan looked worried again. Gabby and Angela had stayed the night; they didn't want to be far away.

'Oh, Dan, what can we do?' said Bridie. 'There's no way our Sean would do anything bad to anyone, let alone those wee children.'

'I know that, girl. There's nothing we can do but say a prayer. I think that's what Sean would want us to do,' added Dan. 'At least Molly is away and doesn't know anything about what's happening. She hasn't rung us, so it mustn't be on the news over in Spain. Kevin rang me about five times today wanting to know what's happening. I wasn't able to tell him anything because nobody is telling us anything.'

'Stop fretting yourself, Bridie. It'll do you no good,' said Gabby. 'I know Sean better than anyone. He will make it through, and everybody will understand.'

'Oh, I hope you're right, Gabby. I don't think I can take much more of this.'

'Come on, everybody, say the rosary with me,' insisted Dan.

Bridie took some solace from Dan's words. She hadn't the inclination to wonder at his newfound conversion. They all knelt down on the floor. Bridie led them off. 'Our Father who art in heaven . . .'

Sean tried to feed Alice, but she wasn't hungry. Mary liked the potato mash, especially when Sean added loads of butter. Alice watched as her sister ate; then she took some prompting from Mary and started to nibble. Sean was pleased. 'We'll have toast and marmalade after this, okay?' he said. Alice smiled just a little.

'Hey, look what I found – a deck of playing cards,' said Fonsie, triumphantly holding a used deck of cards.

'Can I use them to play cards with the children?' asked Sean.

'Sure,' said Fonsie, handing the deck to Sean.

'Give them here first,' said Dino, grabbing them from Sean's hand. 'I like the odd game of patience.' He sat at the table and opened another bottle of beer.

Sean glanced at Fonsie, who shrugged his shoulders. Sean was getting worried that Dino was drinking too much. What happened if he got drunk? He tried to clear that thought from his mind and went back to nursing the children.

About an hour later, Sean felt very tired. He gave the children some milk and lay down on the floor beside them. He was surprised that he was able to shut his eyes. He had barely nodded off when Dino kicked him in the side and threw the deck of cards on top of him.

'Here, you can have them. Fonsie, you keep watch while I grab some shut-eye.' Dino lay himself down in a corner using a cushion for a pillow, and within minutes he was asleep, the beer having had its effect.

Sean waited for about an hour, then shushed at Fonsie to get his attention. 'Fonsie, Fonsie,' he whispered. 'Let us go now while he's asleep.'

Fonsie opened his eyes wide and suddenly looked terrified. 'I can't do that, Faddah. Dino would kill me on the spot – no questions. No, Faddah, I'm sorry.'

'Then let the children go at least.'

Fonsie looked at them, then back at Sean. 'They'd freeze out there on their own. We're in the middle of nowhere, Faddah.'

Fonsie was right, thought Sean again. He looked at them. They were only toddlers. It was hopeless. If he tried to make a run for it, Dino would wake up, and . . . he couldn't bear to think about it. Sean put his head down into his hands and started praying.

Good Friday.

Dawn broke, and Frank hadn't shut an eye. The thermal-imaging display showed a hazy three bodies inside. *It must be the priest and the two children, but we can't be sure,* thought Frank. *The children are definitely in there; they have to be.*

Another three hours went by. Frank sipped some lukewarm coffee and then jumped when he heard, 'Movement,' come through on his earphone. One of the SWAT team reported a door opening at the cabin. Frank held his breath waiting for more information. 'Gunman sighted. Photograph taken. Gunman taking a leak. Gone back inside. Over.' Frank looked at the screen. A moment later it revealed a photograph displayed with the name Alphonsus Murphy – Convict #77639920. *One of the escapees,* Frank thought. *That means there's a good chance that the second guy is in there too. Then who's the third person, and where are the children? Why aren't they showing on the infrared?* Frank was troubled.

Another two hours went by. Finally, he saw Bill stealthily making his way over towards him. 'Okay, we now know that one of them is one of the escaped convicts. We can presume that the other one is in there too. We'll need to wait until we can confirm that for sure. The third image must be your priest,' said Bill.

'But where are the children?' asked Frank.

Bill responded, 'The imaging is a bit fuzzy. It could be for a number of reasons. If they have a fire burning in there, it would disrupt the scan. Remember that thermal imaging works on heat being radiated. Too much heat gives us different readings. We have to wait until it's clearer. It'll soon be midday, and the weather is favorable. The dark clouds help. If we get thunder, then all the better; it'll mask our approach. We don't have too much time, Frank. I hope you are ready to give us the all-clear to take them down.'

Frank looked at his watch. It read midday. 'I need to do something. Give me a half hour.'

'All right, but make your mind up, Frank. We've only get one shot at this – literally.'

Frank made his way back to his car. He reread his files again. There was something still bothering him about this priest. He couldn't find any evidence against him. It was all circumstantial, hearsay, innuendo, nothing concrete. Sure, the papers and social media wanted to hang him out to dry, but he couldn't do that. Then a cold shiver ran up his spine. Could he order the killing of an innocent man? He looked again at his files. There it was. He needed to contact that man.

Frank took out his phone and keyed in the number he had written down. The phone rang. A couple of rings later, a voice said, 'Hello, this is Father Rice. How can I help you?'

'Father Rice, this is Chief Detective Frank Brady of the Galway Gardaí. I'm in charge of the case involving a friend of yours, a Father Sean Robinson.'

'Father Sean – is he okay? Have you found him?'

'No, Father Rice. That's why I'm calling you. Can you help me?'

'Yes, of course, anything. What do you need to know?'

'I understand you were at Father Robinson's mass last Sunday. Is that correct?'

'Yes, that is correct.'

'Am I right in saying that . . .' – Frank checked his notes one more time – '... that he said, "This is my last sermon"? Is that correct?'

'No, he never said that. He said, "This *could* be my last sermon." He also said to the congregation that this *could* be their last day on earth. There's a big difference, detective.'

'Indeed,' agreed Frank. 'So he wasn't implying that he wouldn't be there next Sunday . . . that would be Easter Sunday?'

'Not a bit of it. I'm still expecting him to show up.'

Frank bit his lower lip, thinking. 'Father Rice, can you enlighten me as best you can about your friend, Father Robinson?'

'I'd be happy to.'

Frank spent the next twenty minutes hearing about Sean as a child prodigy, how he had spent his time at Maynooth College enthralling the students and lecturers with his brilliance, and how he had ended up in the seminary at Nottingham, duly impressing everybody there also, including his archbishop.

'So you see, detective, Father Robinson is not a child molester or anything like it. He's a philosopher, a genius.'

Frank raised both eyebrows and shook his head softly. 'I want to thank you for your insights, Father. You've been a great help.'

'It was not a problem. Any time, detective. Please keep me informed, will you?'

'Of course,' said Frank, and they hung up.

Frank thought long and hard about what he had just heard. He thought about the only other evidence against the priest, that being his regular visits to the prison, which could hardly qualify as real evidence. Wasn't a priest supposed to make prison visits? He exited his car and gradually made his way back to Bill.

'I really don't know, Bill. I can't convict this man to die when I have no evidence against him.'

Bill looked at Frank and said, 'I'm not a judge or a jury, Frank. I just do my job – which is to take out the bad guys. I thought that was your job too?'

'I bring the evidence, Bill. The jury and the judge do the rest. In this case, I'm being asked to be judge, jury, and executioner!'

They both looked up to the sky as they heard the rumble of thunder. It still hadn't rained, but it was threatening to.

Sean played snap with the children, but he could see he was having trouble keeping their interest.

'I'm going outside for a leak. Get ready to go, Fonsie,' said Dino.

'Go where?' asked Sean of Fonsie.

'I only do what I'm told, Faddah. Sorry.'

Frank heard another message on his earpiece 'Second convict. Photo confirmed. Taking leak. Gone back inside.' Frank looked at the screen and saw a picture of Dino with the text, 'Daniel Dempsey – Convict #77639921.'

Bill came rushing down the small slope. 'Okay, that's it, then, Frank. We've confirmed the identity of the two convicts. The third one has to be the priest. The children must be in a corner drowned out from our picture by a fire or something.'

'But we don't know if it's the priest or not, Bill.'

Bill looked over at the cabin. 'Not confirmed, granted. But we have to assume it, Frank.' Bill was looking annoyed. 'My men are experts – you know that. We get one shot whenever the three of them are behind that curtain. We have to shoot all three regardless if we are to have any hope of rescuing those little girls. Understood?' Frank was afraid – nervous and afraid. 'Frank, understood?!' said Bill harshly.

'Understood.' And Frank sat down behind the dead tree.

Dino tried texting Harry again. 'Why isn't he replying to me?' He was getting angry and frustrated.

Sean was getting more worried. He turned to the children and told them that they were going to play a game of hide and seek. They looked with wide eyes. They seemed to want to do something. Sean told them he was going to get the nice man Fonsie to close his eyes and try to find them. They nodded delicately. Sean told them to get under the bunk bed and not to move until he told them to come out. They nodded again, indicating they knew how to play this game. Sean covered them with the blanket.

Dino was nervously peeping through the curtain. 'I bet that bastard called the cops. I bet that the cops are probably outside already waiting to shoot us.'

'Harry wouldn't do that, Dino. Besides, it's only . . .' – Fonsie looked at his watch – 'coming up to three o'clock. Give him another couple of hours.'

Dino turned angrily. 'He said he'd be here at midday. That's what he said. Its three o'clock, and there's no sign of him.'

Sean walked slowly over towards the window to join them. He was sullen.

Dino turned. 'Where do you think you're going?' he said, pointing his gun at Sean, who moved in between them, with Fonsie on his right and Dino to his left.

'We have thermal confirmation. Three bodies in sight. Target is confirmed. Permission to shoot?' Bill looked at Frank. 'Call it, Frank.'

Frank stared blindly at the screen. He could see the three images clearly. They were moving closer together. He turned to Bill. 'Do it.'

'Copy,' said Bill into his mike.

A hail of gunshots rang out. Frank could see the window and the curtains shatter and rip. He looked at the thermal camera and saw immediately that the three images hit the ground.

Bill shouted, 'Go, go!' as three units of his SWAT team moved in from three angles. Frank followed closely behind Bill.

Fonsie opened his eyes, and his hand reached out to join Sean's. Sean whispered, 'You will not die yet. You still have a job to do for me. Will you do it?'

Fonsie whispered, 'Yes, Faddah, anything.'

Sean whispered some more. Then Fonsie closed his eyes, and his hand fell back down. The door was kicked in. Bill and his team entered while his second team moved through the open back door.

'Clear!' one of his men shouted.

'The back door was open, sir!' shouted one of the other men.

'Did you see anybody escape?'

'Negative, sir,' Bill's men recounted.

'Then why in blazes are there only two bodies on the floor?'

Frank and Bill looked behind them. There was no third body. Then Frank said, 'There!' He pointed to under the bed, seeing a child's foot peeping out. 'Medics, now, quickly!' shouted Frank as a team of medics made their way over to the children, grabbing them in their arms, wrapping aluminum foil blankets over them, and rushing them outside to a waiting ambulance.

291

Frank looked down at Fonsie and Dino. The doctor said, 'This one's dead,' pointing to Dino. 'This one's still alive but only just,' he said as he listened to Fonsie's heartbeat.

Bill shouted, 'Get the chopper here now! Take him to Galway City Hospital. Go, go, go!'

'Tell me what's happening here, Bill?' asked Frank, looking very perplexed.

Bill looked around. Before answering, he blared into his microphone, 'I want a cone cover to within two miles. Ignore the lake. Do you copy?'

'Copy that.'

'I don't know what to tell you, Frank,' said Bill. 'There were three bodies. You saw that. Now there's only two. It beats the crap out of me.'

'Maybe there weren't three bodies at all. Maybe your equipment was confused. We never saw a priest, did we?'

Bill opened his eyes, and shaking his head from side to side, said, 'No, no, we can't say we actually saw a third person, and we cannot confirm it was a priest.' He looked at Frank full in the face. 'But we both know there was a third person in here, Frank!'

Frank arrived back at the office and saw that his team members were crowded around the television. Frank was giving his press conference.

'We can confirm that today we apprehended the abductors of the two Doyle children. Thankfully both children were unhurt. One of the abductors was shot dead by our special Garda forces. The other one is in intensive care under twenty-four-hour guard. We hope to be in a position to interview him shortly.'

'Where was the priest?' shouted two or three of the reporters at the same time.

Frank held his hands aloft to quiet them. 'I can confirm that there was no third person in the cabin. Father Robinson was not there. If anybody has any further information regarding Father Robinson, they should report it to their nearest Garda station immediately. Thank you. That is all for the moment.'

Frank then rushed through the crowd of reporters. 'Turn that thing off and get back to work,' said Frank. 'And well done, everybody,' he added as he sighed, sitting himself down in his chair.

'Coffee, boss?' asked Pluto.

'Please, Pluto, and add something strong to it.'

'Got it, boss.'

'What happened, Frank?' asked Rhode, sitting himself down.

'Eh, no "well done there, Frank"?'

'You're not a child, Frank, but well done anyway.'

'Thanks,' Frank replied sarcastically. 'You heard it yourself on the TV. We got the bad guys, and we rescued the children. Mission accomplished.'

'But where the hell is the priest?'

Frank turned to the window, thought some more, then said, 'I have absolutely no idea. Maybe we'll get some information from this Fonsie guy – if he recovers. Maybe one of the children will enlighten us, but I wouldn't hold your breath. Those kids are traumatized and won't be saying much to anybody for a long, long time. So who knows? I can tell you this,' he said as Pluto put the strong coffee in front of him. Frank turned, smiled, and, clicking his mouth while nodding his head, said, 'It's way outside of my jurisdiction, and that's a certainty.'

The next day, Saturday, Frank and Pluto arrived at Christy's house on the main street. Frank looked at the house and rang the doorbell.

'Have you got the check?' asked Frank.

'Sure have, boss. Here in this envelope – thirty smack-a-rooskies.'

There was no answer, and Frank tried again, this time banging on the door at the same time as ringing the bell. 'Mr. Welch, it's Detective Frank Brady. We have something for you. I know we're a little late, but better late than never, as they say,' he shouted.

There was still no response. Frank tried the doorknob, and the door opened slightly. He pushed it further, and both men were taken aback as they saw Christy Welch dangling from a rope in the main hallway. He was dead.

'Holy crap,' said Pluto.

'Call an ambulance! Get the homicide crew in here, quickly!' bellowed Frank.

'On it, boss,' added Pluto, running outside.

Frank looked at the dangling body. He could tell he had been dead a while, at least twenty-four hours. 'Why did you do it, son?' said Frank to himself, shaking his head.

Pluto came rushing back. 'They're on their way, boss. What'll I do with his cashier's check?'

Frank looked at Pluto, then back at the dead body. 'Leave it on the sideboard, I suppose. He was the one who earned it.'

Easter Saturday.

Peter shuffled through the pews, fixing the prayer books and making sure the kneelers were back in place. He sat down, hunched over the pew, and whispered to himself that these weren't normal times by any stretch of the imagination. If the past few days were anything to go by, then tomorrow's Sunday mass would have crowds far greater than the capacity of the church.

Peter had arranged to add an additional two masses – one at seven a.m. and the other at nine a.m. He had decided only that afternoon about the seven a.m. mass, and he didn't know if anybody knew about it. He had managed to put up notices around town telling people about the other two masses and saying that everybody was welcome to worship. He knew that the majority of those attending were hoping to get some gossip or maybe a newsflash, but they were in for a disappointment. Little did he know that the events of the past week would hurtle him from a sleepy town in the West of Ireland onto the world's stage, that he would become a celebrity overnight as people clamored for information about him, his community, and of course the whereabouts of . . .

'Father Wilson.' A voice startled him from behind interrupting his thoughts. Peter turned around to find Lee Thomas standing in the center of the aisle.

'How did you get in? The church is locked.'

'One of your assistants let me in.'

'Who?'

'He didn't tell me his name. Father Wilson, I know you are an extremely busy man, and I promise not to take up too much of your time, but can you help me with some questions I have?'

'What sort of questions?'

'My name is Lee Thomas. I work for the *New York Times*, and my editor sent me over to interview you.'

Peter looked the intruder up and down and motioned him forward with his hand. 'Please take a seat. I've been expecting you.'

Lee shuffled his way up towards the priest, thinking that Dick must have been in contact. He obviously had told Father Wilson to expect him.

'You've come a long way. Can I offer you some refreshment? I'm sure I have something in the vestry.'

'No, thank you, Father. I've been well looked after by various people throughout the day.'

'Have you been here a few days, then?'

'No, I arrived earlier today, and I met with the family of Father Robinson. They were very accommodating, both in words and deeds.'

'How are the Robinsons?'

'They seem complacent enough, considering everything that has gone on these past few days. Mrs. Robinson is convinced her son is alive but not convinced that he will be returning, for some unknown reason. The fiancée is the one who is most upset, but overall the whole family appears to be remarkably calm – satisfied that the children have been found safely and that their son has been vindicated.'

'Well, then, what can I do for you?'

'As you know, Father, these past few days have gotten the world's attention. People are clamoring for news about your friend. I have to say that today has been more than a revelation to me. I've spoken to many people today who hero-worship this Father Robinson. Some are calling him a prophet, a miracle worker. It's my job to seek the truth about these rumors, be they fact or innuendo.'

'You are apparently skeptical about the things you've heard.'

'It's my middle name,' said Lee, smiling to himself.

'Where would you like me to start?'

'Why not when you and Father Robinson first met? That would have been at the Galway church, correct?'

'I think we should start with a prayer.' Peter crouched down on the kneeler and invited Lee to join with him. Lee was surprised but cooperated, kneeling down alongside him. Father Wilson spoke aloud:

'Heavenly Father, grant us the wisdom to do your will and the strength to see it through. Have mercy on us, and grant us eternal life through Jesus Christ, our Savior. Amen.'

Lee was staring at Peter when the priest opened his eyes.

'Where did you learn that prayer, Father?' asked Lee open mouthed.

'It was a prayer that Father Sean always recited, day and night. Why do you ask?'

'Well, my wife. . .' Lee paused, looked up at the altar, then back at the priest. 'It doesn't matter, Father. It just reminded me of somebody. Can we go on with your story?' Lee took out his phone, muted it, and pressed the recorder button, and said, 'Tell me a little bit about your own background, Father.'

'My background is as simple as Sean's. Sean, as you probably know, was adopted, having been abandoned as a baby at the doorstops of the hospital over in Ballinasloe.'

'Yes, I heard about that from his mother. So you'd never met or heard of Father Sean before meeting each other at the church in Galway city?'

'No, that's where I first met him. From the outset, we became more or less inseparable. He had an imposing way about him. He definitely stood out from the crowd. Everybody liked him. He was always giving and caring, he never got into any trouble, and of course, he was extremely clever. It was obvious to everybody from the outset that he was destined for bigger things.'

'What do you mean?'

'Sean showed himself to be somebody who had more wisdom than the books we read. I remember him talking to parishioners and captivating them, as well as me, with his different understanding of how the Bible can be referred to in today's terms. He would explain that the demons that Jesus exorcised from those who were possessed were no different from the madness that inflicts people today when they go on killing sprees. It was as if he knew how to translate the Gospels in an effortless way so that everybody could easily understand. He made us think anew about everything.'

'Did you witness any miracles?' interrupted Lee.

'Ah, miracles. People are always looking for signs, wonderments, and Hollywood explosions. It's no good unless Quentin Tarantino is directing and has Jesus being blown from the tomb to the background cacophony of the "Hallelujah" chorus – is that what you mean, Lee?'

Lee raised his eyebrows, creased his forehead, and said, 'I don't mean to be disrespectful, Father. If I'm to report any of this, I do need to have some sort of evidence that there is – or was – some type of divine intervention where Father Robinson was concerned.'

Peter smiled and continued. 'I cannot give you any physical evidence of any miraculous events, but I can tell you of events that your readers – or even you – might find miraculous. Would that suffice?'

'Yes, that would be great, Father.'

'Probably the first time I noticed anything especial about Sean was in his demeanor. He had a "way" about him, as the Irish would say. He had presence.' Peter corrected himself by saying, 'I seem to be speaking in the past tense.' He looked up at the altar. Then, taking a deep breath, he continued. 'From the very first moment we met, I liked him. I enthused with him . . . yet he didn't say or do anything much. He had a way of bringing out the best in you . . . in everybody. It's hard to explain it. It wasn't that anything out of the ordinary happened during our first year or so together, but . . .' Peter trailed off.

'Go on, Father,' encouraged Lee.

'I never really noticed anything until I heard about Bishop Benny's wife. She had been very sick; she was practically dying. Then one night, Sean said he would visit her. Practically the next day, Martha, the bishop's wife, had fully recovered. Come to think of it, she almost nearly genuflected whenever she came into contact with Sean. Nobody, especially the bishop, ever spoke of it afterwards, but I sensed that something had happened.

'Then there was the time that Gabby came to our rescue – sort of out of the blue – one evening as we were attempting to deposit some monies in the bank. He disposed of those ruffians who were trying to rob us. Then of course there was the little girl, our housekeeper's niece. She had polio, a very bad form of polio, and she . . .' Peter stopped as he thought of that day. 'She walked up the aisle of the church and received Communion as if it had been a normal occurrence to her. Then Vinnie told me about Haiti, and of course there was the phone . . .' He trailed off again and stooped low, putting his head in his hands.

'Are you okay, Father?'

Peter looked up at Lee. 'My friend, do you want all of the details?'

'Yes, Father, I do – please.'

Some four hours later, Peter sat back, exhausted. Lee had taken off his jacket and had barely said two words during the past number of hours. He knew that this man, this priest, had to be telling the truth. He couldn't have made this stuff up. Lee had had too much experience dealing with tricksters and gangsters to know when a man was lying or not. The trouble was, Lee didn't know what to do with it.

'Tell me, Father. Do you honestly – in your heart of hearts – believe that this Father Robinson performed miracles?'

Peter turned to Lee and without any hesitation said, 'There is absolutely no doubt in my mind that Father Robinson performed the miracles I told you of. He is categorically divine.'

Lee leaned back in his seat. 'Wow! That's as clear and concise as I could expect anybody to be, Father. I think I have enough. I want to thank you most sincerely for giving me your valuable time.'

'It was my pleasure, Lee.' The two men walked in silence towards the front door. 'Tell me, Lee, you said that my assistant let you in, is that correct?'

'Yes, Father, he said he was your assistant.'

They walked up to the door. Peter took a bunch of keys from his pocket and said, 'You see, the reason I ask is that I don't have an assistant. I work here on my own with my wife. You say that he unlocked this door for you?'

Lee looked cynically at Peter, answering, 'Yes, that's right.'

'Therefore this door would be unlocked; isn't that correct?'

Lee looked at the door, then the lock, and assessed, 'Yes, that would be correct. Why?'

'There is only one main front door key – and I possess it, nobody else.' Peter took the key and turned it in the lock. There was a loud clunk as the key moved the bolt. 'You see, this door has been locked all the time.'

Peter looked up at Lee, who looked with curiosity and wonder. Peter pulled open the heavy door, and as Lee passed him to exit, Peter placed his hand on Lee's shoulder and said, 'Lee, I have good news for you. Your daughter is healthy and will live a long and peaceful life.'

Lee turned just as Peter smiled. He slowly closed the church door and locked it. Lee stood there in silence, staring at the church door. He turned and walked – and turned back again. 'How . . .?' He shook his head, trying to take in what had just occurred, what he had just heard.

Lee flicked his phone off record and mute. He saw that he had twenty-three missed calls and fourteen messages. He frowned and said, 'What the . . .?' He dialed his voice mail and heard, 'Daddy, Daddy, oh, where are you? Please call me. Oh, Daddy, this is incredible.' Every message said more or less the same thing. They were all from Maggie.

Lee flicked forward and saw one from Barry, then three from Des. He listened to Barry's message first. Barry was excited too, but more controlled than Maggie. He was saying something about a miracle. He stopped that recording and moved to Des's. Surely Des would be able to explain clearly what the hell was going on. As he played back Des's message, he turned pale and had to take a seat on the nearest wall. He listened as Des told him that the disease was gone.

He hung up and speed-dialed Des. After about thirty seconds, he heard, 'Lee, where the hell have you been? We've been trying to get hold of you for hours!'

'I'm sorry, Des. I was working on this case here in Ireland. What's going on, Des?'

There was a huge silence at the other end. Lee thought they had been cut off. 'Des, Des, are you there?'

'Yes, I'm here, Lee. I'm hesitant because I don't know how to say this to you. Maggie . . . your daughter is . . . cured. She's totally cured!'

Lee let his shoulders fall. This was getting too much for him. 'Des, what do you mean she's cured? What are you talking about?'

'I'm sorry, Lee. I know how this must sound to you, but about five hours ago, I got the results of the latest MRI which showed no trace whatsoever of any cancer in Maggie's body. I've never seen anything like it in my life. Lee . . . she's fully recovered. The cancer's gone . . . and I've no idea why.'

Lee rubbed his face over and over again. *What are they saying to me? How can this be happening? This is insane!*

'Des, tell me again, how can this have happened?' Lee looked up at the crucifix standing high on the steeple tower. He looked down again at his phone. There was still silence from Des. Lee thought back; he had entered the church about five hours ago, the same time that Maggie started to feel better! 'Des, let me ask you another question. Are you saying, or are you thinking, that this is some sort of miracle?'

There was no answer. Lee could hear Des breathing. He allowed another minute to pass by. 'Des, I need an answer!'

'Lee . . .' Des stuttered, 'I know you don't want to hear this, but . . . for no other logical reason, then I'd have to say that a miracle has taken place. That's as good an assumption as any.'

Lee breathed in heavily and out quickly. 'Put Maggie back on, Des.'

A short few seconds later, Lee heard, 'Oh, Daddy, Daddy, it's a miracle. It's Mom. It's God. Oh, Daddy, I love you so much.'

Then the tears flowed down Lee's face. The tears were uncontrollable. He shook with tears. His very body broke down as if he had become possessed with grief. 'Oh, Maggie, oh, Joanna . . . I don't know anything anymore. I love you both too. Help me, help me!'

'Daddy, come home. I need you. Come home to me, please.'

Lee finally stopped crying. He had nothing to blow his nose into, so he wiped his tears on his coat sleeve. 'Yes, yes, I'm coming home, my darling. I'll be home just as soon as I can. I love you, my precious. I so love you.'

They hung up. Lee couldn't take much more anyhow. He stared again with welled tears back at the church he had just left. He looked up at the cross set against the contrasting moonlight. Finally, he managed to drag himself upwards and turned towards the entrance gate.

'Lee, Lee, are you all right? It's Anderson . . . Anderson Cooper, CNN.'

Lee looked up and refocused his eyes. 'Anderson, what are you doing here?'

'Following you, Lee. We were in the city earlier, and I spotted you and wondered what you were doing here. It's not often you get to see the great Lee Thomas in action. I saw that most reporters are camped outside the church in Galway waiting for something to happen. I got my driver to follow you here. What's going on, Lee? You've been inside for about five hours.'

Lee looked back at the church and then at the CNN communications vehicle parked outside. 'Do you have computers and the ability to transmit inside of that thing?'

'Sure do. Why? What's on your mind?'

Lee stepped closer to the truck. He thought of something. He turned excitedly to Anderson. 'Will you let me inside your truck? I need to write my report for Dick back in New York. Anderson, if you do this for me, I promise you that I will let you interview me. I'll give you the greatest scoop of the year, maybe even the century.'

Anderson looked at how animated Lee had become. 'Gee, Lee, of course. Can't you just give me a hint?'

'No hint. Trust me, you won't be disappointed. What time is it now?'

Anderson checked his watch. 'It's coming up on one a.m. Why?'

'That makes it eight p.m. in New York. It gives me enough time to make tomorrow's edition. I need to do this now. Can you show me inside?'

Anderson nodded his head, smiling. 'Come on up.'

They climbed the few steps into the back of the truck. There were computer screens throughout and all sorts of communications equipment. Lee looked around, and two of the screens had pictures on them. Lee stopped dead. 'Who's that there?' he said, pointing to the left-hand picture.

Anderson looked where Lee was pointing and said, 'That's one of the escaped convicts, the one who was in a coma. He died a few hours back. The other guy was shot dead at the cabin. Why?'

Lee opened his eyes wide in disbelief. 'But that can't be.' He looked out through the window back at the church, then back at the screen again. 'That's the guy who opened the church door for me,' he said softly.

'What'd you say, Lee? No, that's not right. You went into the church on your own. I saw you. Look – here, let me rewind the tape.'

Anderson pressed some buttons, and the timer went back five hours. He stopped, and the tape showed Lee walking up the footpath to the church. When he arrived at the door, he did seem to turn and talk to somebody – but there was nobody there! The door opened, and Lee walked in.

'That can't be. I saw that man there,' said Lee, pointing at Fonsie on the screen. 'He opened the door for me.'

Anderson began to show concern. 'Are you sure you're okay, Lee? Would you like me to get you something?'

Lee blinked a number of times; then he turned to Anderson. 'Coffee. Lots and lots of coffee. Thank you, Anderson.'

'There's pots of decent coffee over there,' he said, pointing.

'Stay outside, Anderson, and don't let anybody inside, okay?'

'Okay, Lee, I'll do as you say.'

Lee grabbed one of the chairs and pulled his phone from his pocket. He speed-dialed Dick. It rang a few times; then Dick answered. 'Talk to me, Lee. Tell me you have something.'

'Can I make the front page of tomorrow's edition?'

'Holy crap, Lee – you're not telling me you have something for me, are you?'

'I believe I have the scoop of the century, Dick. Have you anything going for tomorrow?'

'No, Lee. What have you got for me?'

'Let me send you a thousand words. Then you can tell me if you want more. How's that?'

'Okay, send it – but hurry, man.'

Lee sat there in front of the screen for what seemed like ages. The myriad of thoughts raged throughout his mind. Where did he start his report? He listened to his recordings and read and reread his notes. Then his fingers started working:

Maybe God Was an Irishman!

Lee 'The Skeptic' Thomas

I have just returned from Ireland, having been sent there to investigate the goings-on in the western city of Galway and the small rural towns of Tuam and Ballinasloe.

I didn't hold out much prospect of being able to achieve what I was sent to do. I went there as your special agent to unravel the possible fraudsters who had turned into criminals, to defrock part of the Anglican church that was protecting a fraudster. I was looking forward to the challenge.

Did I achieve what I set out to do? The answer is yes. But instead of finding cheats and fraudsters, I found a people who were genuine in their disclosures to me. Instead of taking their word for it, I checked and double-checked their responses and answers against one another. And what did I find? I found the truth.

Further on in this report, you will find an in-depth account, written by our chief crime correspondent, Bill Canon, giving explicit details of the criminal aspects of this case as only Bill Canon can do. My attention is centered solely on the religious and possibly divine part of the story.

If you ask me if I saw any miracles, my answer would have to be no. If you ask me if I experienced any miracles, my answer would be an emphatic and resounding yes.

I arrived at Shannon Airport yesterday around midday. I started my investigation in Ballinasloe, the "birthplace" of the prime suspect, Father Sean Robinson. I've put quotation marks around the word "birthplace" because this was where he was found, not born. You see, Sean Robinson was a mere infant when his adoptive mother, Mrs. Bridie Robinson, stumbled upon our protagonist on a fateful evening as Halley's Comet bid its farewell to planet earth for another 76 years.

Turn to pages 2, 3 & 4

See our Sunday magazine for the crime report relating to this article.

Lee pressed the send button. His full five-thousand-word report was delivered. Dick was deliriously happy. Lee was drained.

Lee opened the door to find Anderson Cooper still sitting there. 'Did you do it, Lee?'

Lee smiled. 'I did it, Anderson, thank you for being so patient. What time is it?'

Anderson checked his watch. 'It's coming up on six-thirty. Are you ready to do the interview?'

Lee smiled. 'Of course I am. I made a promise, didn't I?'

Anderson and his assistant set up the camera and the sound equipment. Lee answered all of Anderson's questions. Anderson raised his eyebrows in shock most of the time as Lee recounted his story. A half hour later, it was done.

'Gee, Lee, that's incredible. Do you honestly believe everything you told me?'

Lee smiled again. 'Every blessed word, Anderson.'

Lee walked up the church pathway.

'Where are you going, Lee? The airport is that way,' Anderson said, pointing in the opposite direction.

Lee turned and said, 'I'm going to mass. It's Easter Sunday.'

To be continued...

Thank you for reading. If you liked my book, I would appreciate it, if you would post your review on Amazon. Its also a great encouragement for me to know that my readers like what I write.

You can also follow me on

www.amazon.com/Bernie-Donnelly

 Bernie Donnelly

berniedear

Maybe God was an Irishman

Book Review – SPR December 2016.

"The complexities of religion, faith, love and tragedy tangle in the pages of *Maybe God Was an Irishman*, an entertaining and insightful novel by Bernie Donnelly. With an overflowing cast of peripheral characters and multiple story lines that brilliantly overlap, this is an expansive novel that stretches across oceans and philosophies, making it an addictive read for anyone who appreciates clever writing and heartfelt narratives.

Initially, it is difficult to determine who the protagonist of the story is, but that is Donnelly's way of setting the stage for what is to come. Readers are soon introduced to Sean, an orphan who grows up between these chapters, eventually facing the hard choices of an Irish life, namely working at a pub or joining the priesthood. Having overcome the difficulties of an unusual childhood, he must soon tackle an even more challenging decision – making a life with Linda, a woman he could easily love, or leaving her behind for a much higher calling. With Sean as such a core element of the story, the novel seems to be headed for a religious turn, as the title might suggest, but at its core, this book is about the tough choices and moments in any life – secular or otherwise.

The chapters of the book are biblically themed and cleverly relate to the progression of the story, from The Marriage Feast (elaborate wedding) to The Disciple (Father Sean urging Vinnie to go and help the suffering masses in Haiti). The connections are subtle, and the chapters help readers put themselves in the right mindset for what they are about to read. Without being heavy-handed, the book is highly spiritual, and focuses on the moments of grace and potential salvation that can be found and embraced, if one is willing to see them.

Book-ending the novel is the story of Lee "the Skeptic" Thomas, who readers are introduced to at the very start of the book. He is an investigative journalist for the NYT, who has personally experienced unimaginable tragedy in his life. However, his cynicism is shattered when he witnesses the truth of so-called "miracles" in Ireland, specifically in the work and life of Father Sean, whose birth was signaled by Halley's Comet, another infamous "star" heralding legendary arrivals.

The writing is clean and honest, and despite having a bevy of different characters, Donnelly keeps the stories straight and easy to follow. There are very few grammatical errors or repetitive syntax, and the pace of the story is consistent and engaging; in other words, once you dive into this complex piece, it will be difficult to put down. The colloquial language is subtle, but helps establish a believable context for the tale. Furthermore, the depiction of relationships – both difficult and easy – shows that the author has an insightful and comprehensive grasp on human nature.

As a whole, the novel centers on the real-world wonders that certain people are able to achieve through kindness, compassion, patience and self-sacrifice. Perhaps there is such a thing as divine intervention and the gentle nudging of God, but the tangible miracles of good-hearted humans are often even more powerful. The end of this novel will leave readers uplifted and refreshed – spiritually, emotionally and philosophically – regardless of one's particular religious beliefs or opinions. That is the sign of a truly great book, and a very talented writer."

Other Books by the same author;

DEAR
DAUGHTER

Bernie Donnelly

ISBN: 1523883251
ISBN 13: 9781523883257
Library of Congress Control Number: **2016902624**

REVIEWS

DEAR DAUGHTER
Bernie Donnelly
ISBN: 978-1-5238-8325-7; March 2, 2016

*This debut work of "creative nonfiction" relates an Irish entrepreneur's
tumultuous professional and personal life.
The author opens with an ingenious framing device: he has just
received an email from his estranged adult daughter. Her
brief, polite message asks a simple question: "why did you leave me?"
The narrative that follows is his detailed response,
relating his life before and after his separation from his children. The
son of a film projectionist and a factory worker, he
fights his way to the upper echelons of the software industry and
ultimately becomes a multimillionaire. His strategies
are gutsy, and his distinctive personality is his greatest asset: he's
forceful, driven, occasionally oblivious, and very
funny. In addition to his business triumphs and defeats, he goes
through two marriages, the births of multiple children, a
battle with cancer, and the loss of his father. His tale is also loaded
with humorous tales that cover everything from a
bacchanalian trip to South Africa to his own man-hating dog.
Throughout all of these accounts he shines as an eminently
charming narrator...*

Prologue

It was another beautiful morning on the Gulf Coast of Florida, just like every other morning. I always liked routine. I always felt that a person who had a routine was, generally, a happy person, and that morning I was a very happy person.

I put the kettle on for my early morning cup of Irish tea, a habit that I didn't want to break. Well, I tried to, but I couldn't get used to the American cup of coffee thingie. After popping my usual two pills of aspirin and my medication, I sat down to do my usual news reading and e-mail checking on my computer. It was during that process when I saw a message from someone I hadn't heard from in forever, someone I had only seen for barely two hours over the previous twenty-five years. It read:

Hi there,
Sorry if this comes out of the blue, but I was wondering if I can ask a question? I suppose I might have asked it before, but seeing as how I better express myself in writing. . .
I'm just wondering why you left me?
I don't want you to think I am angry with you or that I blame you, I'm not even upset about it, but I want to stop asking myself this "why" question. I won't be annoyed or upset with whatever answer you give me; it will be the right answer because only you can really answer this question.

So there it is: why did you leave me?

Again, my apologies if this takes you by surprise, but I have to send this question out there: maybe you could answer it,

all the best,

Lora

Lora was the youngest of four children from my first marriage. She had two other sisters and an older brother, the oldest child being seven when I left in 1990.

How do I respond to Lora's question? I thought about it every waking moment. My wife was excited for me because she, more than anyone, knew how much I had missed my children. My wife tried her best to get me started on my reply, but she knew that only I could try to explain to Lora why I had walked out on her and her siblings all those years ago and had never been in contact with them since.

So I made my decision: I was going to tell her the truth. I had no idea how she was going to react, and I had no idea where the truth was going to take me. I replied thus:

No apologies necessary whatsoever, Lora. I'm delighted you asked. It's a profound question that demands a concise answer.

I want to make sure I explain myself properly to you, but you will need to understand that it requires a long and detailed response. Is that okay with you? It will take the form of a book, and I hope you will be able to follow me on my journey.

Love Dad

She responded almost immediately:

Sure, thanks for agreeing to this.
all the best, Lora

Oh yuck! This didn't sound good; it didn't sound good at all. She wasn't helping me. It seemed like a very cold response. Why no "Love, Lora" or no "Okay, Dad? "

It didn't get my pulse racing, but the more I thought about it, the more it made sense. I wasn't her dad, so how could I expect her to respond as if I were?

So I sent the following email:

Lora, I don't know anything about you and, as a result, I don't know how strong you are or whether you are capable of handling what I need to say to you. This is very much to my chagrin because, as much as you've been troubled about me "leaving you," I'm asking you if you "care" how much I've been troubled about never having seen you, been around you, or known anything about you? Does it matter to you that I've never known my youngest daughter, continually seeing normal parents every day of my life as they watch their children growing up in front of them, wondering what it would have been like to be a part of their every living moment - good and bad? Does it matter to you that I have suffered just as much as you because, while you were just a child growing up, I was your dad watching from a distance, not being able to be a part of your life? You see, as much as I want to explain "the leaving" to you, it troubles me that maybe you don't care how I was feeling when I left you, what events occurred leading up to my departure, how troubled I was living with your mum, and all the crazy things that happened to me that just don't happen to normal people living normal lives!

I don't want to upset you anymore than you have been already, and the truth could upset you. I have to explain your father to you, and I don't know if you care or are interested in me enough to want to understand.

Is this what you want to hear?

Love, Dad

She replied the same day:

Hi there,

I know writing this will be hard for you. I am asking you to be honest with me. Let's face it: I am a stranger. However, I know what our perspectives and situations are. We are different. I was a child, and I didn't know you so I didn't know what I was missing. Naturally, I understand that it must have been more difficult for you. I have no children, but the mere thought that I would not see my nephew again would crush me.

I have heard only briefly about what you went through around that time. Naturally, I would prefer to hear it from you because only you can explain your feelings. My mom will obviously be a (substantial) part of your answer. I know this. I understand this. However, you two had a completely different type of relationship to the one that I have had, and continue to have, with her. On top of that, it was almost thirty years ago; I doubt either of you are the same person today. I understand your reluctance. You don't know me, and I am not unaware of the upset that I have caused by merely asking this question. So it's your choice. As for my interest in you, if I didn't want to know you as you were and as you are now, I wouldn't have e-mailed.

All the best, Lora

So that was it then, a perfect response from a very intelligent lady who I didn't know. Yes, as she so succinctly pointed out, we were strangers, so it should be easy for me to tell her the truth - a perfect truth - at least as I remembered it.

So I responded:

Lora,

I am going to tell you everything. I've told nobody everything. This'll be a no-holds-barred exposé of my life leading up to my exit from yours. It's the only way I can explain myself to you and, thereby, explain my actions. You have to know all about me if you want to understand how I affected your life, and then you can come to your own conclusions. You will be shocked, but I believe you can take it - maybe more so than anybody. It will be a first for me, also. To do this, it helps knowing that we're strangers because I can talk to you in that context, not as your father, which would be awkward.

As a result of this decision it will take me a lot longer to reply, but so what? We have plenty of time, and I need to do this correctly. I want to take my time to ensure that I have the timeline correct and that I don't miss anything pertaining to the events in my life that affected me, leading up to my frame of mind when I left.

My only hope is that, as a result of doing this, we will no longer be strangers.

Dad

And so it was time to remember.

Chapter 1

You see, Lora, two years prior to receiving your email, I decided to clean up my office. As I was going through my old files, a postcard fell from a folder. It was from my eldest son Jack, your brother. He had sent me that postcard around ten years before asking me how I was and giving me his contact details. I examined that card for hours, and when my wife awoke, I told her that I'd sent an e-mail to Jack at the address on the card and asked him to contact me. I also let him know that I would love to hear from him. She was surprised but excited for me, and so we waited to see if I would get a response.

I waited for days, checking my e-mails every hour, thinking that it was almost impossible that he would have received my e-mail because the address he had used was a very old one from a provider that had probably long gone out of business. I had no other way of finding out where he was because there was nobody I knew who would give me information about him because I was persona non grata in Ireland.

Then, about a week later, lo and behold and hallelujah! A response arrived.

Hi Dad,

Still using this address. Better way to get me though is through this new email address.
So I hear from my sources that you are living in Florida now. How long have you been there, and how did you end up this side of the pond?
I am currently living in Ashland, a small town in Southern Oregon. I have been married for almost a year and a half to Angelina; she is from here.
Anyway, I hope you are healthy and happy.... Jack

Holy crap-a-rooskie! It was an e-mail from Jack; I hadn't seen him in over twenty-four years, apart from a brief encounter when Jack's teacher had contacted me about Jack when he was about twelve. When I met with the teacher, he explained that he had asked his students to write about what they wanted in their lives, and Jack had simply written "my dad." I choked up when he told me that, and then he told me that Jack was waiting for me in the adjoining room. When I saw him, I couldn't stop crying. I bawled out loud in front of the little fella as he sat and stared at me. I repeatedly told him I was sorry, and that I loved him so much. As the uncontrollable flood of tears streamed down my face, I asked him how he was doing at school, and he barely said two words. I think he was in so much shock at seeing his dad break down.

As I left him I promised to see him often but, of course, I never did. The reasons will be explained later. Now that we were back in contact I was determined that Jack and I would never lose each other again.

He made it very easy for me to get to know him. He called me "Dad." Wow, none of my children had ever called me Dad before - not since I had left. We started to exchange lots of e-mails, and I tried to remember what a father should do, trying not to be overanxious, but I couldn't help myself. I was more than thrilled to have another opportunity.

I had missed all of the great events in his life up to this point, but at least I could be around for of his future events - if he'd let me. I was not going to let him slip away, ever.

Eventually, I needed to hear his voice, so I gave him a call. I was like a child when I first heard his manly voice. I had no idea what he would sound like. I had rehearsed everything I wanted to say, all of the questions I wanted to ask, but I forgot everything as soon as I heard his voice.

He was calm, relaxed, and mature, and he made it easy for me to engage. It wasn't long before a year had gone by, and as we approached our second year, I decided I had to see him in the flesh. I told him I wanted to visit him and his wife in Oregon for my sixtieth birthday, that it would be the best present I could ever have. He was taken aback but was delighted at my suggestion, so we organized everything for the trip.

My wife and I flew into Portland, Oregon, about two days before we were due to meet Jack. When the day came, we drove down to meet him. I was nervous, and I didn't know what we should do when we met, so in true inspirational Irish style I decided we should go to the pub to calm everybody's nerves, especially my own.

We waited outside the hotel, and only having a photograph he had sent me, I looked up and down the street wondering what he would look like in person. Then I saw him on the other side of the street, and he saw me. My god, he was huge, about six feet four, and I couldn't take my eyes off him as we awkwardly embraced. He asked me what we wanted to do, and I said we should go to a pub, even though it was only ten in the morning. I never thought that would be a problem; the Irish never had a problem finding an open bar. Jack said he thought he knew of one place, so we walked around making small talk as he looked up the bar owner that he knew. He invited us in, and we sat down and had a few beers while the girls had coffees. Finally, we were relaxed.

This wasn't going to be a time for a deep conversation; it was too soon for that. This was about seeing one another in person. The other stuff could wait. We spent the day together having lunch at a local vineyard, eating pizza, and drinking wine while a tree protected us from the glorious sunshine. We chatted, laughed, and made small talk, mainly because neither of us was sure how it would go or how we should react. But it was a start - a great start - especially for me and, I hope, for him, too. Not wanting to screw things up by overstaying our welcome, I suggested that my wife and I should return to the hotel because I was tired, and we planned on meeting the next day for breakfast before heading back home to Florida. The next day was even more relaxed. The girls were great. They both knew this was a unique occasion, and they got on great together, which made everything so much easier for Jack and me.

Before we met for breakfast I decided to look around town. I was in a store when I decided to buy Jack a hat, one of those cool fedoras that I thought would suit him. It was a great success. He said it was his favorite type of hat, and that he had recently lost his old one, so I was thrilled. He then produced a card and a present that he had bought for my birthday. I choked up. It was the first present I had ever received from any of my children.

After that, things were so much easier between us, and even though we had spent only two days together, it felt great that we had broken the ice. We're still getting to know one another, and it doesn't matter if it takes the rest of my life, at least we've started.
Jack reintroduced me to his eldest sister May who has since given me two grandchildren I plan on meeting next year. I haven't seen May in about twelve years. We had arranged to meet in a local hotel near her university in Dublin, but in my excitement I forgot to bring any money, so I thanked the Lord that she didn't want anything to eat or drink. We ended that meeting with her not wanting to be beside me and both of us finding things a bit awkward. We never saw each other again, not because we had a fight, but because we were simply strangers. But things have greatly improved with May and me over the past two years, and we speak often.

So, Lora, that brings you up to date regarding my relationships with Jack and May. I am barely into a renewed relationship with my two eldest children, and now you have laid this on me. How the hell do I reply and not lose you again? It's not as if May or Jack hasn't asked me similar questions, but they never pursued it as graphically as you are now.

Lora, because you know nothing about me and, subsequently, nothing about my family or the people around me, I thought it would be a good idea to give you a little background to how I grew up, the people I met along the way, and the things that happened to me because those are the things that molded me into what I am today. Once you hear these stories, I hope to explain myself to you satisfactorily, and then I will explain why I left you. Whether my explanation is satisfactory, only you can judge.

Chapter 2.

My ninth birthday was the first time I nearly died. We had a small party at the house, and I was drinking an orange soda. I somehow bit off a chunk of the glass. It got caught in my throat and protruded through both sides. I remember exactly where I was standing in the kitchen as I saw my father turn blue in the face as he reached toward me, forced my mouth open, and retrieved the glass from my throat. Everyone panicked except my father. He stopped the bleeding by slapping a lump of Vaseline across my throat. He then poured me another orange soda as if nothing had happened, and everybody went about their business. But I'll tell you this: I'd never seen anybody look as scared as my father did that day.

I hated school—every living, breathing, fart-filled moment. The Irish school buildings were always cold, damp, and filthy, as were most of the teachers. The Christian brothers were as "Christian" as ISIS. Most of them were alcoholics. Some should have been imprisoned, and none was the least bit friendly. They were incapable of imparting knowledge that would make you think, that would bring out your skills, or that would even encourage you to be something. They ruled with the terror of the strap or the ruler in the spirit of the Roman legions. You were their slaves, and they were your masters. The Irish governments of the day were happy to have a cheap educational solution, thanks to the Christian Brotherhood, and the brothers used the power ceded to them to great effect.

There was never a day I looked forward to, never a moment of happiness beyond staring at the hands of the clock, waiting for them to reach four so I could escape. The lay teachers were just as bad as the brothers, with one or two exceptions. There was the English teacher who continually punched students with his ringed middle finger for no reason whatsoever as he patrolled the classroom, and, boy, it hurt. There was the geography teacher who had a major lice problem and would flick the crawling beasts off his arms on to the nearest unsuspecting student. The math teacher continually picked his nose in front of us, and we all ducked when he flicked the snot at us. The science teacher scared the shit out of us. He appeared to be seven feet tall to us twelve year olds, and he only had one bloody piece of magnesium to demonstrate a chemical reaction, which ensured that none of us would be joining NASA anytime soon. They tried to teach us physics and civics, but they soon gave up.

There was an Irish language teacher who took such a major dislike to me that he would immediately say "Donnelly, out!" It became so routine that whenever he entered the classroom I immediately made my exit, saving him the bother of ordering me out. Many years later I was in a restaurant when he strolled in and, I swear, I automatically stood up to leave; that's how much of a hold those teachers had on us.

We had no sporting facilities, no fields, nothing. There was only a concrete yard where running competitions were held, which I always won (preparing myself for the great escape). I was so good that the school entered me in a national athletics competition in Croke Park—a major Dublin venue—but I was so petrified that as I approached the finish line in first place, I suddenly stopped because nobody had told me there would be a cord to indicate the finish line. So as I stopped dead, another runner crossed the line, breaking the cord and finished first. The teacher-in-charge crucified me on the journey home. That teacher was my Irish language teacher, the guy who always told me to get out of his class, hence the ridicule and displeasure I had to endure from him for the rest of my school life.

An honorable mention must go to the history teacher who arrived during our final year. He was a breath of fresh air because, as we opened our boring textbooks, he asked us what we thought of World War II. He actually sought our opinion. We gazed at him with shock and awe. We wondered when the men in white coats would be arriving to take him away. It was like that scene from *Dead Poets Society* when Robin Williams tells the class to rip up their books, except this was seventeen years prior to that movie, and our hero was serious about getting us to discuss World War II.

Then again, I couldn't blame the teachers entirely when I considered the rabble they had to deal with. We were sorted into "A", "B," and "C" classes based on intelligence and how bad you smelled. Thankfully, I was always in the "A" classes because I was constantly clean and well-dressed. The lay teachers were usually from outside the city, "culchies" as they were known, and they didn't have a clue about how to treat city boys. They expected us to follow Gaelic games or talk about hurling or Irish football, even if we had no interest in any of it. They considered us totally subservient, so they never treated us with the slightest hint of respect.

I recently discovered that a principal from the junior school had been molesting young boys for years. One poor chap, a man in his fifties, recently committed suicide. He had been abused and had to live with that dark secret all his life. The animal that did that to him has since died; may he never rest in peace.

We knew we could never tell any of this stuff to our parents because they simply wouldn't believe us; instead, they would tell us that it must be our fault, and that we should always do what the teachers told us. So it was no wonder the teachers got away with the awful things they did; they were protected by the society around them.

Those Irish schools were nothing like the ones you attended or what kids attend now. Those schools shed no light on our talents. It was only after I finished school that I realized I had a talent for math, and that I loved history and English.

I kept to myself, changing friends often and steering away from trouble. I didn't have an outgoing personality; it only developed after I left school and started working. I always passed my exams, but I didn't shine in any subject. I stayed below the radar and waited for it to be over. What a waste of fifteen years . . . When I finally finished high school I walked up the street and, without turning around, I said aloud, "Thank God that's over," and I never thought about the place again. We tried to have a school reunion once, but it didn't work. We never tried again as I guess nobody wanted to relive those days. Sean was my best friend. We often played together, and on one summer day, he arrived at my house and wanted me to come out and play. My father took me to the movies instead. I don't know why, but Sean started climbing the big tree up the road, and he fell, breaking his leg. I found out when I got home, and we went down to St. Michael's Hospital the next day to see Sean. He had developed an infection and died a few days later. Everyone was shocked. My father blamed the hospital, saying it was a dirty place and, as a result of Sean's death, he would never consider taking us there, no matter the emergency. I didn't understand. I just wanted to see my friend, but the next thing I knew I was going to my first funeral. I couldn't make sense of the fact that even my grannies were still alive, yet my best friend was dead at thirteen. I think of Sean often.

A couple of years went by, and I had made new friends. One day we went down to the beach for a swim. There was a spring tide, high and rough. Neither my friend nor I could swim, and we hadn't seen the sea so rough before. I decided to test how deep the water was, so I jumped in, only to be taken out about fifty feet by a riptide. In a matter of seconds, I was way out of my depth, and I sank like a rock. This would be my second unintentional attempt to leave this world. It's true that you come up and down twice when you're drowning, and then you stay down the third time. I came up the first time to see my friend laughing his bollocks off, thinking I was messing about. I went down the second time, and my lungs started to fill with water. When that is happening, you don't have time to be scared. Somehow, I surfaced again and managed to blurt out "Help!" a couple of times before sinking again, and there would be no coming up.

Three blokes dived in when they heard me scream. They were great swimmers and managed to drag me out by my hair, my small nuts, and my leg, and proceeded to pump the water out of me. Strangely, after I got my breath back, my first thoughts were that my parents would find out and kill me, which was stupid, really, but I didn't want them to hear about it. To this day, even though I taught myself to swim, I totally panic if I go outside my depth.

That very same day I returned to the beach because somebody told me I must conquer my fear, that I must go back into the water. But that time I never made it to the water because I slit my foot on some broken glass and had to be carried to the first aid hut. I was spilling blood everywhere.

I was never good at sports except running and boxing. Whenever they picked street football teams, I was the last to be picked, alongside anybody else with an infirmity, which didn't do anything to develop my nonexistent ego. I liked running because I could be by myself, and I was fast. I took up boxing when I was about sixteen because I knew I needed to defend myself as it was a rough town in those days. I had a good trainer who taught me how to fight but, above all, he taught me restraint, and that has served me well ever since.

I always said hello to everybody. It didn't matter who you were; Bernie would always bid you the time of day. I did that from the time I could talk and walk. My mother told me that I would often go missing when I was around five or six years of age. She would go looking for me, and she would always find me in one of the neighbors' houses eating cookies and having a soda. I used to do the same on the streets. On the way to school we used to pass an old man on his donkey with his cart full of pig shit. The stink was awful, and he'd have his young kid on the back of the cart helping him. The kid obviously never went to school, and the two of them always waved at me and gave me a big smile. The other lads would jeer and ask why I was talking to those knackers, but I ignored them because, as far as I was concerned, they were nice people.

Fast forward ten years, and I was walking home from my summer job as a bartender downtown, and I got caught on the wrong side of the road as ten or so thugs were approaching me. One thing you never do is cross the road in the face of such a threat—that would be suicidal because they would know you were scared. You just had to ride it out and hope to Jesus you got through the gauntlet unscathed. Well, they saw me, and I basically said my prayers because I was doomed. I was going to get a good hiding at one o'clock in the morning. I was in the middle of them being shoved around when, all of a sudden from a dark doorway a voice said, "Leave him alone; he's with me." They all looked at a guy with a lit cigarette as he stepped forward into the moonlight.

"Oh, didn't know that, sorry," one thug said, and off they went.
The bloke with the cigarette looked at me and said, "You're a bit outside your neighborhood, aren't you?"
I said yes and thanked him.
"You'll be all right now," he said, and he went on about his business.
Of course, it was that kid who used to ride the donkey cart with his father all those years earlier. I met him again some thirty years later at a charity golf outing. He had become a multimillionaire who owned a number of pubs and newspapers.
At that golf outing he asked, "Do you remember me?"
"Of course I do. You saved me from a hammering one night."
"Do you know you were the only person who ever said hello to me or my dad?"
"No, I didn't know that, but I'm glad I did."
"And you never knew my name, did you?"
"No."
"Maybe we should leave it that way."
"Maybe we should."

And I never saw him again.

You can continue reading this book by purchasing it on Amazon. Thank you.

Author Profile

Bernie Donnelly was born in Dublin in 1953. He formed his own software company at the age of twenty-nine and had operations in Ireland, England and India.

Following the sale of his business in 1999, he spent some years in Portugal, and in 2008 he emigrated to the U.S.A., arriving in Sarasota, Florida, where he remains to this day. He became a U.S. citizen in 2014.

He is an avid reader of biographies and history and has travelled extensively.

CPSIA information can be obtained
at www.ICGtesting.com
Printed in the USA
LVOW10s0207090817

544325LV00018BA/900/P